Resist and Persist

Resist and Persist

*Essays on Social Revolution
in 21st Century Narratives*

Edited by AMANDA FIRESTONE *and*
LEISA A. CLARK

McFarland & Company, Inc., Publishers
Jefferson, North Carolina

Library of Congress Cataloguing-in-Publication Data

Names: Firestone, Amanda, 1982– editor. | Clark, Leisa A., 1968– editor.
Title: Resist and persist : essays on social revolution in 21st century narratives / edited by Amanda Firestone and Leisa A. Clark.
Description: Jefferson, North Carolina : McFarland & Company, Inc., Publishers, 2020. | Includes bibliographical references and index.
Identifiers: LCCN 2020012672 | ISBN 9781476676678 (paperback : acid free paper) ∞ ISBN 9781476639826 (ebook)
Subjects: LCSH: Motion pictures—Political aspects—United States—History—20th century. | Motion pictures—Social aspects—United States—History—20th century. | Social problems in motion pictures. | Television programs—Political aspects—United States—History—20th century. | Telvision programs—Social aspects—United States—History—20th century. | Social problems on television.
Classification: LCC PN1995.9.P6 R47 2020 | DDC 791.43/6581—dc23
LC record available at https://lccn.loc.gov/2020012672

British Library cataloguing data are available

ISBN (print) 978-1-4766-7667-8
ISBN (ebook) 978-1-4766-3982-6

Front cover image © 2020 Shutterstock

Printed in the United States of America

McFarland & Company, Inc., Publishers
 Box 611, Jefferson, North Carolina 28640
 www.mcfarlandpub.com

To those who resist

"Any human power can be resisted and changed by human beings. Resistance and change often begin in art, and very often in our art, the art of words."

—Ursula K. Le Guin (2014 speech at National Book Awards)

Acknowledgments

This book could not have existed without the input and support of so many wonderful people. We begin by thanking our wonderful contributors, who have generously given of their time and expertise to produce insightful and diverse essays. Special thanks go to McFarland editor Susan Kilby for always being there to support us through the processes, pitfalls, and issues that are inherent in working on an edited collection. Additionally, we need to give a big shout-out to Alisha Menzies for stepping in at the last minute to offer much-needed help in the final hours of this project. We wish to thank all of our friends, family members, and colleagues who stood by us during the ups and downs over the many months we worked on drafts, edits, changes, and challenges.

Table of Contents

Preface

AMANDA FIRESTONE

When I was a child, one of my favorite films was *Mary Poppins* (1964). I especially loved the number "Sister Suffragette," performed by Mrs. Banks (Glynis Johns), who marches around the family home, putting Votes for Women sashes onto the housekeeper, cook, and the (departing) nanny. Of course, as a kid, I had no idea that the people and events embedded in the song's lyrics were actual parts of history, but I did find a kind of joy in a vague notion of women's empowerment.

Fast forward about 15 years to my time as an undergraduate student at Penn State. By that time, I was beginning to come into my intellectual and political own as a feminist. I relished taking courses that revealed to me the histories of my foremothers who worked, struggled, fought, and suffered in order to make deep-rooted social changes. Learning about the first wave of feminism was revelatory, and after seeing the film *Iron Jawed Angels* (2004), I became obsessed with learning about the suffrage movement.

There were a lot of times when I daydreamed that I could have been part of something so momentous and historic. In 2004 the opportunity came for me to participate in my first big protest event: the March for Women's Lives in Washington, D.C. My excitement was palpable, and I eagerly asked my mom if she also wanted to take part in the event. She happily agreed, and we rode the coach bus from State College to D.C., absolutely buzzing with anticipation.

To help contribute to my visual solidarity, I specifically ordered a t-shirt from Ani DiFranco's Righteous Babe online shop that featured lyrics from her spoken word piece "Self Evident": "Here's a toast to all the nurses and doctors who daily provide women with a choice, who stand down a threat the size of Oklahoma City just to listen to a young woman's voice." (I still own the shirt.) I wasn't alone in my desire to *show* that I was part of the group. Lots of folks wore printed shirts for women's organizations, shirts that had the march's logo, and tons of shirts, buttons, and badges that were clearly homemade. All of this in addition to the colorful cardboard signs, both printed and homemade, that sprung up in the mass of people. When my mom and I exited the bus and were directed into the swelling crowd, I was stunned with sensory overload and a profound understanding that I was part of something important.

Frankly, the rest of the day is a blur. We walked with the crowd, moving down Pennsylvania Avenue toward the central gathering point where a stage was erected. Prominent celebrities, politicians, and organization leaders took turns at the mic, sharing information, their thoughts, and experiences with the group. As we moved, we easily got into the groove of things as we joined in call and response chants and songs. We shouted repetitive slogans in support of the cause. We cheered and clapped and laughed with each other and the hundreds of people surrounding us. At several points we saw anti-choice protestors, and although the two factions shouted at each other, reportedly there were no actual altercations that day.

Back on the bus, I fell asleep almost immediately as we started the journey home. When I did wake, although I was still exhausted, the frenetic energy of the day returned to me. Up to that point, it was one of the most exciting moments of my life. And I pledged that in the coming weeks, I would become more politically engaged and active in my community. I planned to join the local chapters of NOW and NARAL Pro Choice and assiduously stay on top of political news so that I could be better informed about the goings-on of the nation, especially in regard to things that I felt passionately about.

While I began in earnest, I am sorry to say that I did not follow through on any of my plans. My mom drove back to my hometown the next day; I returned to my classes, and quotidian life swept me away. Soon enough, my memories of the march experience were a dim background hum compared to all of the other things that pressed forward. Still, my passion for American women's history and women's studies grew, and I threw myself into reading and discussion that broadened my understanding of both. Through my education, I learned about subtler ways to resist and to push back against the system in addition to highly visible, public tactics like organized marches.

That for me is the key here. There are many ways to resist. Participation in social change is often about the small gestures that compile over time rather than the grand ones. I think back to *Mary Poppins*. Winnifred Banks is an ardent supporter of her cause, but it's clear that her visible support for it is problematic inside of her household. "Ellen, put these [sashes] away, you know how the cause infuriates Mr. Banks." Her Votes for Women paraphernalia is whisked away. Although she may struggle to negotiate her progressive political ideals in her traditional marriage and home life, Mrs. Banks continues to attend meetings. She remains active and resists her husband's desire for comfortable conformity. At the end of the film, once Mary Poppins has worked her magic and the Banks family is happily together, Mrs. Banks has another important moment of resistance: "A proper kite needs a proper tail, don't you think?" She quickly affixes one of the Votes for Women sashes to the mended kite as the family leaves 17 Cherry Tree Lane, thus quietly but firmly making her suffragette status visible and clear.

When we initially brainstormed this book in spring 2018, we talked about the many ways that we noticed people participating in resistance: reusing bags when shopping instead of getting plastic bags, boycotting certain companies or brands, pushing for important language changes to be more intersectional and inclusive, mobilizing social media to keep people accountable, voting with dollars by choosing more conscientious purchasing, and being an ally by offering different types of support to struggling people or organizations, just to name a few. It occurred to us that if we noticed this apparent growing trend, then surely other scholars had also discerned it. We were not disappointed.

When we sent out the call for essays, we received nearly 60 abstracts in response. As always, we were impressed by the breadth of subjects covered in the submissions. Even so, we knew there were significant gaps, and although we wished we could have accepted every proposal, there was a finite amount of space for the project. Once we were in the thick of things with authors turning in second and third drafts, we continued to prompt them for additional insights because inevitably *something else* had happened that was relevant to the subject. We doled out extra words where we could, trying to keep the information as up to date as possible until we reached a point of no-more-edits return.

Our contributors look to real-life events, fictional popular media, and sometimes combinations of the two in order to demonstrate how social resistance imbues every facet of Western, largely American, culture at this specific moment at the end of the 2010s. Their work is insightful, thought provoking, and most importantly, inspiring. We wanted to create this book in order to bring together scholarly voices to critique circumstances and experiences that even in the moment reveal themselves to be profoundly culturally relevant. Collections like this are an example of how scholars can write resistant research in the face of subjects that are difficult and also deeply personal. We all stand together. To paraphrase Mrs. Banks, side by side, we march forward into the mire, knowing that our actions can make a radical, positive difference for future generations.

WORKS CITED

DiFranco, Ani. "Self Evident." *So Much Shouting So Much Laughter*, Righteous Babe Records, 2002.

Mary Poppins. Directed by Robert Stevenson. 1964. Walt Disney Studios Home Entertainment, 2009.

Section I
"They're already here. You're next"

Amanda Firestone

The frantic quotation that titles Section One of this edited collection is taken from *Invasion of the Body Snatchers* (1956). The character Dr. Miles J. Bennell shouts this at drivers as he hysterically runs through moving traffic near the end of the film. He is trying to warn them, in vain, of the already in-process invasion. Most people ignore him and no one believes him, except us—the audience, because along with Miles, we watched the world unravel as the truth was revealed that aliens have slowly but surely replaced humans with imperfect copies.

Critics have read the film simultaneously as an anti–Communist text and one which challenges McCarthyistic conformity (Hagopian). The fever-pitch paranoia that imbues the film asks audiences to intellectually engage with hypothetical scenarios in which their families and friends are duplicitously replaced. Although this threat came from outer space, the real horror is that it's happening "right here, in any town USA, and it's happening to *us*" (Maltin, emphasis added). In the mid–1950s, the dichotomy of resistance to Communism—or anything that didn't speak directly to hegemonic American ideals—and blanket conformity, which violently suppressed people and communities in terms of religious practice, personal identity, and intellectual engagements, was strong. Not for the first time, nor for the last, was the country deeply divided across political and ideological lines.

There is a tendency within the general rose-colored cultural memory of the Fabulous Fifties to remember it as a simpler time. Collectively, at first thoughts, we tend to think of it as a time of economic prosperity, one when upward social movement was easily attainable; a time in which people were more invested in achieving the new middle-class American dream. And while the recognition of diversity among Americans was becoming more transparent, there was also an assumption that Americans were becoming more homogenous. Men knew how to be men and women knew how to be women. People (though there were increased opportunities) knew their place, and what's more, they appeared to be happy in them. The glowing and dreamy ether that surrounds the 1950s negates the true complexities and sociopolitical hardships that actually shaded people's daily lives.

This idealized version of that era is supremely supported by the media technology that took the nation by storm: television. According to the Library of Congress, "In 1950, only 9 percent of American households had a television set, but by 1960 that figure had reached 90 percent" ("Television"). Family sitcoms of the day presented what supposedly was the American family at its best through shows like *I Love Lucy, Father Knows Best, Leave It to Beaver,* and *The Donna Reed Show.* Shows like these included very few minority characters (Desi Arnaz is, of course, the exception) and few designations of class distinctions apart from the middle class. The other popular genre at the time was the Western, and it provided an ahistoric version of the "Wild Wild West" that more accurately represented 1950s ideals than those of the 1850s. All Americans with TV access had a finite programming list to view, which meant that millions of people didn't see themselves or their life situations represented on the screen. Reality was much broader and perhaps darker than these conservative shows' scripts conveyed. Yet, it is those gray and grainy images that persist as the false beacon of what life was really like at that time.

Fortunately, we have things other than sitcoms and Westerns to provide a more well-rounded and accurate depiction of that era. While entertainment TV gave audiences escapist fantasies, there was also news programming. Initially, news broadcasts were about 15 minutes long and didn't garner the numbers for viewing audiences that other shows did (Mickelson 3). But, as the medium's technology became more sophisticated and news shows were able to broadcast both live and edited footage, people across the nation began to rely on the information delivered to them via rabbit ears rather than over the radio.

This was the way in which an American public began to bond over their shared experiences. This included events that were challenging and divisive for people. Unlike those shiny sitcoms, news media of the time reveal a nation in a tenuous state. In fact, in 1989 I.F. Stone, a left-wing investigative journalist, published a collection of his columns and editorials that he called *The Haunted Fifties.* The title paints a very different image than when compared with the moniker "fabulous." The contents of the book expose a grim portrait of the country, and Stone includes articles about Communism, freedom of speech, government warmongering, Civil Rights, and anti–Semitism. Several pieces decry the escapades of Senator Joseph McCarthy and the related committees that forced Americans to testify, once more helping us make touch with interpretations of *Invasion of the Body Snatchers.* Stone writes in 1953,

"Investigations have been fundamental but the kind of investigations utilized in this *witch hunt* are something new in American life. [...] The idea that a committee of Congress could interrogate Americans on their political beliefs is a revolutionary excrescence not a fundamental of American government in the past" (20, emphasis added).

Through the venue of his *Weekly* newspaper, Stone showed his opposition and resistance to the growing corruption that he witnessed in Washington, D.C., throughout the 1940s and '50s. He took it upon himself to reveal a different version of the story rather than the one that was wielded by powerful bureaucrats or carefully primped and preened by public relations experts. Other journalists took up the call, and in 1954 Edward R. Murrow produced "A Report on Senator Joseph A. McCarthy" for his news program *See It Now*. The broadcast, consisting mostly of video and audio of McCarthy's own speeches, denounced the senator's actions. Murrow famously says near the end of the broadcast:

> [McCarthy's] primary achievement has been in confusing the public mind as between the internal and external threats of Communism. We must not confuse dissent with disloyalty. We must remember always that accusation is not proof and that conviction depends on evidence and due process of law. We will not walk in fear, one of another. We will not be driven by fear into an age of unreason if we dig deep into our history in our doctrine and remember that we are not descended from fearful men, not from men who feared to write, to speak, to associate, and to defend causes that were for the moment unpopular.

His strong and stirring words echoed across the country, and it's clear that his broadcast and message resonated with people. Apocryphally, Murrow went to lunch at Sardi's in Midtown Manhattan the day after the program aired and was greeted with a standing ovation by the patrons there.

These small examples offer some insights into the necessity for resistance, especially in the midst of a brewing crisis. Though I began with the science fiction film *Invasion of the Body Snatchers*, the sensibilities displayed by the fictional character Miles and the real-life journalists Stone and Murrow are similar. All three see their communities in peril; they see neighbor spy on neighbor, and friends become enemies. Their passionate mission is to tell others what is happening and why it's necessary for everyone to become involved. Miles could only shout at people in passing cars, and Stone started with a limited readership of just five thousand people (Stone 3). Murrow reached the widest audience, both in his broadcasts and subsequent repetitions and reprintings of his words. In essence, everything that begins with a shout has the potential to become a roar.

The essays in this first section of the book also speak to this same ideal. The subjects within these pages expose the grimy and distorted and hidden underbelly of contemporary American society. Each author has chosen a subject that is absolutely of this moment in the 2010s. In the face of instantaneous and intense scrutiny, facilitated by the ever-reaching scope of media production and consumption, resistance becomes both normal and public. The movies we watch and the TV shows we binge on weekends, the documentaries that magnify our efforts and issues, the social media hashtags that blow up our phones, these things show us a world outside of our own lived realities.

Within the stories that we tell are reflections of who we are and what we believe in during a particular time and place. They can project our fantasies of the world that we wish we could live in, just like those sitcoms and Westerns from the 1950s. However, increasingly it appears that our stories reflect what we fear about our world and perhaps provide subtextual tools to help us cope with what might be coming. For example, the Netflix series *Jessica Jones*, as described by Caroline Hovanec, suggests that the world can be a rather dark and traumatic place for women to exist in. Hovanec sees the series (and especially the character Jessica) through the lens of the noir aesthetic—it is dark, rough, and terrifying. Ultimately, Hovanec determines that injustice in the world is unending, yet we are obligated to help in instances in which it is revealed to us.

Meagan Thompson's essay provides the real-world perspective of the troubling and often dangerous encounters that women experience. Thompson examines the collective power of social media in the context of the growing #MeToo movement. Finding a visible and vocal community also means that people become willing to share their own stories, even if painful and difficult, in a move toward solidarity with an aim to make important social change.

Connectivity is necessary for people struggling through deeply rooted, often institutionalized, oppressions, and Alisha Menzies' analysis of Jordan Peele's *Get Out* examines the importance of shared community experience. Respectability politics are a crucial survival tactic for Black Americans, and the ability to codeswitch, especially in white dominated contexts, is key in navigating life. For the character of Chris, his employment of respectability politics while at the country home of his white girlfriend's family allows him to negotiate their increasingly bizarre behaviors. Menzies provides deft commentary about some of the realities for Black Americans, particularly Black men.

The character Chris in *Get Out* must eventually resort to violence in order to survive his ordeal. Violence is often understood as a necessary part of social resistance, and it is sometimes discussed as a moral grey area. Jason Buel and Kristi Kouchakji approach the subject of violence through the instance in which noted white supremacist Richard Spencer was punched—twice—during on camera interviews. The footage has lived a long life through satire, which sets the punches to music in memes, and these memes have opened conversations about the ethics of punching Nazis and the requisite intolerance of white supremacist ideologies. Satire is the focus of our last essay in this section about the film *The Death of Stalin*. Sabrina Mittermeier points out that although the film is set during 1953, its events mark strange and disconcerting parallels to recent history, specifically the Trump administration. The use of Stalinist Russia communicates the importance of understanding how those historic events, even those re-created or constructed, implicitly connect to contemporary times. For audiences watching the film, there's a distinct impression that there is a danger of repeating events if the populace is not actively creating a different trajectory.

Miles Bennell in *Invasion of the Body Snatchers* attempted to make the people around him aware of the dire situation. Journalists I.F. Stone and Edward R. Murrow also worked to inform the American public of the realities of the prejudice and discrimination facing people. Our authors in this section expertly point to media texts and recent historical examples that reveal the darker parts of contemporary life. In their own ways, each of the essays is an effort to expose significant social injustice and prompt a decisive call to action. Don't be next.

Works Cited

Hagopian, Jack. "Film Notes—Invasion of the Body Snatchers." *New York State Writers Institute*. 2019. www.albany.edu/writers-inst/webpages4/filmnotes/fnf03n6.html.

Invasion of the Body Snatchers. Directed by Don Siegel. Walter Wanger Productions, 1956.

Maltin, Leonard. "Leonard Maltin on Invasion of the Body Snatchers." *YouTube*, uploaded by American Film Institute. 05 Oct. 2009. www.youtube.com/watch?v=vDtFX4UINEM.

Mickelson, Sig. *The Decade That Shaped Television News: CBS in the 1950s*. Prager, 1998.

Murrow, Edward R. "Edward R. Murrow: 'A Report on Senator Joseph A. McCarthy.'" *YouTube*, uploaded by KD. 10 Nov. 2014. www.youtube.com/watch?v=-YOIueFbG4g.

Stone, I.F. *The Best of I.F. Stone*. Public Affairs, 2006.

"Television: Moving Image Section—Motion Picture, Broadcasting and Recorded Sound Division." *American Women: A Gateway to Library of Congress Resources for the Study of Women's History and Culture in the United States*, 18 June 2013. loc.gov/american-women-moving-image/television.

Jessica Jones, Film Noir and #MeToo

Caroline Hovanec

International Women's Day in 2018 made noise across the world, from rallies in New York and Los Angeles to strikes across Spain to protests in Manila and Delhi. In cities like Seoul, #MeToo was the watchword; at the Academy Awards the previous Sunday, "Time's Up" resounded among Hollywood stars fed up with their industry's sexism (Povoledo, Minder, and Joseph). Netflix observed International Women's Day by dropping season two of *Jessica Jones*, Marvel's noir-inspired series about a sharp-tongued, whiskey-swilling, female private eye with superpowers. The show's first season, three years earlier, had been hailed as a feminist triumph, and on the eve of the new season critics and headline editors alike had a common reaction. *NPR*: "'Jessica Jones' Returns, Her Rage Especially Resonant in the #MeToo Era" (Bianculli). *Variety*: "'Jessica Jones' Team on Genre Show's Timeliness, Being Ahead of the Curve on #MeToo" (Bitran). *Entertainment Weekly*: "Why Marvel's Jessica Jones is the Superhero for the #MeToo Movement" (Li). *The Daily Beast*: "'Jessica Jones' Is the #MeToo Superheroine We Need Right Now" (Madison).

The first season of the show (2015) focused on Jessica's reckoning with Kilgrave, a handsome, urbane, British, and chillingly evil villain with mind control powers. A year before the show begins, Kilgrave had controlled and raped Jessica in a vile simulation of a romance. When he returns, preying on an undergraduate track and field star named Hope Shlottman and ordering her to kill her parents, Jessica vows to take him down and defend Hope's innocence. Season two explores the mysterious origins of Jessica's superpowers; in one especially timely subplot, Jessica's best friend Trish Walker, a child star turned talk show host, confronts a film director who had offered her a role in exchange for sex when she was 15 years old.

It's easy to see the connection between these plotlines and #MeToo, the movement to speak out about sexual violence that took the world by storm in late 2017. Me Too originally started in 2007, when Tarana Burke, the founder of a nonprofit that helps survivors of sexual assault and harassment, coined the term as a shorthand for her movement (Garcia). As a social media phenomenon, the phrase began trending on Twitter in October 2017 when the actress Alyssa Milano tweeted, "If you've been sexually harassed or assaulted write 'me too' as a reply to this tweet" (@Alyssa_Milano). The accusations against Harvey Weinstein, the Miramax mogul who allegedly harassed and assaulted dozens of women in the film industry, had just been made public, and Milano and others wanted to show their support for his accusers (Garcia). Though both seasons of *Jessica Jones* were written before #MeToo became household words, the show's exploration of sexual violence, trauma, and survival seems especially acute in the #MeToo era.

Jessica Jones' feminist intervention in the conversation about sexual violence is entwined with its film noir aesthetic. The term "film noir" originally referred to a group of moody, pessimistic black-and-white American crime films produced in the 1940s and '50s. But as Ian Brookes explains, many critics now see noir as a cinematic style, a set of common themes, or even a mood, which extends beyond the original golden age of the '40s and '50s into the present (11–12). Noir style is recognizable by "low-key lighting, chiaroscuro effects of light and shade and unusual shadow patterns ... [and] distorted effects through devices such as canted camera angles (Dutch angles) or unconventional camera positions" (Brookes 35). Its mise-en-scène is likely to feature wet city streets, neon lights, and sketchy bars or hotels (Brookes 35). The film noir narrative typically features a private detective haunted by the ghosts of his past, a sultry and mysterious femme fatale, a deeply corrupt cast of criminals, and an unhappy or ambivalent ending (Brookes 35). Thematically, noir is obsessed with the specter of a "world too corrupt for [its protagonists] to change or even understand" (Alpers). And, as Wheeler W. Dixon discusses, the genre is also preoccupied with the inexorability of fate, its small characters overpowered by bigger forces (55).

Set in a seedy, shadowy New York City, *Jessica Jones* expertly deploys noir tropes: compromising photographs, broken glass, cynical loners. Most importantly, the show appropriates the paranoid mood of film noir and places it in a new context. Noir is known for putting its (anti)heroes in a fatalistic, corrupt world they cannot fully redeem. But in *Jessica Jones* it's the female survivor, rather than the traditional male P.I., who most vividly experiences and understands this corrupt world, and who finds her paranoia realized— someone really is out to get her. The near-omnipotent Kilgrave offers an eerily prescient representation of the powerful alleged serial predators, including Weinstein and Bill Cosby, whose victims were silenced, gaslighted, or blacklisted over the years. *Jessica Jones*, I argue, uses film noir elements to vindicate the "paranoia" of sexual assault survivors. This paranoia is in fact a knowledge about patriarchy that is just beginning to enter public consciousness.

What survivors know is that patriarchy, like other systemic cultural phenomena (capitalism, white supremacy), really does often operate in a conspiracist way. In the case of Weinstein, as Ronan Farrow has reported, the years-long cover-up involved the aid of many underlings, the use of covert intelligence-gathering firms, and (allegedly) pressure from NBC for Farrow to drop the story (Farrow, "Harvey Weinstein's Army of Spies"; Koblin). "Conspiracy theory" has traditionally been the province of men, male characters, and masculine fictional genres like the political thriller, as Sianne Ngai observes (298–299). She describes paranoia as a belief that one is caught in a large, powerful, impersonal system, and that even apparent coincidences are evidence of that system's workings; an example is Fox Mulder of *The X-Files*, a brilliant male detective who is uniquely capable of apprehending the shadowy machinations of government (298). But, Ngai argues, conspiracy theorizing and paranoia can also be useful for feminism, because feminists need an "abstract and holistic" concept like patriarchy to produce knowledge about how gender inequities work in our society (300–301). The #MeToo movement has produced new public knowledge about sexual harassment and assault by revealing that the hidden, "shameful" experiences of survivors are overwhelmingly common; *Jessica Jones*, meanwhile, uses noir elements to reveal that women's fear of powerful men is justified, not *merely* paranoid.

Jessica Jones firmly establishes its noir aesthetics in its opening scene. This scene, which finds Jessica performing her job as private investigator, features a wet blur of lights against a dark city night, indistinct views of illicit couples embracing, and a moody saxophone soundtrack, punctuated by the click of Jessica's camera and a pause for each photo she takes. In voiceover—a classic noir technique—Jessica establishes her cynical perspective on a sordid, corrupt world: "New York may be the city that never sleeps, but it sure does sleep around. Not that I'm complaining. Cheaters are good for business. A big part of the job is looking for the worst in people. Turns out I excel at that. Clients hire me to find dirt, and I find it" ("AKA Ladies Night"). Jessica's pessimistic view of humanity—that people are untrustworthy, sinful, fallen—is typical of noir, which, Dixon argues, is concerned with themes of "hopelessness, failure, deceit and betrayal" (1). And as viewers will gradually discover, it is an outlook shaped by Jessica's traumatic experience. Flashbacks to Jessica's life pre–Kilgrave will reveal that while she has always been sarcastic and a bit dark, she also once believed in heroism; after Kilgrave, she no longer does.

Next, the opening scene cuts to the hallway outside Jessica's office, and to a moment that is, as Aleah Kiley and Zak Roman have noted, straight out of *Chinatown* (1974) (47). The moment is borrowed from the neo-noir film via the *Alias* comic books on which the Netflix series is based. As in *Chinatown*, it portrays the confirmation—in glossy full-page photos—that a client's wife is cheating on him, as well as the client's horrified reaction to having his worst fears substantiated.

Equally important, though, is how this opening scene *differs* from *Chinatown*; Jake Gittes, the P.I. protagonist of the 1974 film, aims to establish a fraternal rapport with his devastated client, offering him a glass of whiskey and uttering the famous line, "What can I say, kid? When you're right, you're right, and you're right." Jessica's client, in contrast, chooses to "blame the messenger," and Jessica offers no sympathy, throwing him through her glass door when he gets out of hand. A high-angle shot displays shards of glass and photos fluttering to the ground, before Jessica peers down at the client through the broken window, declaring, "And then there's the matter of your bill" ("AKA Ladies Night"). The scene establishes Jessica's super-strength, but more importantly, it also shows that the kind of easy-going masculine bond Gittes can establish with clients is not available to Jessica. As a woman P.I., she has to be twice as tough, twice as strong, and twice as impersonal. Gittes can afford to be charming and convivial, but Jessica drinks alone.

This revision of *Chinatown*'s opening scene foreshadows the way that *Jessica Jones* revises noir more generally. Traditionally, film noir centers on a male P.I., a figure disillusioned with the official justice system, and a *femme fatale*, an alluring mystery woman who tempts him from the righteous path (Kaplan 2–3). The question of how *Jessica Jones'* gender swap intervenes in film noir is a matter of some debate. Brian Fuller and Emily D. Edwards interpret the show as concerned with the typical dilemmas of film noir—especially determinism, as emblematized by Kilgrave's mind control, versus individual agency, as emblematized by Jessica. Daniel Binns, on the other hand, argues that Jessica is best understood as a P.I. who herself becomes a *femme fatale*, using her sexuality to destroy Kilgrave (23–25). While Binns offers evidence for his reading, it's also important to realize that the creators did not intend Jessica's character to be a *femme fatale*. As showrunner Melissa Rosenberg declared, "if you look at any female cop character or detective they always end up in a bandage dress playing the honeypot—in high heels trying to lure the suspect in. We started off by saying 'I'm not doing the honeypot.' I will never do the honeypot" (qtd. in Dekel). By focusing on a female P.I. rather than a *femme fatale*, *Jessica Jones* takes the traditional paranoia of film noir—the sense that the protagonist is caught in a web he is only beginning to understand—and turns it into a specifically female paranoia, oriented around the threat of sexual violence and the machinations of powerful, corrupt men, which Jessica seeks to expose.

Kilgrave's "mind control" power is really a power to speak and make things so. He tells a person to do something, and they are compelled to do it. It is a power that renders familiar safeguards—security teams, police officers, guns, deadbolts, trusting only those you know—useless. Jessica understands this, which is why her response to discovering that Kilgrave is still alive is an intensified paranoia. When her estranged friend Trish asks Jessica to move into her apartment to hide from Kilgrave, Jessica is quick to disabuse her of this illusion of safety:

> TRISH: I have a security system, a doorman, I have an actual lock on my door—
> JESSICA: You think I'll be safe there? I'm not safe anywhere. Every corner I turn, I don't know what's on the other side. I don't know who's on the other side. It could be the cabbie who's gonna drive me into the East River, okay? It could be the FedEx woman. It could be a talk show host who was my best friend ["AKA Ladies Night"].

Jessica's paranoia is soon vindicated: Kilgrave really is out to get her, not to drown her in the East River but to "win her back" as a sexual partner.

Like many violent men in the real world, Kilgrave's crimes reflect his frustrated sense of sexual entitlement. Gender studies scholar Jamilla Rosdahl points out that Elliot Rodger, the UC Santa Barbara killer motivated by romantic rejection, frequently expressed anger at women for not desiring him: "he made numerous references to his expensive taste, glasses, clothes and car. He couldn't understand why these powerful attributes weren't appealing to girls." In the cases of Rodger and of Alek Minassian, the "incel" (involuntary celibate) who, inspired by Rodger, killed 10 people in Toronto in 2018, the abstract, intangible ideology of masculinity produces real, material violence (Gismondi). Kilgrave's polished appearance, obsession with Jessica, and brutality connect him to Rodger and Minassian. As with these "incels," Kilgrave lashes out violently when he is denied the sexual attention he feels entitled to.

The show's portrayal of male power may seem overdramatic—after all, mind control doesn't really exist—except that powerful men really do have an array of techniques at their disposal to control and silence their victims: traditional male privilege, authority over hiring and firing, expensive settlements, nondisclosure agreements, prestigious lawyers, a rumor mill to discredit any victim with the temerity to speak out. In the wake of the #MeToo movement, there are too many examples here to name, but the most relevant is Harvey Weinstein. Jodi Kantor and Megan Twohey report that, to the public, Weinstein appeared to be "a liberal lion, a champion of women and a winner of not just artistic but humanitarian awards." Behind the scenes, however, he allegedly sexually harassed and assaulted women in the film industry routinely for decades, before being forced out in late 2017 and arrested in May 2018. Ronan Farrow describes the producer's treatment of women as "an open secret" among Hollywood insiders. Farrow's sources say that Weinstein's victims and abettors were afraid of him, believing that he would "crush" them, destroying their careers and reputations, if they failed to comply with his demands ("From Aggressive Overtures").

One victim, Lucia Evans, told Farrow that years after Weinstein assaulted her, she saw him again while walking in Greenwich Village. "I remember getting chills down my spine just looking at him. I was so horrified. I have nightmares about him to this day," she said (qtd. in Farrow, "From Aggressive Overtures"). Her words testify to the enduring effects of trauma on survivors, especially the fear that can bubble up even in ostensibly safe places, like a crowded street, when they are reminded of their abusers.

Jessica Jones represents these effects of trauma, as critics including Melissa Wehler have explored, through the use of flashbacks. Flashbacks, Wehler argues, are a cinematic technique to represent the subjective experience of post-traumatic stress disorder (PTSD). They are also a staple of film noir, where they signal the irreversibility of the past and conjure a sense of fatalism (Pippin 38–39). In *Jessica Jones*, flashbacks gradually uncover Jessica's history with Kilgrave. Upon realizing, in the pilot, that Kilgrave is reenacting his relationship with Jessica through Hope, Jessica turns pale and dizzy; she runs outside and begins running down the street, muttering to herself "Birch Street. Higgins Drive," a calming mantra she has been taught by a therapist. The cinematography of this scene, which includes a handheld camera, rapid panning, and a lowered frame rate to achieve a choppy, blurry effect, aims to capture Jessica's subjective experience of PTSD, which can turn even an ordinary street in broad daylight into a waking nightmare.

Though Kilgrave is more of a lone operator than Weinstein was, he routinely uses his powers on bystanders to get at Jessica, creating a far-reaching web of power while concealing himself. In this regard, he can be seen as an *homme fatale*, a male equivalent of the "spider women" who entrap the heroes in typical noir films. The moment that Jessica realizes his web's true extent draws heavily on the techniques and mood of noir. Tracking down Kilgrave to his hideout at the end of episode three, Jessica descends two staircases and fights off a series of goons to discover, deep in the heart of the apartment, a dark purple room covered from floor to ceiling with full-page photos of herself, taken all over New York without her knowledge. Jessica circles the room as, in its center, a printer continues to produce more photos, culminating with one that reads, on the bottom, "SEE YOU LATER." The pictures are physical evidence of Kilgrave's obsession; they also echo Jessica's own use of photography as a private investigator. The surveiller recognizes, in a deeply uncanny moment, that she herself is the target of surveillance. In the next episode, Jessica discovers that Kilgrave has manipulated her neighbor Malcolm into following her and taking these photos, confirming her fear from the pilot that with Kilgrave on the loose, she cannot trust anyone ("AKA It's Called Whiskey").

Again, Kilgrave's omnipotence might seem unrealistic, merely the stuff of superhero fiction, except that, as Farrow's article "Harvey Weinstein's Army of Spies" demonstrates, alleged predators like Weinstein really do exercise a startlingly similar network of power. As Farrow reports, Weinstein hired the intelligence firms Kroll and Black Cube to dig up dirt on his accusers and the journalists working to expose him. One investigator befriended Rose McGowan, using a false name and pretending to be a women's advocate from an investment firm. Other operatives created extensive and personal dossiers on McGowan, Rosanna Arquette, and even the New York–based journalist Ben Wallace, searching for information that might discredit them. Farrow closes his article by quoting McGowan, who directly compares her experience to a noir film: "It was like the movie 'Gaslight'.... Everyone lied to me all the time.... I've lived inside a mirrored fun house" ("Harvey Weinstein's Army of Spies").

Against these forces sowing skepticism and suspicion, *Jessica Jones* emphasizes the importance of believing victims, as critics including Valerie Estelle Frankel have pointed out. The public may disbelieve Hope and Jessica's accounts of a villain whose words compel obedience, but viewers never doubt for a second. Making Hope and Jessica authoritative sources of knowledge about Kilgrave seems even more important in retrospect, in the wake of the Brett Kavanaugh Supreme Court hearings in September 2018. Professor Christine Blasey Ford testified that Kavanaugh had attempted to rape her in 1982. For Congress and for much of the nation, her word was simply not believable—she was accused of being a liar, a partisan saboteur, or, in Orrin Hatch's view, simply "mistaken" about what had happened all those years ago (Burr). Kavanaugh's confirmation represented a serious blow to the #MeToo ethos of believing women, revealing that for large swathes of the American population, women like Ford are diabolical or hysterical *femmes fatale*, not reliable authorities on their own experience.

In this climate, *Jessica Jones* affirms women's testimony about sexual assault. Further, the show vindicates female paranoia, recognizing it as not just justified, but also a form of knowledge about a patriarchal world. The detective has long been a figure of knowledge production or discovery, from Conan Doyle's Sherlock Holmes to Christie's Hercule Poirot to *Law and Order: SVU*'s Olivia Benson. But Jessica's epistemological work—to find, understand, and expose Kilgrave, and to clear Hope's name—is inflected by both her P.I. skillset and her experience as a survivor of sexual violence. Together these afford her a knowledge about Kilgrave that manifests as paranoia. Likewise, long before Farrow, Kantor, and Twohey made Weinstein's alleged abuses public knowledge, his victims knew something about how Hollywood works, and more broadly, about how patriarchy works, that defied common sense but was nevertheless true. They knew that, beneath the surface narrative of Hollywood progressivism lies an underbelly not just of abusers, but of people who enable and cover up for abuse, making it difficult or impossible for victims to get justice for even the most harrowing of violations.

For Jessica, "justice" would mean not just killing Kilgrave, but exposing his crimes and establishing Hope's (and, implicitly, her own) innocence. One of the show's most compelling moments in this regard occurs in episode eight. At this point, Kilgrave has purchased Jessica's childhood home and outfitted it to look exactly as it did when she was young—an act that, like his surveillance of Jessica, reveals his obsession with her, and a violation of her coping mechanism of naming the streets near her old house to quell PTSD symptoms. Jessica has agreed to move back to the house with Kilgrave to prevent him from hurting any more innocents (and to carry out a secret plan to get him to confess on tape, so that Hope can be acquitted). The plotline speaks to a common issue that victims of sexual and domestic violence face: if they do anything that appears, to outsiders, like they are going along with their abuser, then many people will doubt their testimony. Indeed, Weinstein and his operatives, according to Farrow, believed that they could use photos of McGowan hanging out with Weinstein and smiling to convince the public that her allegations against him were untrue ("Harvey Weinstein's Army of Spies").

Though Jessica is living with Kilgrave, and thus might appear to be consenting to a relationship, she is still disgusted by him. When he attempts to take her hand, she jerks away.

> KILGRAVE: We used to do a lot more than just touch hands.
> JESSICA: Yeah. It's called rape.
> KILGRAVE: What? Which part of staying in five-star hotels, eating in all the best places, doing whatever the hell you wanted is rape?
> JESSICA: The part where I didn't want to do any of it! Not only did you physically rape me, but you violated every cell in my body and every thought in my goddamn head ["AKA WWJD?"].

This is a moment that many critics have identified as crucial to the show's critique of rape culture. As Kiley and Roman argue, "By directly naming her experience as rape, she shifts the assault of mind control from the symbolic realm into the real world experience of gender violence. Jessica's refusal to back down from naming her experience is a pointed moment of resistance and agency in the show" (55). Calling rape rape, instead of veiling it in a fog of euphemisms and "he-said-she-said," is rightly seen as a major achievement of the show, especially considering, as Melissa C. Johnson points out, that its source material, the *Alias* comics, demurs on this issue—Jessica specifically does not describe her experience as rape there (Bendis and Gaydos).

By labeling Kilgrave as a rapist, the scene testifies to a "faith in exposure" (Sedgwick 130). Cultural criticism has often operated in a paranoid mode, looking to diagnose why books, films, and shows are "problematic." In recent years, though, some critics (most notably Rita Felski) have begun to doubt that exposing problems is really a useful way of mitigating them. As Eve Kosofsky Sedgwick points out, the paranoiac or paranoid critic believes that the exposure of hidden evils is itself the goal (130). But "while there is plenty of hidden violence that requires exposure there is also, and increasingly, an ethos where forms of violence that are hypervisible from the start may be offered as an exemplary spectacle rather than remain to be unveiled as a scandalous secret" (Sedgwick 140). Sedgwick made this point in 2003, but it seems even more relevant today under a U.S. regime led by a president who has bragged about "grab[bing] women by the pussy" and openly flirted with white supremacist groups. There's nothing hidden about those forms of sexism and racism; they are a public spectacle. Nevertheless, the accomplishments of #MeToo and related movements suggest that mainstream American culture is witnessing a major feminist reckoning with the power of exposure to combat sexual violence. Bill Cosby has been convicted; Weinstein has been convicted; a number of other accused predators have lost their jobs. Exposure is not itself justice, and it is no guarantee of justice, but it has brought a measure of reckoning, however delayed and partial, to many survivors.

In the final scene of *Jessica Jones* season one, Jessica sits at her desk with a bottle of whiskey, listening to and deleting a series of voicemails from would-be clients. People are still in trouble; women are still in danger; domestic violence is still common. It's still Chinatown out there. It's a pessimistic ending typical of late noir; eliminating Kilgrave has not redeemed the corrupt world. But then Jessica's friend Malcolm answers her phone: "Alias Investigations. How can we help?" ("AKA Smile"). Knowing about patriarchy and sexual violence is not easy, and it clearly weighs heavily on Jessica. But for her, for viewers, and for those participating in the #MeToo movement, it's a life-changing knowledge. Once you see the conspiracy, you see it everywhere, you can't unsee it, and you're obligated to help.

WORKS CITED

"AKA It's Called Whiskey." *Jessica Jones*, season 1, episode 3, *Netflix*, 20 Nov. 2015.
"AKA Ladies Night." *Jessica Jones*, season 1, episode 1, *Netflix*, 20 Nov. 2015.
"AKA Smile." *Jessica Jones*, season 1, episode 13, *Netflix*, 20 Nov. 2015.
"AKA WWJD?" *Jessica Jones*, season 1, episode 8, *Netflix*, 20 Nov. 2015.
Alpers, Ben. "Jessica Jones and the Film Noir P.I." *Society for U.S. Intellectual History Blog*, 5 05 Dec. 2015, s-usih.org/2015/12/jessica-jones-and-the-film-noir-p-i/.
@Alyssa_Milano [Alyssa Milano]. "If you've been sexually harassed or assaulted write 'me too' as a reply to this tweet." *Twitter*, 15 Oct. 2015, 1:21 p.m. twitter.com/alyssa_milano/status/919659438700670976?lang=en.
Bendis, Brian Michael and Michael Gaydos. *Jessica Jones: Alias*, vol. 4, no. 25, Marvel, 2016.

Bianculli, David. "'Jessica Jones' Returns, Her Rage Especially Resonant in the #MeToo Era." *NPR*, 08Mar. 2018, https://www.npr.org/2018/03/08/591889803/jessica-jones-returns-her-rage-especially-resonant-in-the-metoo-era.

Binns, Daniel. "'Even You Can Break': Jessica Jones as Femme Fatale." *Jessica Jones, Scarred Superhero*, edited by Tim Rayborn and Abigail Keyes, McFarland, 2018, pp. 13–27.

Bitran, Tara. "'Jessica Jones' Team on Genre Show's Timeliness, Being Ahead of the Curve on #MeToo." *Variety*, 20 May 2018, variety.com/2018/tv/news/jessica-jones-netflix-marvel-me-too-1202816973/.

Brookes, Ian. *Film Noir: A Critical Introduction*. Bloomsbury, 2017.

Burr, Thomas. "Sen. Hatch Says Christine Blasey Ford Is 'Mistaken' in Accusing Supreme Court Nominee Brett Kavanaugh of Assault." *Salt Lake Tribune*, 17 Sept. 2018, www.sltrib.com/news/politics/2018/09/17/sen-hatch-says-christine/.

Chicago Tribune Staff and KT Hawbaker. "#MeToo: A Timeline of Events." *Chicago Tribune*, 23 Jan. 2019, www.chicagotribune.com/lifestyles/ct-me-too-timeline-20171208-html story.html.

Chinatown. Directed by Roman Polanski, Paramount Pictures, 1974.

Dekel, Jon. "How Marvel's Jessica Jones Pairs Feminism with Superhero Noir." *National Post*, 20 Nov. 2015, nationalpost.com/entertainment/television/how-marvels-jessica-jones-pairs-feminism-with-superhero-noir.

Dixon, Wheeler Winston. *Film Noir and the Cinema of Paranoia*. Rutgers University Press, 2009.

Farrow, Ronan. "From Aggressive Overtures to Sexual Assault: Harvey Weinstein's Accusers Tell Their Stories." *The New Yorker*, 10 Oct. 2017, www.newyorker.com/news/news-desk/from-aggressive-overtures-to-sexual-assault-harvey-weinsteins-accusers-tell-their-stories.

_____. "Harvey Weinstein's Army of Spies." *The New Yorker*, 6 Nov. 2017, www.newyorker.com/news/news-desk/harvey-weinsteins-army-of-spies.

Felski, Rita. *The Limits of Critique*. University of Chicago Press, 2015.

Frankel, Valerie Estelle. "Battling Bluebeard, Fighting for Hope: The Heroine's Journey." *Jessica Jones, Scarred Superhero*, edited by Tim Rayborn and Abigail Keyes, McFarland, 2018, pp. 203–220.

Fuller, Brian, and Emily D. Edwards. "Integrity, Family and Consent: The Ontological Angst of *Jessica Jones*." *Jessica Jones, Scarred Superhero*, edited by Tim Rayborn and Abigail Keyes, McFarland, 2018, pp. 161–188.

Garcia, Sandra E. "The Woman Who Created #MeToo Long Before Hashtags," *The New York Times*, 20 Oct. 2017, www.nytimes.com/2017/10/20/us/me-too-movement-tarana-burke.html.

Gismondi, Melissa J. "Why Are 'Incels' So Angry? The History of the Little-Known Ideology Behind the Toronto Attack." *Washington Post*, 27 Apr. 2018, www.washingtonpost.com/news/made-by-history/wp/2018/04/27/why-are-incels-so-angry-the-history-of-the-little-known-ideology-behind-the-toronto-attack/.

Johnson, Melissa C. "*Jessica Jones*' Feminism: AKA *Alias* Gets a Fixed-It." *Jessica Jones, Scarred Superhero*, edited by Tim Rayborn and Abigail Keyes, McFarland, 2018, pp. 133–144.

Kantor, Jodi, and Megan Twohey. "Harvey Weinstein Paid Off Sexual Harassment Accusers for Decades." *The New York Times*, 5 Oct. 2017, www.nytimes.com/2017/10/05/us/harvey-weinstein-harassment-allegations.html.

Kaplan, E. Ann. "Introduction." *Women in Film Noir*, edited by E. Ann Kaplan, British Film Institute, 1980, pp. 1–15.

Kiley, Aleah, and Zak Roman. "'AKA Occasionally I Give a Damn': Mirrored Archetypes and Gender Power in *Jessica Jones*." *Jessica Jones, Scarred Superhero*, edited by Tim Rayborn and Abigail Keyes, McFarland, 2018, pp. 44–63.

Koblin, John. "How NBC and Ronan Farrow Ended Up in a Feud Over Weinstein." *The New York Times*, 4 Sept. 2018, www.nytimes.com/2018/09/04/business/media/nbc-ronan-farrow-harvey-weinstein.html.

Li, Shirley. "Why Marvel's Jessica Jones Is the Superhero for the #MeToo Movement." *Entertainment Weekly*, 7 Mar. 2018, ew.com/tv/2018/03/07/marvel-jessica-jones-season-2-feature-metoo/.

Madison, Ira. "'Jessica Jones' Is the #MeToo Superheroine We Need Right Now." *The Daily Beast*, 8 Mar. 2018, www.thedailybeast.com/jessica-jones-is-the-metoo-superheroine-we-need-right-now.

Ngai, Sianne. *Ugly Feelings*. Harvard University Press, 2005.

Pippin, Robert B. *Fatalism in American Film Noir: Some Cinematic Philosophy*. University of Virginia Press, 2012.

Poveledo, Elisabetta, Raphael Minder, and Yonette Joseph. "International Women's Day 2018: Beyond #MeToo, with Pride, Protests, and Pressure." *New York Times*, 8 Mar. 2018, www.nytimes.com/2018/03/08/world/international-womens-day-2018.html.

Rosdahl, Jamilla. "Elliot Rodger: When Sexual Rejection Turns Deadly." *The Conversation*, 27 May 2014, theconversation.com/elliot-rodger-when-sexual-rejection-turns-deadly-27205.

Sedgwick, Eve Kosofsky. "Paranoid Reading and Reparative Reading, or, You're So Paranoid, You Probably Think This Essay Is About You." *Touching Feeling: Affect, Pedagogy, Performativity*, by Eve Kosofsky Sedgwick, Duke University Press, 2003, pp. 123–151.

Wehler, Melissa. "The Haunted Hero: The Performance of Trauma in *Jessica Jones*." *Jessica Jones, Scarred Superhero*, edited by Tim Rayborn and Abigail Keyes, McFarland, 2018, pp. 145–160.

Digital Activism and Storytelling

Exploring the Radical Potential
of the #MeToo Movement

MEAGAN THOMPSON

On October 15, 2017, actress Alyssa Milano tweeted, "If you've been sexually harassed or assaulted write 'me too' as a reply to this tweet," along with an image of her own addition, "Me too." Milano's tweet specifically responded to the ever-growing allegations against Hollywood producer Harvey Weinstein; a way to show the world the staggering number of women who face the realities of sexual violence every day. I tweeted the words "me too" upon seeing the post, remembering occurrences of gendered and sexual harassment I experienced, from being catcalled on the street to being groped in a crowded room. I watched as my Facebook, Instagram, and Twitter feeds were flooded with #MeToo statuses, posts, and images. Some were just the hashtag, like mine, a phrase of solidarity and witnessing. Others posted longer testimonials, accounting their stories ranging from workplace sexual harassment to violent sexual assault. I had never seen so many of my family and friends engaging with the same viral hashtag movement, across so many different populations. There was no discrepancy among age, race, ethnicity, sexual orientation, or geographic location. The women of my life were coming together to say that they, too, had experienced sexual harassment and assault.

Within hours, it was clear that not just my family, friends, and coworkers were engaging with the hashtag. According to the Associated Press, there were more than 12 million "Me Too" posts on Facebook alone within the first 24 hours of Milano's tweet. Social media analytics firm, Crimson Hexagon, reports hundreds of thousands of tweets with #MeToo each month since

October 2017. The PEORIA Project at George Washington University also collected data to study the number of "conversations" surrounding sexual harassment and assault taking place on Twitter and noticed a huge uptick after Milano's October 2017 tweet (Olheiser). Michael Cohen, chief data scientist for the PEORIA Project, noted that what is even more striking about this Twitter "moment" is its sustainability, putting it on par with other social media movements like #BlackLivesMatter (Olheiser). Like Black Lives Matter, #MeToo is a chance for people who have been violated, oppressed, and silenced to use their voices, tell their stories, assert their humanity, and find ways of healing through community and collectivity—mediated through digital spaces. As a performance mode, storytelling builds community as it negotiates power relations and the daily navigation of trauma faced by marginalized populations; when storytelling happens on social media platforms that are widely accessible, it allows for more populations to participate in the conversation. However, it must be recognized that some stories are often deemed more valuable or believable based on race, gender, sexual orientation, socioeconomic class, ability, and other identity factors. For this reason, it is the responsibility of those with more privilege to uplift the voices and stories of those most marginalized, so that all populations can experience the potential for restorative justice and healing.

The #MeToo movement is the embodiment of the 1970s feminist slogan, "the personal is political." As a hashtag movement, it is the modern-day enactment of the belief that lived experience is valid, and personal stories can inspire political action. Originally founded in 2006 by Tarana Burke, the organization "me too" is a call for "empathy through empowerment" which seeks to support and raise the voices of survivors of sexual assault and violence ("Me Too"). Their mission is "to uplift radical community healing as a social justice issue" ("Me Too"). The hashtag exists as an extension of a social movement grounded in real-world experiences and is connected to a grassroots collective fighting for justice from continuous every day and institutionalized oppression and trauma. The ways in which #MeToo foregrounds attention to community as a form of restorative justice and healing from legacies of trauma are representative of digital activism's potential to construct collective identities, rooted in protest, through social media and expressive communication (Gerbaudo and Treré 866). It is especially representative of the power of expressive communication and digital storytelling as its digital presence is predicated on inviting survivors of sexual harassment and assault to share their stories on social media.

While #MeToo stories and posts are shared on multiple social media platforms, the hashtag has the most engagement on Twitter, the site where #MeToo was born. Twitter is arguably one of the 21st century's most democratic platforms for storytelling, and its ease of access and mission to share information with a wide audience makes it one of the most popular social media platforms in the world. Social activists have turned Twitter into a space for digital activism, where they can share meaningful stories of trauma and pain, but also of hope and possibility, as a performance of activism. In his book, *The New Digital Storytelling: Creating Narratives with New Media*, Bryan Alexander suggests that many view Twitter as an unlikely source for meaningful storytelling because of its branding. Their logo is a cute blue bird, and "tweeting" is a somewhat silly name for sharing information. However, Twitter users have seen past what Alexander calls the platform's "self-abnegation" to find a vehicle for open-access, user-driven storytelling (61). With the use of hashtags, pioneered by Twitter as a means of categorizing topics, activists can "tag" their tweets to be part of an automatically curated conversation about specific events or concerns. Digital activists use hashtags as a tool to collect stories about social justice issues, often collecting large numbers of tweets and going viral in the process.

The #MeToo movement follows in the legacy of cyberfeminism, first defined by Sadie Plant in the 1990s as the mode of feminist discourse and practice that exploits existing information technologies to subvert dominant power structures (Luckman). Now often seen in the form of "hashtag feminism," much in part because of the rise of democratized technologies like Twitter, feminists across the world can collect and protest against sexist, misogynistic, and oppressive systems. These feminist hashtags—viral sensations spreading across social media platforms—allow women to share their experiences with everyday sexism, violent assaults, and the realities of living with a marginalized identity. Over the past decade, we have seen such movements as #YesAllWomen, #YouOKSis, #WhyIStayed, and #SayHerName, all representative of a history which privileges personal experience and storytelling as viable political practice, a view long espoused by feminist, queer, and critical race theorists. Professor of women's and gender studies Catherine Fosl reminds us that "marginalized groups have historically looked often to their personal experience as the basis for larger social claims," citing African American literature's roots in slave narratives and feminist theory's foundation in women's autobiographies (220). E. Patrick Johnson asserts that storytelling is a quotidian form of self-fashioning, and personal narratives testify to the power of voice, self-determination, and tenacity in overcoming oppressive and traumatic realities ("The Beekeeper"). He writes, "The politics of resistance is manifest in vernacular traditions such as performance, folklore, literature, and verbal art" ("'Quare' Studies" 127). Participating in viral feminist hashtags is a contemporary tradition that places one within a larger cultural context and conversation, a way of claiming one's agency through language.

It is worth noting that hashtag feminism as a form of protest has been criticized as "slacktivism" because it is seen as a removed way to perform activism without facing real-world consequences. However, these objections deny the complexities of political action and the forms it can take. Protest and political action are not just marching in the streets and calling one's senators to vocalize dissent. Participating in digital activism in the form of hashtags works to build community and raise awareness, often acting as the catalyst for further political action. As such, the act of storytelling is often only a first step, as activism cannot stop at raising awareness, but it is a vital form of participating in social and political change. In their work on the viability and validity of personal narratives to stoke and enact political change, Catherine Fosl and Veronica Barassi focus on oral stories, either in-person or digitally recorded speeches delivered to a large audience. These stories, Fosl argues, engage "the performative aspects of personal narratives to instigate social and political action, specifically as they establish intimacy and physical presence with the listener" (Fosl 221–222). The majority of the #MeToo posts are written narratives, and short ones at that. Even longer Facebook posts or Twitter threads confine storytellers to a limited and restricted space. What matters in these stories, then, is not the length, or even the "quality" of the post. The rhetorical moves of the writer are not necessarily judged, nor are extensive details even required for a "successful" #MeToo post. The posts are powerful because they are the stories of a population typically silenced, ignored, questioned, and doubted, finally being told. Many of those who shared their stories using the hashtag expressed relief and determination in no longer keeping the stories to themselves. Brianne Hendricks shared on Twitter, "I was a child too scared to speak. Though the anxiety and blame still haunt me, I am no longer that child. I will not be silent. #MeToo."

As more and more #MeToo posts are shared, they build a collective narrative that speaks to the prevalence of rape culture, defined by Emilie Buchwald, Pamela R. Fletcher, and Martha Roth in *Transforming a Rape Culture* as "a complex set of beliefs that encourage male sexual aggression and supports violence against women. [...] In a rape culture both men and women assume that sexual violence is a fact of life, inevitable" (1). One #MeToo tweet says of rape culture, "I am not sure I know a woman who has not been assaulted or raped, groped, molested, harassed, or threatened. #MeToo" (@rensaysthings). The sheer number of #MeToo posts within the first day of the hashtag's appearance certainly speaks to this sentiment. The success of #MeToo is not only in a single poster's story, then, but the sheer quantity of total posts, shared across generations and locations. The single user's sharing of the hashtag counts toward a collective story, where one story by one poster becomes a drop in the bucket, one of hundreds, one of thousands, one of millions, across social media platforms. With this collective story comes a community of survivors, where solace can be found. Paula tweeted, "Best

Thing: Finding out we are not alone and have all dealt with this / Worst Thing: Finding out we have all dealt with this #MeToo." Other users shared notes of solidarity, like Shannon Taylor's tweet that has more than 4,600 favorites: "It's been 5 years since I have been raped. To fellow survivors: / You will / -Trust again / -Love again / -Feel safe again / -Be you again #MeToo." These tweets encapsulate the heart of #MeToo, survivors recognizing themselves in each other, sharing messages of solidarity and hope in the face of trauma.

However, we cannot deny the sometimes paradoxical, and dangerous, realities of utilizing technologies to speak out against sexual violence when said technologies are rampant with unchecked harassment, particularly against people of marginalized gendered and racialized identities. In a 2017 study conducted by Pew Internet Research Center, more than 40 percent of adult internet users reported being harassed or abused online, to include being called offensive names, threatened, stalked, and/or assaulted. Within that group, women were twice as likely to experience severe forms of harassment. Additionally, African American and Latinx[1] internet users were about 20 percent more likely to experience harassment than white internet users (Duggan). This gender, racial, and ethnic disparity in who is affected by online harassment and abuse makes Twitter a seemingly unlikely place for such minority populations to safely express their negotiations with daily and institutional traumas and oppression, or to use it as a viable platform from which to launch, grow, or participate in social activist movements. For this reason, I read Twitter as a site of struggle, alluding to Black Feminist Patricia Hill Collins' theory of the dialectic of oppression and activism, where art, criticism, and activism are sites of struggle that also function as tools to resist that struggle. In her work, she describes this dialectic as "the tension between the suppression of African-American women's ideas and [their] intellectual activism in the face of that suppression" (3). As a white woman, I take up Hill's words with caution, but I suggest this dialectic of oppression and activism can be read into #MeToo because the original movement's vision was, and continues to be, a platform for, particularly, "young women of color from low wealth communities" to find restorative justice through community ("MeToo"). Further, those most affected by harassment, both online and off, are people of color.

Tension does exist between Burke's intentions for the movement and who has the most visibility within the #MeToo movement. A significant part of rape culture is the prevailing image of the "perfect victim," typically a white cisgender woman who is violently attacked by a stranger. Sexual violence and its victims are, of course, much more nuanced than this. *Huffington Post* reported that 64 percent of transgender people will experience sexual assault in their lifetime, and trans people of color are 1.8 times more likely to be sexually assaulted than the general population. Further, 70 percent of assaults are committed by people the victim knows (Vagiano). Despite these statistics, the societal perception of "real victimhood" is skewed, often resulting in most victims being doubted and further harassed for speaking out about their assault. In September 2018, Dr. Christine Blasey Ford told her #MeToo story, accusing Brett Kavanaugh, Supreme Court nominee, of sexual assault. Blasey Ford's lawyers wrote in an open letter to Senate Judiciary Committee chairman Senator Chuck Grassley that, while she had received a tremendous amount of support, Blasey Ford "has been the target of vicious harassment and even death threats. As a result of these kind [*sic*] of threats, her family was forced to relocate out of their home. Her email has been hacked, and she has been impersonated online" (Abramson). In June 2019, E. Jean Carroll accused President Donald Trump of sexually assaulting her in 1996. This news was reported by the *New York Times* not on the front page, but in the Books section, as Carroll made this accusation for the first time in her forthcoming memoir. Carroll's accusation was originally treated as a publicity stunt, and Trump belittled the rape accusation by stating, "She's not my type" (D'Antonio).

Blasey Ford and Carroll, who are white cisgender women with relative social and economic privilege as a professor and journalist, respectively, have been leveled with vitriolic harassment, doubt, and even mocking jokes. If these women are not exempt from harassment and disparagement when accusing someone of sexual assault, then it is to be expected that people with less social and economic privilege will not be free from it either. For this reason, some have spoken about the challenges of launching a campaign protesting harassment against women on a site where women—particularly women of color—were regularly harassed, especially when the women at the forefront of the #MeToo movement at the conception of the hashtag were wealthy white women. There was similar backlash against the predecessor to #MeToo, #WomenBoycottTwitter, a collective response to actress Rose McGowan's temporary suspension from Twitter when she included a phone number in a string of tweets responding to allegations against Weinstein (Bowles and Buckley). This boycott, which many white feminist allies participated in on October 13, 2017, was purportedly "in protest of women's voices being silenced," according to the movement's shared infographic. This protest, and its participants, largely ignored similar harassment and suspension issues when they were reported by women of color. April Reign, the organizer of the viral #OscarsSoWhite, commented, "White women have not been as supportive as they could have been of women of color when they experience targeted abuse and harassment" (Garcia). When, two days later, Milano launched the #MeToo movement, she and her fellow #MeToo tweeters faced similar criticism, particularly because the name (and its purpose) was created by

Tarana Burke, a woman of color, for marginalized communities facing sexual harassment and assault.

Shortly after Milano's original "me too" tweet, Burke addressed her worries about this co-optation of her movement, which had gone unrecognized by mainstream media until Hollywood's involvement (Garcia). Burke told the *New York Times*, "I felt a sense of dread, because something that was part of my life's work was going to be co-opted and taken from me and used for a purpose that I hadn't originally intended." Even after Milano credited Burke in a *Good Morning America* interview, the mainstream representation of #MeToo continued to focus mainly on white women. When *Time* magazine named the "Silence Breakers" as the 2017 Person of the Year as a nod to those speaking out using this hashtag, Burke was not featured on the cover. In a released statement following *Time*'s announcement, Burke asked us to remember and support our most vulnerable communities and those most likely to be victims of sexual violence: women, people of color, indigenous people, trans and queer folks, those in low wealth communities, and any intersection thereof. A year later, especially with Burke's involvement, the official organization continues to speak out for these communities. We have also seen some corporations begin to participate in these conversations as they piggy-back onto the #MeToo movement, such as Twitter itself and its #HereWeAre campaign, which Twitter highlighted in a commercial that aired during 2018 Academy Awards, capitalizing on the social and political movement started by the success of #MeToo.

The commercial featured Denice Frohman performing her poem *#SheInspiresMe*. In the ad, a diverse group of women pose in front of the camera in black-and-white moving and static clips. Their images are overlaid with the poem's words, flashing across the screen at varying speeds. Frohman celebrates powerful women, rejoicing in their voices, their bravery, their audacity: "i heard a woman becomes herself / the first time she speaks / without permission ... when a woman tells her own story / she lives forever" (Frohman). Frohman writes with embodied language, asserting the agency and capaciousness of womanhood, performed on and by the body. It speaks to the mission of #MeToo, claiming the personal and political power of storytelling, where words become riots and stories establish a woman's humanity. The minute-long video was a striking break from the opulent Oscars ceremony, with its simple monochromatic color scheme and a single voice heard clearly over an otherwise silent commercial. The ad's tone complemented the ceremony's commitment to speaking out about the #MeToo movement, during which there were many references to the movement, from Jimmy Kimmel's opening monologue to the video introduction for Best Supporting Actress which featured women in film professing their anger.

At the end of Twitter's commercial during the ceremony, the words

#HereWeAre flashed across the screen to encourage social media engagement with viewers. Twitter also launched a newly designed hashtag with a golden Venus "female" symbol. While the ad—and Frohman's poem—was widely praised and appreciated for its message celebrating the voices and work of women, Twitter, as the producer of the ad, faced criticism. Author and activist Luvvie Ajayi tweeted a perfect summation of the conflicting thoughts about it: "This #HereWeAre Twitter commercial just gave me chills. That was stunning. Now. Twitter, we shall await your continued work to make this platform safer for women who look like those in that commercial." As Ajayi indicates, harassment on Twitter goes largely unchecked, especially when the victims are women of color. For this reason, the commercial can only be viewed as an initial step and cannot be the only action Twitter takes to show solidarity with and support of women. Without further actionable steps, it can be seen as another "slacktivist" movement. While #HereWeAre is still appearing on Twitter, it does not carry the same weight as #MeToo, because Twitter continuously fails to take the action to protect its users. In other words, #HereWeAre maintains its "slacktivist" status because the organization behind the hashtag did not mobilize to enact change. The #MeToo movement, on the other hand, progressed beyond storytelling to form coalitional organizations whose goals are to transform rape culture for all people.

The 2018 Hollywood awards season, during which Twitter's #HereWeAre ad aired, saw the launch of one such organization, Time's Up. In an open letter addressed to the members' "sisters," the organizers announced their commitment to "holding our workplaces accountable," establishing a legal fund and network of advocates for women to speak out and fight against sexual harassment in the workplace. The coalition of women behind Time's Up includes Tarana Burke and Alyssa Milano, as well as other celebrity actresses, directors, and producers. Joined by lawyers, agents, and entertainment executives, Time's Up operates on an "action plan" with quantifiable and measurable goals. This organization responds to the concerns of hashtag activism and storytelling as protest addressed by Francesca Polletta in *It Was Like a Fever: Storytelling in Protest and Politics*. She details the importance modern Americans place on storytelling in creating empathy and identity, while also questioning their viability or significance in enacting material change, either socially or politically. Polletta is concerned with the limited range of voices who can share their stories, who can share their stories on their own terms, and whose stories will be believed. These factors depend upon the medium, context, and individual storyteller. Thus, a movement like #MeToo depends upon its storytelling platform on democratized technologies where more people have access and power to share their stories, and where they gain power in numbers. Further, she warns that storytelling as a form of actionable protest, particularly for marginalized groups, is not necessarily the holy grail of political reformation or transformation. Rather than letting the storytelling be the end-all-be-all of a political movement, Polletta suggests storytelling should be the catalyst for political action and the formation of coalitional organizations, like Time's Up.

As a political organization responding to the stories of #MeToo, Time's Up continuously engages in protests against sexual assault and amplifies the voices of those communities already doing this work. Their first public protest took place during the 2018 Golden Globes, when members and allies wore all black to the first awards show of the season, many also wearing signifying pins. While their first public display of solidarity was met with some Twitter criticism that it was a performative empty gesture, it was a defining moment of community and protest. In response to the Time's Up call for all celebrities to wear black on the red carpet, actress Viola Davis said, "I think it's a coming out. You know, it's all of these women just embracing their authentic voices and standing in solidarity with each other" (qtd. in Gonzales). In the spirit of #MeToo, where people from different backgrounds came together to speak on common experiences, the first Time's Up protest was a symbol of community. Davis continued, "One of the things I want to express to the public: I think people feel like Hollywood could be out of touch at times. But for me I'm here because I hear the voices of women who said *me too*, which, one of them was me" (qtd. in Gonzales, emphasis added). Here, Davis highlights the connection between #MeToo and Time's Up by telling the people who shared their stories that using this hashtag had power to influence change and inspire political action.

Time's Up is a direct consequence of #MeToo, an example of an organization inspired by and connected to a digital activist movement based on personal storytelling. The members of the Time's Up coalition are leveraging their social, political, and financial capital, which affords them more actionable power than a grassroots or hashtag movement. When they announced their support of the #MuteRKelly campaign, a movement calling to end corporate sponsorship of R. Kelly in the face of several sexual assault allegations, Time's Up amplified the voice of a grassroots movement. In so doing, they used their considerable privilege to bring attention to a population of victims that goes largely unheard, (young) women of color. By backing already existing movements, Time's Up exemplifies the value of solidarity, which was the ultimate goal of #MeToo, to create a community of survivors. Taken together, #MeToo and Time's Up, we can see the effect of storytelling to enact political change. The stories shared through #MeToo are only one part of a larger movement. They are valuable contributions that serve as a rallying cry for further political action, especially for those whose voices are frequently marginalized and silenced.

Because so many people shared, and continue to share, their experiences living in rape culture with #MeToo, the hashtag becomes representative of a shift in cultural awareness, where we now live in a so-called "#MeToo era." The rise in allegations of sexual harassment and assault is not because there are more cases now than ever before. Rather, victims of sexual harassment and assault are coming forward now more than ever before. Even if they are not officially reporting their assaults, they are sharing their stories in a larger cultural conversation, thereby holding the perpetrators accountable. #MeToo has forced society to take notice of rape culture, to listen to accounts of sexual harassment and violence. The telling of the stories cannot guarantee belief in them, nor can they guarantee political or social change. However, there is power, still, within the very act of telling the story. #MeToo embodies the importance of uplifting the voices of marginalized people, speaking out against institutionalized silences, and rejoicing in the power of everyday storytelling.

When Blasey Ford accused Brett Kavanaugh of sexual assault, people began tweeting with the hashtag #WhyIDidn'tReport in an act of solidarity similar to #MeToo. Blasey Ford's testimony sparked another storytelling movement that expanded beyond the digital sphere. After sharing her story at the hearing to determine how these allegations would affect Kavanaugh's confirmation, two women protesting the nomination confronted a senator who was wavering on his vote. Ana Maria Archila and Maria Gallagher crowded Arizona Republican senator Jeff Flake on an elevator, recounting their own stories of rape. When Flake looked to the ground, Gallagher demanded, "Look at me and tell me that it doesn't matter what happened to me" (CNN). Their stories, told with indignation, were shared widely, retweeted from CNN's account alone more than 60,000 times. While Archila's and Gallagher's stories may not have been the leading factor in Flake's decision to call for an FBI investigation into Dr. Ford's claims of assault, these women's stories were heard loud and clear by people across the nation. Despite Blasey Ford's testimony and the national protests against Kavanaugh's nomination, the Senate confirmed Kavanaugh's nomination to the Supreme Court.

Not everyone can confront their senator in an elevator, demanding him to look them in the face when they speak, nor must every survivor share their story in front of a government hearing. But with Twitter and digital activism, everyone can tell their story and add it to the cultural conversation. Told enough times, and by enough people, perhaps the nation will take notice. One person's story can be the tipping point in an individual's actions, and a collection of stories can be the catalyst for a political movement. Even if a shared story does not have an actionable outcome in the political arena, it still holds weight as part of a necessary dialogue between, about, and for survivors of sexual and gendered violence. The very act of storytelling, in the case about and against rape culture, pushes back against the dominant narrative that sexual violence is inevitable and only happens to certain people. Storytelling is a vital step in both the healing process and in dismantling the status quo.

Author and *New York Times* columnist Lindy West describes the real change these acts of (digital) storytelling can inspire. In an essay about #MeToo, she writes, "After decades of debates and doubts and dissertations and settlements and nondisclosure agreements and whisper networks and stasis and silence, all of a sudden, in one great gust, powerful men are toppling." Here, West summarizes the brilliance of effective Twitter activism. #MeToo, as a social activist movement mediated through Twitter and other social media platforms, is a *public* reckoning of normalized and institutionalized legacies of oppression and trauma. Accounts of sexual harassment and assault are now part of an ongoing mainstream conversation and are inspiring positive and transformative action at the individual and collective level.

NOTE

1. I use "Latinx" to recognize individuals of all genders within the Latino/a community.

WORKS CITED

Abramson, Alana. "Read the Letter from Christine Blasey Ford's Lawyers Requesting an FBI Inquiry into Kavanaugh Allegation." *Time*, 19 Sept. 2018. https://time.com/5400239/christine-blasey-ford-investigation-letter/.

Ajayi, Luvvie (@Luvvie). "This #HereWeAre Twitter commercial just gave me chills. That was stunning. Now. Twitter, we shall await your continued work to make this platform safer for women who look like those in that commercial." *Twitter*, 4 Mar. 2018, 5:51 p.m.

Alexander, Bryan. *The New Digital Storytelling: Creating Narratives with New Media*, ABC-CLIO, LLC, 2011.

Barassi, Veronica. *Activism on the Web: Everyday Struggles Against Digital Capitalism*, Routledge, 2015.

Bennett, Jessica. "Behold the power of #hashtag feminism." *Time*, 10 Sept. 2014. https://time.com/3319081/whyistayed-hashtag-feminism-activism/.

Bowles, Nellie, and Cara Buckley. "Rose McGowan's Twitter Account Locked After Posts About Weinstein." The *New York Times*, 12 Oct. 2017. https://www.nytimes.com/2017/10/12/arts/rose-mcgowan-twitter-weinstein.html.

Buchwald, Emilie, Pamela R. Fletcher, and Martha Roth, editors. *Transforming a Rape Culture*. Milkweed Editions, 1993.

CNN (@CNN). "Women confront Sen. Jeff Flake after he says he'll vote yes to Kavanaugh: "That's what you're telling all women in America, that they don't matter. They should just keep it to themselves because if they have told the truth you're just going to help that man to power anyway." *Twitter*, 28 Sep. 2018, 6:46 a.m.

Collins, Patricia Hill. "The Politics of Black Feminist Thought." *Black Feminist Thought: Knowledge, Consciousness, and the Politics of Empowerment*, 2nd ed., Routledge, 2015, pp. 1–19. PDF.

D'Antonio, Michael. "'She's not my type' tells us all we need to know about Trump." *CNN*, 27 June 2019. https://www.cnn.com/2019/06/27/opinions/carroll-rape-allegation-trump-dantonio/index.html.

Duggan, Maeve. "Online Harassment 2017." *Pew Research Center: Internet & Technology*, 11 July 2017. https://www.pewinternet.org/2017/07/11/online-harassment-2017/.

Fosl, Catherine. "Anne Braden, Fannie Lou Hamer, and Rigoberto Menchu: Using Personal

Narrative to Build Activist Movements." *Telling Stories to Change the World: Global Voices on the Power of Narrative to Build Community and Make Social Claims*, edited by Rickie Solinger, Madeline Fox, and Kayhan Irani, Routledge, 2008, pp. 217–226. Print.

Garcia, Sandra E. "The Woman Who Created #MeToo Long Before Hashtags." The *New York Times*, 20 Oct. 2017. https://www.nytimes.com/2017/10/20/us/me-too-movement-tarana-burke.html.

Gerbaudo, Paola, and Emiliano Treré. "In Search of the 'We' of Social Media Activism: Introduction to the Special Issue on Social Media and Protest Studies." *Information, Communication & Society*, vol. 18, no. 8, 2015, pp. 865–871.

Gonzales, Erica. "Women Open Up About Wearing Black on the Golden Globes Red Carpet." *The New York Times*, 7 Jan. 2018. https://www.harpersbazaar.com/celebrity/red-carpet-dresses/a14773793/celebrities-wearing-black-golden-globes-quotes-2018/.

Hendricks, Brianne (@BrianneIsHere). "I was a child too scared to speak. Though the anxiety and blame still haunt me, I am no longer that child. I will not be silent. #MeToo." *Twitter*, 15 Oct. 2015, 7:21 p.m.

Johnson, E. Patrick. "The Beekeeper: Performing Southern Black Women Who Love Women." Old Dominion University Office of Intercultural Relations and Gay Cultural Studies, 13 Mar. 2018, Old Dominion University, Norfolk, VA. Lecture Performance.

_____. "'Quare' Studies, or (Almost) Everything I Know About Queer Studies I Learned from My Grandmother." *Black Queer Studies: A Critical Anthology*, edited by E. Patrick Johnson and Mae G. Henderson, Duke University Press, 2005, 124–157.

Luckman, Susan. "(En)Gendering the Digital Body: Feminism and the Internet." *Hecate*, vol. 25, no. 2, 1999, pp. 36–47.

Me Too, me too. Movement, 2018, metoomvmt.org.

Milano, Alyssa (@Alyssa_Milano). "If you've been sexually harassed or assaulted write 'me too' as a reply to this tweet." *Twitter*, 15 Oct. 2015, 1:21 p.m.

Olheiser, Abby. "How #MeToo Really Was Different, According to Data." *The Washington Post*, 22 Jan. 2018. Accessed 16 Mar. 2017. Web.

Paula (@therealpaulah). "Best Thing: Finding out we are not alone and have all dealt with this/Worst Thing: Finding out we have all dealt with this #MeToo." *Twitter*, 15 Oct. 2017, 6:41 p.m.

renm (@rensaysthings). "I am not sure I know a woman who has not been assaulted or raped, groped, molested, harassed, or threatened. #MeToo." *Twitter*, 15 Oct. 2017, 8:10 p.m.

Taylor, Shannon (@HeyThereImShan). "It's been 5 years since I have been raped. To fellow survivors: / You will / -Trust again / -Love again / -Feel safe again / -Be you again#Me Too." *Twitter*, 15 Oct. 2017, 6:36 p.m.

Time's Up. *Time's Up*, 2019, timesupnow.com.

Vagiano, Alanna. "30 Alarming Statistics That Show the Reality of Sexual Violence in America." *Huffington Post*, 5 Apr. 2018. https://www.huffpost.com/entry/sexual-assault-statistics_n_58e24c14e4b0c777f788d24f.

West, Lindy. "We Got Rid of Some Bad Men. Now Let's Get Rid of Bad Movies." *The New York Times*, Opinion, 3 Mar. 2018. https://www.nytimes.com/2018/03/03/opinion/sunday/we-got-rid-of-some-bad-men-now-lets-get-rid-of-bad-movies.html.

The Perils of Performance

Performing the Politics of Respectability as Resistance in Get Out

Alisha Menzies

According to bell hooks: "Socialized to believe the fantasy, that whiteness represents goodness and all that is benign and non-threatening, many white people assume this is the way black people conceptualize whiteness. They do not imagine that the way whiteness makes its presence felt in black life, most often as a terrorizing imposition, a power that wounds, hurts, tortures is a reality that disrupts the fantasy of whiteness as representing goodness" ("Representing" 340). In recent memory, perhaps nothing exemplifies this quote better than Jordan Peele's 2017 debut horror film *Get Out*. It centers on what happens when a Black man, Chris, in present day United States visits his white girlfriend's seemingly liberal and welcoming family for the first time.[1] *Get Out* received universal acclaim among film critics and diverse audiences, both nationally and internationally. According to the *Internet Movie Database*, the film grossed more than $250 million worldwide against a modest $5 million budget ("Get Out"), becoming one of the most critically and commercially successful Black directed films of all time (Harris).

Immediately after the film's release, media outlets and cultural critics exploded with commentary and theories about the meaning of the film. For some, *Get Out* is a psychological thriller that defies easy classification and pushes viewers to reconsider what a horror film is, while other critics claim that the film's depiction of white benevolent racism and racial anxiety makes *Get Out* feel more akin to documentary nonfiction. Mostly aligning with the latter description of the film as a Black woman, and understanding popular culture as a site of public pedagogy (Giroux 346), I am drawn to how *Get Out* cinematically influences and contributes to the public understanding of racial histories and the effects of racialized gender performance in the United States. In light of this, my analysis focuses on Chris' ability to strategically perform respectability politics (a Black American gender performance conforming normative ideals for masculinity and femininity to increase social standing) in predominantly white spaces as a means of survival.

Films such as *Night of the Living Dead* (1968), *Candyman* (1992), *Tales from the Hood* (1995), *Eve's Bayou* (1998), and *Beloved* (1998) have similarly used tropes of horror to explore race relations and the Black experience in the United States. More pointedly, these films' narratives focus on the fascination and repulsion of the Black body in the white imagination. I extend the analysis of *Get Out* and build on existing scholarship that examines media representations of whiteness and racism (Griffin 184). In this analysis, I position the politics of respectability and Black masculinity scholarship as conceptual lenses to analyze this film. I argue that in this contemporary moment, *Get Out* challenges us to consider the utility of respectability politics as a discourse that still aligns with antiquated and binary notions of racialized gender, sexuality, and class. *Get Out* provokes viewers to consider the possibilities of performing respectability to protect the vulnerable Black body.

In a plot that begins as a play on *Guess Who's Coming to Dinner* (1967), after several months of dating, Chris and his girlfriend Rose determine it is time for him to meet her family, who live in a secluded, wooded, mostly white suburb. However, Rose decides not to inform her parents that Chris is Black prior to arriving for their weekend getaway. Initially, Chris reads the effusive politeness and kind gestures of Rose's surgeon father, Dean, and hypnotherapist mother, Missy, as an effort to overcompensate for the anxiety they are experiencing that, unbeknownst to them, Rose was in a relationship with a Black man. As soon as they meet Chris, both Dean and Missy work to establish their liberal political views and colorblind credibility. For example, while giving Chris a tour of his home, Dean reveals to Chris that he voted for Barack Obama in both the 2008 and 2012 presidential elections. However, Chris quickly realizes there is something suspicious in the open-minded façade they present, and he becomes acutely aware of the robotic creepiness of the Black staff that resides in Rose's parents' home. As the weekend continues, a series of increasingly disturbing encounters and interactions present him with a truth he could have never imagined. Chris discovers Rose's family runs a racial auction network that lures Black people, more often Black men, to upscale social events mostly held at their home, to then auction them off to their middle-aged, white suburban neighbors. After purchasing the Black people, both buyer and property undergo surgery. The surgery allows the white buyers to live in the Black people's younger, healthier, and racially marked bodies forever. They literally embody Blackness.

In negotiating social, cultural, and class identities in the predominantly white United States, Black people necessarily have employed respectability politics. First coined by Higginbotham in 1993 as "a strategy to counter white racist constructions of Blackness, gender performance, sexuality, and class" (41), historically, the politics of respectability was framed as a strategic form of self-representation positioned as impression management that Black Americans used to assimilate with white middle class heteronormative gender and sexual codes. To counter racist stereotypes, Black Americans have performed respectability through conservative dress, using Standard English rather than Black Vernacular English in the presence of white people or in racially mixed spaces, and promoting proper etiquette. The idea was that executing behavior and values emphasizing morality would help Black Americans access and secure social acceptance, political equality, and safety in predominantly white spaces.

Performing respectability is not primarily defined by typical class status markers: material wealth, education, and occupation. As a result, respectability promotes a sense of agency for Black Americans because class visibility is linked to specific behaviors. In other words, while performing respectability articulates class difference, it is primarily defined through behavioral terms. Here, I evoke news footage of Black men and women wearing their "Sunday's best" calmly being hauled to paddy wagons, attacked by dogs, pummeled by police billy clubs, and being knocked down by water hoses during Civil Rights demonstrations in the 1950s and 1960s. Black Americans maintaining dignity and decorum in the midst of police brutality and socially sanctioned violence from white civilians calls attention to savagery and mistreatment of Black Americans. The performance of respectability in these circumstances serves as a visual presentation of Black Americans' attempt to mitigate the impact of racism in their public and private lives.

Black scholars assert that we must not demean or negate the politics of respectability as an effective strategy for both social and political advancement. Historically, for many Black Americans, the politics of respectability has served as the primary mechanism to leverage power in dominant white society. Thus, although respectability politics has a historical trajectory dating back to the 19th century, it remains a prominent discourse Black Americans use in our current political moment to resist both social and systematic racial discrimination. Yet, the politics of respectability has become a target for contempt in discussions in popular media about Black identity and representation in the United States. Black scholars, public intellectuals, and activists argue that "respectability will not save us" (Smith). They see the current expectations and parameters of respectability for Black people as flawed, harmful, and ineffective. Brittany Cooper states: "In the 1890s post reconstruction context in which this strategy was codified, after the U.S. government abandoned black people to the violent terrorism of the post–Civil War

South, such thinking makes sense, however in the 21st century this thinking does not make sense. In this contemporary moment such thinking reinforces the myth of Black respectability as the antidote for anti-black rhetoric and violence." In turn, for both Black women and men performing respectability involves a constant self-disciplined practice of surveillance of both self and white Americans that has the goal to function as a survival mechanism from racial discrimination. The story of respectability politics in the United States is one of Black people constantly questioning if their images are polished, sanitized, or acceptable enough for white society. In other words, do certain representations make "us" look bad in front of "them"? Therefore, while performing respectability articulates class difference, it is primarily defined through behaviors. As a result, respectability promotes a sense of agency for Black Americans because integration and assimilation in white middle class society is linked to specific behaviors.

Because Chris is the primary Black protagonist in *Get Out*, he serves as an example to deconstruct the tedious nuances of the politics of respectability. While Chris and Rose refer to his racial identity, his racial identity is not explicitly discussed by any other characters in the film. Throughout the film, viewers watch as Chris navigates the assumptions of stereotypical Black masculinity while consciously performing respectability. For example, when Rose's older brother, Jeremy, joins the family for dinner he decides he needs to get to know the man dating his little sister better and, to her chagrin, he proceeds to tell multiple stories that embarrass Rose. What begins as a seemingly harmless conversation reminiscing about sibling rivalry, teenage high jinx, and first kisses suddenly takes a sinister turn. Dean decides to change the subject and discuss sports with Chris. The camera zooms in on Jeremy sizing up Chris' physical frame from across the table. As he intensely gazes at Chris, Jeremy leans in and asks Chris in a low voice, "are you a MMA fan?" (*GO*).

As everyone at the dinner table looks around uncomfortably, Chris slowly engages Jeremy's question, making eye contact with him the whole time. He asks, "what do you mean, like UFC? Yeah, nah, too brutal for me" (*GO*). As soon as he states this, Dean quickly turns his head toward Chris, indicating he is surprised by his answer. Chris' response could be minimalized as a guy whose demeanor is too mild and meek to enjoy the violent nature associated with MMA. But, Dean's surprise at Chris' remark is demonstrative of a white man's expectation of a *Black* man's brutality and enjoyment of physical engagement. Juxtaposed against Jeremy's intense verbal aggression, Chris' carefully chosen words in this scene reinforce scholars' notions that the performance of respectability is a willful assertion of agency (Neal). As a Black man immersed in a completely white space, Chris' decision to verbally disengage Jeremy's aggressiveness conveys to the audience that he recognizes his body is in a vulnerable space. If Chris matched Jeremy's verbal intensity, Jeremy's aggression would be overshadowed and dismissed. There, in this space, Chris' passive verbal approach confirms his intention to center Jeremy's anger and his humanity.

Despite Chris' calm demeanor and mild responses, Jeremy continues assessing Chris' physicality with searing eyes. Still sitting, Jeremy pushes his body forward and as he intensely stares at Chris' body, he states, "with your frame and your genetic makeup, if you really pushed your body, trained, I mean really trained you know, no pussy footin' around, you'd be a fucking beast." Viewers watch as Chris slowly nods in agreement, never losing eye contact with Jeremy. In a startling moment, Jeremy stands up from the table and demands that Chris gets up. Viewers watch as Jeremy physically grabs Chris by the shoulders and attempts to put him in a headlock. Physically restraining Jeremy, Chris states, "Got a rule ... no play fighting with drunk dude." After a few tension-filled moments, Jeremy releases Chris' shoulders, and declares "I wasn't gonna hurt him" (*GO*).

Studies of Black masculinity in popular culture trace a long history of Black men in the United States presented as hypermasculine, physically aggressive, sexually insatiable, and unruly (hooks, *We Real Cool* 68). Collectively, Black American men have been constructed as a dangerous population that is a threat and potential harm to white femininity because the cultural imagination presumes Black men are "more prone to be guided by base pleasures and biological impulses" (West 27). Thus, what constitutes socially and culturally acceptable performances of masculinity have been defined by performances of white masculinity, which are aligned with restrained sexual practices, subdued violent tendencies, civility, and social conservatism. In turn, the performance of respectable Black masculinity is understood as a grounding of politeness, civility, and social conservatism associated with hegemonic white masculinity (Neal). In this instance, Chris is well aware that he must maintain his composure and civility in the aggressive face of Jeremy's taunts and physical provocations. Despite the tension-filled encounter, when Chris dismisses Jeremy's physical advances, the film presents Jeremy at a clear disadvantage. Chris does not display any inherent anger or violent behavior toward him at any point of their interaction. However, Chris clearly indicates the interaction is over when he *chooses* for it to end, via no violent means.

Despite years of popular culture discourse that constructs notions of Blackness and Black bodies as frightening and dangerous in the white collective imagination, in the essay "Representing Whiteness in the Black Imagination," bell hooks challenges readers to consider the opposite. hooks interrogates the rhetorical framework that whiteness and physicality are aligned with invisibility for Black people in the United States (341). Pointedly, hooks states, "to name that whiteness in Black imagination is often represented as terror: one must face the palimpsest of written histories that erase and deny, that reinvent the past to make the present vision of racial harmony and pluralism more plausible" ("Representing" 339). Hooks also asserts that in U.S. culture white people have been conditioned to safely assume they are invisible to Black people because white supremacy has historically, socially, and systematically accorded them control of the Black gaze ("Representing" 342). For example, in the Jim Crow Era, many southern states had laws that prohibited Black people from making direct eye contact with a white person. A Black person could be sent to jail for *reckless eyeballing*, which was deemed as assault on a white person. Hence, white Americans assume that they are invisible to Black people if they so choose to be. Consequently, hooks argues that Black people have been conditioned to remain silent about representations of whiteness in the Black imagination, especially in connection to the notion of whiteness as terrorizing ("Representing" 341). As hooks states, "Without evoking a simplistic, essentialist 'us and them' dichotomy that suggests black folks merely invert stereotypical racist interpretations, so that black becomes synonymous with goodness and white with evil, I want to focus on that representation of whiteness that is not formed in reaction to stereotypes but emerges as a response to the traumatic pain and anguish that remains a consequence of white racist domination, a psychic state that informs and shapes the way black folks 'see' whiteness" ("Representing" 341).

To put this in perspective, I analyze how *Get Out* serves as a text to deconstruct how the politics of respectability function as a strategy Black Americans use to mitigate the terror of whiteness in the Black imagination in predominantly white spaces. During his weekend visit, Chris is invited to attend the annual garden party the family hosts for their neighbors and friends. As Rose and Chris enter the party, the camera pans out to reveal dozens of upper-class white people mixing and mingling in the backyard. As they cross the lawn, Rose stops to greet her parents' friends, Mr. and Mrs. Green. The couple warmly receive Rose and Chris with handshakes and hugs. As introductions conclude, Mr. Green immediately asks Chris if he enjoys the game of golf. Chris admits to Mr. Green he doesn't have much golfing experience. Mr. Green ignores his response and begins to adamantly share his admiration of Tiger Woods. Chris politely acknowledges Mr. Green's comments and agrees Woods is an excellent player. In a split second, Mr. Green asks Chris to demonstrate his golf stance, despite their previous exchange. This conversation happens because Mr. Green has tokenized Chris' racial identity and demands he display the athletic ability associated with Black masculinity. In moments like these, viewers learn that the easiest way for Chris to diffuse them is with polite civility.

After ending the conversation with Mr. and Mrs. Green, Chris and Rose make their way inside where they encounter Mr. and Mrs. Deets. Immediately after introducing herself, Mrs. Deets walks toward Chris and queries to Rose, "how handsome is he?" as she feels his shoulders and chest. Before Chris has a moment to respond, Mrs. Deets looks at Chris' pelvic area and slyly asks, "so is it true, is *it* better?" Before the audience can hear a coherent response from Chris, the film cuts to yet another conversation Chris is subjected to on the patio. In this moment, Mr. Dray is educating Chris on the commodity of skin tones in U.S. culture. Mr. Dray says, "fair skin has been in favor for the past, what, couple of hundreds of years … but now the pendulum has swung back. *Black* is in fashion" (emphasis added). This conversation proves to be Chris' breaking point and he excuses himself to be alone (*GO*).

The garden party scene is important to understanding how the politics of respectability function in moments of white terror. The interesting aspect of this scene is the ease and casualness with which the white people talk to Chris. They present their questions and comments in a welcoming manner, but because Chris is literally one of the few Black people at the party, the conversations are isolating and position him as the Other. Despite their jovial tone, Chris is well aware that the white people at the party are reading him as Other. His performance of respectability politics is a crucial strategic decision in this moment, because to behave in any other manner would put Chris in a deeply dangerous situation. Viewers watch as Chris is subjected to racial platitudes regarding his athletic ability, sexual stamina, penis size, and the commodity of his Black skin at a dizzying speed. Thus, understanding the vulnerability of Chris' body in this situation is predicated on the audience's ability to recognize that Chris must consciously perform respectability in all three interactions.

Unbeknownst to the white people, Chris is watching them just as assiduously as they are watching him. Indeed, the moments during the garden party in which Chris attempts to snap a few candid photos with his camera point to this. The perspective of the film shifts to emulate Chris' view through the lens of his camera, using the mise en scène to frame the white people that are now beckoning him to join their conversation. As hooks asserts, "some white people may even imagine there is no representation of whiteness in the black imagination, especially one that is based on concrete observation or mythic conjecture; they think they are seen by black folks only as they want to appear" ("Representing" 340). Although the white people interrogating Chris frame their conversation as casual banter, each verbal interaction implicates historical scripts of Black masculinity associated with physical prowess, hypersexuality, and fetishization. By not explicitly talking about Chris' racial identity, the white people he interacts with assume Chris does not read more into their racist innuendos. In turn, they feel comfortable enough to ask and say whatever they want to Chris, revealing how racist they are. Thus, performing respectability positions Chris on moral high ground. He does not verbally or physically lash out at anyone despite the intense scrutiny he is under, nor does he dignify any of the racist stereotypes to which he is subjected. At this point in the film, Chris' measured tones and polite responses mark his Black masculinity as palatable and ensures that his Black body aligns with their understanding of hegemonic (read: white) masculinity. Chris' performance of respectability during this interaction leads the audience to believe that Chris is in charge of his self-presentation and the interactions in which he engages.

As discussed earlier, most race scholars acknowledge the tenets of the politics of respectability and suggest that it is one strategy of racial uplift used by Black Americans. Higginbotham writes, "the politics of respectability entailed reform of individual behavior and attitudes both as a goal in itself and as a strategy for reform of the entire structural system of American relations" (187). In other words, respectability does not merely equate to an attempt for individual Black Americans to mitigate the consequences of racism and stereotyping in their individual lives. Instead, individual Black Americans who perform respectability collectively help protect Black Americans from white scrutiny. Therefore, respectability politics has two audiences: Black Americans, who were encouraged and challenged to be respectable, and white people, who need to be shown that black people can be respectable (Higginbotham 187).

While the film depicts Chris' performance of respectability mostly through his interactions with the white characters, we must also consider how *Get Out* positions performing respectability for the other Black characters. While staying with Rose's family, Chris only encounters three other Black people. To reveal how the politics of respectability function via the conversations with the other Black characters in a predominantly white space, I consider how Chris' performance of respectability is central to the other Black characters' articulation of racial identity. I approach these scenes paying particular attention to how performing respectability among the other Black characters isolates Chris, rather than brings him closer to them.

When Chris and Rose arrive to her parents' home, her father Dean immediately volunteers to give Chris a tour. As they walk throughout the house, the audience watches Chris balance his reactions to Dean's unsettling, awkward, and overzealous statements about "culture," as he shows Chris different ethnic artifacts he has acquired through his travels. As Dean continues his home tour toward the kitchen he states, "my mother loved her kitchen dearly, so we keep a piece of her in here." It quickly becomes clear that the "piece" Dean is referring to is a Black woman standing at the kitchen island. She is wearing bright yellow rubber gloves and a collared light gray maid's uniform. Chris acknowledges Dean's comment, but only responds by raising his eyebrows. Dean states, "Georgianna, this is Rose's boyfriend Chris." After the brief introduction, Georgianna and Chris greet each other in polite and measured tones, never losing eye contact with each other (*GO*).

As Dean leads Chris to the scenic outdoor property, they walk by a Black male groundskeeper raking leaves. The man stops what he is doing to acknowledge Chris non-verbally with eye contact and continues what he is doing. As Chris keeps walking, Dean bumps his shoulder and blurts out, "I know what you are thinking … white family, Black servants. I know it's a total cliché." Chris casually counters, "I wasn't going to take it there." Dean then explains that Georgianna and Walter were hired to take care of elderly parents, and he did not want to terminate them after his parents died. He woefully continues, "Well, I hate the way it looks." Taking a measured breath, Chris says, "yeah, I know what you mean." As a consolation, Dean says, "by the way, I would have voted for Obama a third time if I could." In response, Chris smirks and says, "I agree" (*GO*).

Both of these interactions illustrate that Chris quickly realizes that performing respectability in the presence of Dean is important and assumes there is a shared understanding for the importance with Georgianna and Walter. Performing respectability allows Chris to establish an understanding that he acknowledges that Dean is surveilling his interactions with Georgianna and Walter. In turn, Walter and Georgianna's measured pleasantries make Chris assume they also are aware of the surveillance, establishing solidarity.

The next day, when he is walking the grounds, Chris encounters Walter chopping wood. As they are the only two in visual sight (i.e., no white people are around), Chris approaches Walter and states, "they working you pretty good out here, huh?" in a relaxed and familiar rapport. Using "they" is Chris' way of differentiating himself and Walter from Rose's white family. This interaction illustrates that Chris assumes that the mutual performance of respectability between him and Walter the day before is no longer needed in this shared racial moment. The performance of respectability has changed because they are no longer surveilled by wealthy white people. However, something gets lost in translation between Chris and Walter. Walter replies, "nothing I don't want to be doing," as he smiles back. Chris stares at Walter puzzledly and slowly responds, "yeah." Instead of reading this moment as shared identity, Walter continues to perform respectability in a self-monitoring and disciplined manner, discussing his love for Rose's family. By the end of the conversation, it is evident that Chris does not see Walter as a Black male ally, making him feel more alone (*GO*).

On a first viewing, at this juncture in the film, the audience is still uncertain about the full picture of what is happening at this secluded country home. Walter's resistance to dropping the formality of respectability politics sets Chris on edge. It is possible, in this moment, that Walter understands something that Chris does not. Audiences may speculate that the family *is* continually surveilling their interactions; they may have cameras or other recording devices set up that do track Walter and Georgianna's movements and conversations. If so, then the need to persistently perform respectability politics makes sense. And it might be dangerous for Walter to alert Chris to this, therefore squashing his opportunity to approach Chris in that space of mutual racial understanding. Of course, by the end of the film, both Chris and the audience know better.

Just as Chris' private interactions with the few Black household members are unsatisfactory and confusing, his interactions with the white guests at the garden party emphasize his isolation in this place. The comments and physical touches of the other guests fetishize him and reduce him to the stereotypes associated with Black masculinity. Thus, to the party goers he becomes Chris—that Black guy—instead of his individual self. Viewers see Chris attempt to remedy his feelings of isolation with racial solidarity when he approaches Andre Logan King, the only other Black male at the garden party. In a moment when Andre is alone, Chris spots him and greets him, touching his shoulder as he says, "it's good to see another brother around here." This is an explicitly mediated moment to understand how Andre and Chris can potentially interact when they are not in the company of white people. Andre turns around and replies in a formal tone, "yes, of course it is. Is something wrong?" Chris incredulously looks at Andre, indicating that he is not sure why he is being so formal in this moment of just the two of them. Andre ruptures the silent code of racial ally-ship. While his words are respectable and polite, they infer Andre is maintaining a distance from Chris. As Andre's wife, Philomena, joins them, Andre informs her that "Chris was just telling me how he felt much more comfortable with my being here." Viewers immediately see Chris' facial response. He is taken aback that Andre would reveal this in front of his white wife (*GO*).

This is an interesting moment because the tenets of respectability collide. Chris' solution of creating solidarity in a shared racial moment is not successful because Andre's formality throws him off. Moreover, Andre performs respectability when he reveals their conversation to his wife. The audience that requires performing respectability is transposed. Andre violates the tenets of respectability *using r*espectability. In turn, it becomes clear to Chris that Andre is not a Black ally. Lastly, when Chris decides to end his conversation with Andre, he looks him straight in the eye and attempts to give him a fist bump. Instead, Andre reaches his hand out for a handshake. For Chris, even more so than his interactions with the white people, this indicates that there is something dangerous and ominous about the way the white people he has encountered view Black identity. Chris' interaction with the three Black people—Georgianna, Walter, and Andre—make it clear that Rose's home is an unsafe and disturbing place. Chris cannot identify with anyone there, making it clear he is in real danger.

On subsequent viewings of the film, the audience knows from the outset that Chris is the proverbial lamb to slaughter, being led to the butcher's block by his girlfriend—the wolf in sheep's clothing. If anything, the film is more disturbing as second and further screenings allow viewers to more fully understand and experience the white horror that Chris encounters at the country house. Everything about this interaction is designed to size him up as the Black male specimen up for sale in a contemporary, gentrified slave auction. Jeremy's aggressive insistence at dinner for Chris to display his physical prowess is about gauging Chris' response as one that will be docile and malleable rather than overtly challenging and hostile. The family, in the same vein as hooks' observation about white people assuming that they are not being watched by Black people, assumes that Chris is not strategically calculating what is happening around him ("Representing" 342). They do not account for his performance of respectability politics, nor his agency, as a vital part of his existence. As deceitful as they are, they cannot comprehend that Chris, too, performs the role that they hope he will display.

Returning audiences are well aware that Chris is not the first Black person to be put through this farce but with more terrifying results. When Dean says: "my mother loved her kitchen dearly, so we keep a piece of her in here," re-watching viewers know that what he really means is that a literal piece of his mother—her consciousness—is in the kitchen, parasitically nestled in Georgianna's host body. When Walter refuses to have any meaningful conversation with Chris, ostensibly away from the family's prying eyes, audiences know that it is because Rose's grandfather now inhabits Walter's body. He cannot codeswitch to the informal and comfortable conversation and physical posture that Chris expects, because he does not know that this exists. For white people, the recognition that Black people can decidedly transform their behaviors when among white people so carefully from how they live in private contexts is practically unimaginable. This is elevated significantly in the interaction with Andre, who breaks Black social contract by outright telling his wife that Chris is more comfortable with him there. For Chris, this is more than a breach of etiquette; this is a waving red flag that he is truly alone in this place and that something is absolutely wrong (*GO*).

Finally, the garden party is perhaps the most harrowing scene on a repeat viewing. Here, the invocation of the slave auction is clear. Re-watchers know that the white guests who so blatantly comment on his physical prowess, his body, his sexual stamina, and his intellect, are doing so with the hopes that they find him suitable and that they will be able to bid enough in order to make him their host for the foreseeable future. This film takes the concept of *Invasion of the Body Snatchers* to the next level, elevating the current and very prescient concerns of Black Americans embroiled in a systemic, racist system that continues to treat Black bodies as commodities rather than people.

Media are not created within a vacuum. Jordan Peele's vision for *Get Out* is rooted in a specific place and time in American culture. Daily, we are inundated by media that remind us that race relations are tenuous at best. *Get Out* hits back at the growing visibility of seemingly "woke" white people in a so-called postracial world ("I don't see color, I just see people") that claim themselves as allies but continue to prop up and maintain their white privilege in their everyday interactions. These are so well exemplified in *Get Out* by those early scenes in which Dean and Missy are both overly apologetic about their whiteness and their privilege while simultaneously continuing to engage with Chris in stereotypically racist ways. "I would have voted for Obama for a third term if I could" is the newer analog to the well trod "one of my best friends is Black." Lanre Bakare, in a critical review for *The Guardian*, writes: "The villains here aren't southern rednecks or neo–Nazi skin heads, or the so-called 'alt-right.' They're middle-class white liberals. [...] The thing *Get Out* does so well—and the thing that will rankle with some viewers—is to show how, however unintentionally, these same people can make life so hard and uncomfortable for black people."

Overall this critique of *Get Out*'s depiction of respectability through Chris' performance of Black masculine respectability complicates popular discourse and theory regarding the politics of respectability. Depictions of Black men performing respectability suggest that it is a passive act of resistance. As we can see with Chris this presentation continues, certainly for most of the film his performance of respectability presents him as disengaging any acts of aggression that confront him. However, his performance of respectability is tempered by a constant surveillance of the white bodies that surround him, which ultimately works to recenter his agency and resistance. Though dramatized for entertainment the interracial interactions depicted in *Get Out* forces the audience to wrestle with the ignorance of white liberal assumptions that circulate in popular culture. The fact that Peele recognized the need to create a film with a horrific final solution to the subtle arrogance of white privilege reflects a desperate need for critical discussion about the precarious nature of Black male life in U.S. culture. While the audience can revel in knowing that Chris defeats Rose's demented family, the Black male body that is celebrated as victorious in *Get Out* is the same Black male body that faces the consequences of control and discipline in the real world. A recent study found that approximately 1 in 1,000 Black men and boys in America can expect to die at the hands of police, according to a new analysis of deaths involving law enforcement officers (Khan). To put this in perspective, Black men and boys are 2.5 times more likely than white men and boys to lose their lives during an encounter with the police (Khan). These statistics remind us, that in many cases for young Black men, their physical presence in a space is the perceived threat in U.S. culture. There is no presumption of innocence because the threat is inherent in their very being. In *Get Out*, Chris' performance of respectability in white spaces is not merely a plot device, it is his survival mechanism. His performance mediates his humanity; it becomes his response to the inhumanity he faces. While I understand the potential futility of the politics of respectability as a cure for race relations in our contemporary time, I also recognize the multiple ways transgressive possibilities for resistance manifest when performing respectability. While the optics of race permeate the film, we must consider if *Get Out*'s narrative is less about physical binaries between white and Black bodies, and more about resisting white terror, no matter the benign ways it is presented.

NOTE

1. As an act of social political resistance, I choose to capitalize the racial designation Black and decapitalize white as a way of bringing emphasis to Black subjectivity in scholarship.

WORKS CITED

Bakare, Lanre. "Get Out: The Film That Dares to Reveal the Horror of Liberal Racism in America." *The Guardian*, 28 Feb. 2017. https://www.theguardian.com/film/2017/feb/28/get-out-box-office-jordan-peele.

Cooper, Brittany. "Clair Huxtable Is Dead: On Slaying *The Cosbys* and Making Space for Liv, Analise, and Mary Jane." 23, Oct.2015, http://www.crunkfeministcollective.com/2014/10/23/clair-huxtable-is-dead-on-slaying-the-cosbys-and-making-space-for-liv-analise-and-mary-jane/.

Get Out. Directed by Jordan Peele. Universal Pictures Home Entertainment, 2017.

"Get Out (2017)." *Internet Movie Database*, IMDB.com, 1990–2019. https://www.imdb.com/title/tt5052448/.

Giroux, Henry. "Public Pedagogy as Cultural Politics: Stuart Hall and the Crisis of Culture." *Culture Studies*, vol. 14, no. 2, 2000, pp. 341–360.

Griffin, Rachel Alicia. "Pushing into *Precious*: Black Women, Media Representation, and the Glare of the White Supremacist Capitalist Patriarchal Gaze." *Critical Studies in Media Communication*, vol. 31, no. 3, 2014, pp. 182–197.

Harris, Mark. "Will Hollywood Learn Anything from Get Out's Success?" *Vulture*, 1 May 2017. https://www.vulture.com/2017/05/will-hollywood-learn-anything-from-get-outs-success.html.

Higginbotham, Evelyn Brooks. *Righteous Discontent: The Women's Movement in the Black Church, 1880–1920*, Harvard University Press, 1993.

hooks, bell. "Representing Whiteness in the Black Imagination." *Cultural Studies*, edited by Lawrence Grossberg, Carrie Nelson, and Paula Treichler, Routledge, 1992, 338–346.

hooks, bell. *We Real Cool: Black Men and Masculinity*, Routledge, 2004.

Khan, Amina."Getting Killed by Police Is the Leading Cause of Death for Young Black Men in America." *Los Angeles Times*. 16 Aug. 2019. https://www.latimes.com/science/story/2019-08-15/police-shootings-are-a-leading-cause-of-death-for-black-men.

Neal, Mark Anthony. "Coming Apart at the Seams: Black Masculinity and the Performance of Obama-era Respectability." *New Black Man (in Exile): The Digital Home for Mark Anthony Neal*. 7 Apr. 2010, http://www.newblackmaninexile.net/2010/04/coming-apart-at-seams-black-masculinity.htm.

Sandlin, Jennifer. "Popular Culture, Cultural Resistance, and Anticonsumption Activism: An Exploration of Culture Jamming as Critical Adult Education." *New Directions for Adult and Continuing Adult Education* Fall, No. 115, 2007, pp. 73–82.

Smith, Mychal. "Respectability Politics Will Not Save Us: On the Death of Jonathan Ferrell." *The Nation,* 16 Sept. 2013. https://www.thenation.com/article/respectability-politics-wont-save-us-death-jonathan-ferrell/.

West, Cornel. *Race Matters,* Vintage, 1993.

He Did Nazi That Coming

Remix, Resistance and Richard Spencer's Face

JASON BUEL *and* KRISTI KOUCHAKJI

Noted white supremacist Richard Spencer was punched in the face by anti-racists twice while speaking to reporters at an Inauguration Day rally in January 2017. Footage of the second punch, recorded by a news crew, was immediately remixed and set to popular songs by thousands of people. These remixes framed the punch in a positive light, and helped it circulate more widely than it otherwise would have. In most cases, such remixes make implicit ethical arguments for punching Nazis. The circulation of these videos served as a metaphoric punch to Spencer, who told one journalist, "I'm afraid this is going to become the meme to end all memes. That I'm going to hate watching this" (qtd. in Stack). These remixed memes of Spencer getting punched constitute an emerging genre of media that is a form of social resistance in itself. Additionally, they offer a brief respite from the intensity of oppression in contemporary American politics and, in the process, help reframe white supremacist ideas as unacceptable. In this essay, we consider this emerging genre of Nazi punch videos as social action. Such videos are a response to what has become a recurrent rhetorical situation: the need for ordinary citizens to confront overt displays of fascist politics in both online and offline spaces.

Carolyn Miller argues that genres can be understood as indicators of social relations (165). Our analysis of these videos considers two ways that this emerging genre functions as social action: by reflecting cultural expectations in recurrent contexts, and as a set of guidelines for participation in a particular community (Miller 165). These video remixes seek to transform the values of a small subculture (antifascists) into values of the wider culture as a whole. Considering these videos as a reflection of their particular cultural context and as models that sketch out modes of participation, we will show

47

how pairing different songs with the image of Spencer being punched produces new meanings that aid in transmitting antifascist cultural values.

First, we will examine the videos themselves, using four remixes set to the same two songs (M.I.A.'s "Paper Planes" and Phil Collins' "In the Air Tonight") as examples of the conventions that emerge across this genre of video. We will show that the videos craft new relationships between song, event, and viewer, and that they play with the event's timeline in order to turn the raw footage of the event into emotional calls for justice. Inspired by Miller's approach to genre as social action, we then situate these videos in terms of their potential to both mobilize viewers and set the stage for future mobilizations in response to the increasing sense of fear and frustration among marginalized people in the U.S., Canada, and the UK in the post–2016 era (151). Ultimately, we argue that these videos work to condition new modes of resistance on a larger scale, beyond simply re-presenting an action.

We approach this work as emerging scholars whose moral compasses and political ideologies veer strongly to the left. Moreover, as white scholars of settler and mixed settler/non–European migrant descent, who passively benefit from structures of white supremacy and colonialism (and, for one of us, heteropatriarchy), a common theme across all of our work is to not only shed light on these structures, but to think through forms of resistance to them, and to write and work in solidarity with those carrying the heaviest loads of resistance. It should be noted at the outset that we see no moral issue with a singular, performative act of violence against a Nazi calling for or otherwise encouraging violence against marginalized people, nor do we wish to engage at length in debates about "civility"—leaving aside the colonial implications of that term, it is our belief that white supremacists, their ideas, and their enablers have no place in a just society, and that a democratic "civil" society is not possible if it is founded on white supremacist, colonial, and heteropatriarchal structures. It is our belief that calls for "civility" are mobilized more often than not to serve the interests of white supremacist, colonial, and heteropatriarchal structures, which undermines the possibility of any genuinely respectful, good-faith discourse.

Before turning to specific videos, we will first provide an overview of stylistic traits that apply to most of the videos in this emerging genre. The image tracks of these videos generally follow the same pattern: Richard Spencer is facing mostly front, explaining the Pepe the Frog meme to someone standing off-screen to the right of the camera. A masked figure in black enters from the left of the frame and immediately serves Spencer a right hook to the jaw before being pulled back out of frame as Spencer staggers to the right. The camera pans left to follow the puncher's exit before panning to the far right (literally and metaphorically) to follow Spencer's retreat as he brushes back his hair. While some videos include much more of Spencer talking before being punched, and others include much more of his attempt to recover after, these 20 seconds or so are the core of the action as it originally occurred, and the punch the climax of each remix. Regardless of the music chosen, the audio and video tracks are by and large synced up so that the moment of impact where fist meets face occurs in conjunction with the song's most well-known riff or most apt lyric.

It is in the syncing of music and video that creative variations and interventions occur, and to which we turn our attention now. We will look specifically at two remixes each of two songs, M.I.A.'s "Paper Planes" and Phil Collins' "In the Air Tonight," to get a better sense of the different ways remix makers took advantage of the possibilities afforded by the songs chosen. The "Paper Planes" remix video posted to YouTube by a user with the screen name killjoy features none of the events before the punch, and instead opens with a clip from M.I.A.'s original video for the song as she sings the first line of the chorus. The video then cuts to Spencer being punched, repeated in sync with each of the gunshot sounds in the chorus. The effect is that Spencer is being punched repeatedly, several times in quick succession, as additional punctuation to the song's lyrics. The video then cuts back to the M.I.A. original as the chorus continues, and then back to Spencer being punched repeatedly in sync with the song's gunshot sound effect, and so on.

By contrast, the "Paper Planes" remix posted on Twitter by a user named @dunndunndunn begins with Spencer explaining Pepe to someone out of frame, but with the original audio track muted and the song mixed in over it. This allows for a full verse of the song's lyrics to be heard as Spencer is on screen, and, for those who have both heard the song and seen the original event before, creates an additional sense of anticipation as the action unfolds toward the punch and the song unfolds toward the gunshot effect. In this version, too, the punch is looped to repeat with each gunshot sound that punctuates the chorus.

The remixes set to "In the Air Tonight" follow a similar structure in tying music to video. The version posted to YouTube by a user with the screen name J L is fairly basic in its construction. It, too, features a full verse of the song's lyrics over muted video of Spencer speaking, with the punch synced to the first beat of the drum fill that precedes the chorus. The punch, however, is not repeated; instead, the song's refrain plays over footage of Spencer walking away from the camera. Again, for a viewer who is familiar with both the event and the song, there is some comedic and cathartic payoff here, but, at the same time, the simplicity of this remix is disappointing in that it fails to take full political advantage of the opportunities the song's musical structure offers.

The version posted to Twitter by a user named @donswaynos begins with Spencer explaining Pepe immediately before the punch, which is then repeated to each beat of the drum fill. The punch is also repeated to each major beat through the song's most famous lyric, intercut with footage of Spencer walking away. Moreover, in the last two repetitions of the punch, the image has been enlarged to emphasize a "White Lives Matter Too Much" placard visible over Spencer's shoulder in the left of the frame, with the arc of the punch cutting across the frame's horizontal midline and impact occurring in the far-right foreground (again, literally and metaphorically), emphasizing the politics informing the punch remix videos as a genre.

There are literally thousands of other punch remix videos in existence and examining them all would be too much for this space. After reviewing the 108 videos posted by the @PunchedToMusic Twitter account as a sample, in addition to the four detailed above, we have observed that these remixes are all fairly similar in terms of structure. Looking over these videos as a genre, it becomes clear that four factors are key in driving views for these videos: the most-viewed videos leverage a combination of nostalgia, rebellion, and/or celebration in their choice of song; celebrate the punch itself by looping or repeating it in sync with a major beat in the music; establish a comic or ironic relationship to the song's lyrics; and are posted to Twitter rather than YouTube, making it easier to share the remix as well as increasing the odds that it will be seen while someone is just idly scrolling their social media feeds. This is supported by the viewing data for the four videos outlined above: killjoy's version of "Paper Planes," which is intercut with M.I.A.'s video and does not repeat the punch, has at the time of this writing 24,035 views, while @dunndunndunn's version, which is on Twitter and repeats the punch throughout the song's chorus, has 35,400. Even starker is the difference in numbers between the two remixes set to "In the Air Tonight": J L's remix, which has only one iteration of the punch and is on YouTube, has 41,609 views, while @donswaynos's, which repeats the punch to every major beat and plays with framing to underscore the intended message, has 915,900.

It's worth addressing the differences between "Paper Planes" and "In the Air Tonight" to understand why they would be chosen for such remixes and what additional meanings these choices might produce. "Paper Planes," a 2007 song by a woman of color, comments on U.S. gun culture and politics, everyday racism and xenophobia, and post–9/11 travel and immigration restrictions. Matching the song to video of a white supremacist being punched highlights the long history that such ideologies have within social and political structures, and it also suggests that popular resistance—through direct action and cultural production—is one route to dismantling them. The description posted with killjoy's remix outlines exactly this: "don't just like it go out and do something! apathy and acquiescence got us here! fight back with your words and mind and with your fists as a last resort!" [*sic*]. In that sense, the remixes set to "Paper Planes" leverage not only the pleasure in hearing a tremendously popular song from recent years, but also the song's multiple meanings and the pleasure of seeing a white supremacist be met with direct resistance to create a new set of meanings for viewers.

"In the Air Tonight," meanwhile, is a 1981 song by a white man, the lyrics to which are not nearly as well known as the chorus and drum parts and are about anger at the end of a relationship. J L's choice to include a verse from the song in their version of the punch remix is interesting, given that the verse in question is most readily interpreted as a confrontation with someone who has betrayed the singer on a moral and emotional level, raising and recontextualizing questions about social codes of acceptable behaviors. With that said, it is more significant that @donswaynos chose to use only the drum riff and chorus line that the song is most well known for: by doing this, the remix evokes only nostalgia for the song and the emotional pleasures that accompany such a feeling, without calling attention to any personal pain or negativity the audience may be reminded of by hearing a full verse of the song. In this way, recontextualizing the song's most famous refrain and turning it into (literally) a punch line by coupling it with instant replays of the punch makes the remix video a site of multiple pleasures for viewers.

That two such different songs, as well as such a wide range of songs chosen for the videos on @PunchedToMusic (everything from EDM to Britpop to postmodern masterpieces), can be used in such different ways to convey the same argument shows that it is the audio track that offers the greatest potential for impact, and is the driving force of people's engagement. It is not possible to change the events themselves or the way in which they were recorded. It is, however, possible to add or create meaning through choosing a particular soundtrack. It is also possible to play with the sequence of events through looping, repeating, and other visual edits, thus imposing a rhythm that differs from the events as they were initially recorded, and which marries the event more closely to the song chosen.

Looking through the songs chosen for the remixes on @PunchedtoMusic underscores this. The songs chosen are primarily party anthems and/or are about some form of resistance to oppressive structures. And they are predominantly up-tempo, in major keys, and easily recognized by members of the subcultures the songs themselves appeal to. Potential subtextual meanings are then amplified or leveraged through edits that emphasize some aspects of the event or song over others in order to produce new meanings and construct a positive atmosphere around the event itself, implicitly associating pleasure with white supremacists being punched. In some videos, like "Song 2—Blur" and @donswaynos' version of "In the Air Tonight," Spencer's words can at first be heard clearly over or instead of the music. In others, like "Just—Radiohead" or the "Paper Planes" remixes, his words are entirely replaced by the music, or seemingly responded to by the song only starting at the moment of impact. This is also the case with the video on @PunchedToMusic titled "4'33"—John Cage," in which the track—four minutes and 33 seconds of silence—begins at the moment of impact, amplifying the punch's silencing of Spencer's hateful discourse.

It is worth taking a moment here to think through the selection of "4'33"" for one of these videos beyond the obvious gag. One of the many points of "4'33"" is that it transcends genre and has become such an important work in 20th-century pop culture, art history, music history, and sound studies that to use the track at all is to make a point about monumentality. As Alexander Rehding explains, "the cultural function of monuments is to articulate history," and monuments "aim to overwhelm rather than persuade; the message that monuments convey is not subtle but forceful" (70). Moreover, monumentality—particularly in music—is based on "a simplicity that stands up to being stated emphatically, without collapsing in empty rhetoric" (Dahlhaus qtd. in Rehding, 70). Marrying "4'33"," a track which articulated a particular moment in postmodern art and music history and which has since itself become a sonic monument, to Spencer being punched, an act which articulates a particular moment in 21st-century political history (occurring in conjunction with another moment that certain politicians would like to hold up as monumental based on imagined crowd sizes), emphasizes the monumentality of the punch. In addition, one of the other points of "4'33"" is to challenge listeners to listen to room tone—that is, all of the sounds in their environment that make up the sonic background of the moment in which they are listening, and which are often overlooked and labeled as simply "silence"—in other words, to listen to the components of what is considered the "blank" default position against which all other sounds are defined. Metaphorically speaking, this is also exactly what the punch, and the remix videos of it, ask us to do: to listen to what has become normalized as a default position, and to emphatically resist it without collapsing into empty rhetoric.

In all of the other videos (those whose soundtracks include music and lyrics), the song's crescendo is timed to coincide with the punch itself. This also literally and metaphorically silences Spencer. It is a political statement made through the combination of image and audio. With each new video that repeats this pattern, the choice to use music to silence Spencer becomes a genre convention that reflects the values of the community that makes, watches, and circulates these videos. The punch itself is satisfying, but the emotional payoff arises from the combination of music, editing, and mixing choices, where "the right" choices are discovered through trial and error in conversation with a community of people viewing, discussing, and creating these remixes.

The payoff in these videos also comes through what Jane Gaines describes as political mimesis. In her study of the connection between documentary films and social action, Gaines observes the limits of nonfiction media to directly cause audiences to take action. Gaines states that the question of how and whether films lead audiences to take action raises other questions: "What constitutes action? How do we measure that action? What are the signs of political consciousness?" (89). Gaines' answer to the first question lies partly in the concept of political mimesis: the relationship between the bodies on screen and the bodies watching the screen (90). It is such political mimesis, which operates by stirring a somatic, embodied response to the action on screen rather than any appeal to intellect or conscious emotion, that allows activist media to be effective. As Gaines puts it, "we still need to think the body in relation to films that make audience members want to kick and yell, films that make them want to do something *because of the conditions in the world of the audience*" (90, emphasis in original). To that end, she writes that makers of such media "use images of bodies in struggle *because they want audiences to carry on that same struggle* [....] The whole rationale behind documenting political battles on film, as opposed to producing written records, is to make struggle visceral, to go beyond the abstractly intellectual to produce a bodily swelling" (Gaines 91, emphasis in original).

Gaines also writes that songs and music used in activist media "reach audiences at the juncture of the physiological and the psychological [producing] not just affiliation but action" (93). This notion is underscored by activist filmmaker John Greyson's assertion that he used a music video for an original song as a recruiting tactic in two of his 1980s AIDS activist shorts, writing that this was specifically intended as "a danceable club song that also functioned as a call to arms" (262). This is significant because the same thing is happening with these punch remix videos, whether their creators are aware of it or not: by choosing music that different groups of viewers will know as "danceable club songs" and/or "call(s) to arms," and then matching them to "images of bodies in struggle," the creators of these videos are relying on a mimetic effect to underscore the political arguments they are making. Moreover, the wide variety of music chosen for these punch remixes offsets the lack of a shared viewing space, such as a movie theater, where physical proximity to others may have heightened emotional and somatic responses to the material (as was the case for the films Gaines writes about). At the same time, it also works around the fact that the desired viewership for these videos as an aggregate does not come from one pre-existing community or subculture (as was the case with Greyson's shorts, which were made for a queer programming series on a Toronto cable access channel).

In choosing songs that evoke both happier times and/or possible alternative futures on a bodily level beyond the viewer's conscious or intellectual control, and pairing them with footage of Spencer being punched, the creators of these videos are drawing on what Sara Ahmed calls "happy objects." By "happy objects," Ahmed means objects which have come to be associated with happiness in some way and thus have the power to set an expectation of happiness just in being thought of, and which aren't necessarily material but can be places, people, experiences, etc. In the case of these videos, we argue that the songs chosen are already happy objects for different groups of viewers, that images of white supremacists being decisively silenced constitute a second happy object for those who object to racist ideologies. Combining the two produces a new happy object that leverages the feelings already associated with each of its components to produce a range of bodily effects among viewers: joy, justice, catharsis, and so on. As evidenced by the description included on killjoy's video, at least some of these punch remix creators explicitly aim for these new happy objects to move viewers to taking action against white supremacy in their own communities.

Killjoy's username is worth considering in this context. While they may very well have chosen that name for any number of reasons long before making their "Paper Planes" punch remix, it remains apt on a number of levels. The punch represents not just a moment of resistance to white supremacy, creating joy in some, but kills the joy Spencer is clearly taking in being given a platform for his ideas, and also kills the joy that some on the left take in claiming non-violent resistance and a belief in the "marketplace of ideas" as the only path. It arguably also kills some of the joy that the puncher may have felt, given that they risked both retribution from Spencer's acolytes and legal consequences for the act.

As Ahmed writes, people who are killjoys become associated with bad feelings because they point to unjustness in others' good feelings, and they disrupt the social contract of public comfort, i.e., going along to get along (39). In that sense, the puncher, by explicitly rejecting Spencer's good feelings and any means of disseminating them, as well as disrupting comfortable leftist ideals, is in many ways a killjoy. It follows that creators of these remix videos, by turning this moment into a happy object (or a collection of hundreds of variations of the same happy object) become killjoys for those who would prefer to avoid direct action. It is worth noting that the figure of the killjoy is so central to Ahmed's thinking that she herself blogs as feministkilljoys on her site feministkilljoys.com.

The killjoy is a needed figure in this scenario because refusing to let go of suffering and insisting on killing some forms of joy in response to such suffering can, as Ahmed suggests, become the basis for a model of social good. In that sense, the punch delivered to Spencer's face in these videos, despite its violent aspects, remains a gesture of optimism or hopefulness that injustice can be countered and a more just social form built in its place. The remix videos serve as a way of thinking through a path to countering injustice and of attempting to convene a community of resistance around a shared happy object thereby providing an additional way of building an "alternative model of the social good" in the process (Ahmed 50).

With the growing prevalence of social media, contemporary social and political movements are sometimes (wrongly) seen as developing absolutely spontaneously. While these videos may not have led directly to large groups of antifascists roaming the streets in search of Nazis to punch, the videos' ability to amplify the meme of Nazi-punching has become a potential catalyst for a new set of social and cultural standards in which public refusal of explicitly white supremacist ideologies is the expected and accepted response to that particular set of ideas. This speaks to what Paolo Gerbaudo describes as "choreographies of assembly"—the ways that social media are able to give "shape" to the way that people act together offline (4–5). The way that a larger movement takes shape depends on encounters between various bodies and objects as they are drawn together. In this case, such encounters are shaped by emerging media practices such as these remix videos of a Nazi being punched.

These video remixes of Spencer being punched work to reshape public discourse and popular culture's political bent by rejecting both surface-level solutions that do not address root causes of injustices, and reductions of complex situations into simple good/bad binaries, what filmmaker Joshua Oppenheimer calls "Star Wars morality" (qtd. in Behlil 31). As Ahmed observes, "Maintaining public comfort requires that certain bodies 'go along with it,' to agree to where you are placed" (39). These videos celebrate one particular body that unequivocally refused to go along with our uncomfortable slide into fascism. They encourage us to turn our own bodies toward not just the most notable faces of fascism in the U.S. but also toward the faces of those whose ideas have built its foundation. And, just as importantly, they help construct a recognizable "us" out of the bodies that have refused to "go along with it" (Charland). Videos like these help construct a counter public by creating an alternative structure of feeling that channels those feelings toward a more radical politics of direct action; a politics that, by necessity, overflows the electoral process and the sufficiency of words as resistance.

The punch is a gesture of empowerment. The punch itself enacts a killing of joy as a model of the social good. The video remixes of the punch tend to insert a new form of joy all their own. The punch itself shows that the proliferation of fascist ideals need not and must not be passively ignored. The punch does not restore balance to the universe, but it does remind viewers that we can and must work to chip away at politics predicated on overt oppression. The video of this act, then, becomes a "happy object" for people interested in doing anti-racist work. The punch itself is a small act that if it were all alone would have little to no effect on much of anything. But it models a willingness to kill joy—to refuse, in this case, Spencer and the "alt-right's" enjoyment in their perceived triumph—which is absolutely necessary for any sort of resistance movement. As Ahmed reminds us, refusing to let go of suffering and even going so far as to kill joy when that joy erases or is built on such suffering can be an "alternative model of the social good" (50). Pairing the video of the punch with up-tempo music, often party anthems, is part of attaching the image of the event to a preexisting happy object, and it helps create a shared orientation toward the event recorded. It kills the Nazi joy built on the suffering of others and inverts the emotional resonance of the Nazis' presence in public discourse by building joy on top of this momentary suffering that he has been made to endure.

These videos enact a slowing down of the unchecked dissemination of white supremacist ideas. They help to choreograph how a larger slowing down might come into being in public spaces, both online and off. The actual act of punching works, at least temporarily, to de-platform the Nazi by literally silencing him mid-speech and, in so doing, engaging in a détournement of the media attention afforded him. In other words, when the camera moves to follow the puncher, it literally takes the attention off Spencer, who is afterwards only seen from behind and whose words are no longer audible on the original video. The remixed videos of the punch expand to counter-platform Spencer. They first do so by largely refusing to give any time or space to the substance of his ideas, or at least refusing to give them any credence. In this way, they differ from the original un-remixed video clip. They do so secondly by developing a larger atmosphere in which such ideas are no longer accepted in public spaces. This ultimately impacts future public debate and not just Spencer's own ideas but those of other "alt-right" icons as well. These videos also draw viewers into a new set of cultural expectations in which Nazis, white supremacists, right-wing extremists, and the like are seen as a social scourge whose ideologies are not acceptable in this new public sphere. Such visible, direct opposition to white supremacy is especially important in the context of the global rise of the far-right, and the way that the results of the 2016 U.S. presidential election have helped amplify such ideologies.

These videos have not been entirely without controversy, nor has the event of the punch itself. In particular, questions have been raised about the ethics of punching Nazis, the limits of free speech (as it is woefully misunderstood), and whether the videos glorify violence and hatred or sink below the level of appropriate discourse. While ethical conclusions are ultimately up to the reader to draw for themselves and free speech debates are not anything we have space to engage in here, we would like to briefly address the joint questions of violence, hate, and socially acceptable discourse.

First, the primary argument made by these videos is that Nazis (and those with similar views who, for our purposes, we would also consider Nazis) have no place in the socially constructed public sphere and that highly localized action is required to enforce this. Such a localized, highly distributed approach to direct action can also be seen in other ways, such as the nonviolent disruption of Tr*mp administration officials' meals at restaurants. While such actions are often organized, they are not coordinated across local organizations in any sort of centralized national effort. They also require an incredibly high degree of flexibility and almost instant mobilization from the time an opportunity presents itself until that time has passed.

Second, while the punch remix videos do show an act of physical violence, the emotional, somatic, and political appeal they make is based in love as resistance to the hate contained in Spencer's rhetoric, and draw on the songs' status as "happy objects" for a wide range of viewers to condition them to seeing this resistance favorably. Ultimately, this creates an aesthetic that is loving but does not eschew violence. Instead, it reframes violence as something that can serve to defend existing communities and can catalyze new communities-in-potential.

Finally, as anyone who has been active on social media from early 2016 on can attest, words are not always effective as resistance. As Erin Manning writes of non-verbal communication, "These languages are not 'less than' spoken words—they are the more-than of language's expressibility. Spoken words are the selected extraction from the nexus of experience that converge into appearance" (216). In that sense, such acts as ejecting architects of and spokespeople for inhumane policies rooted in hateful ideologies from restaurants and other public spaces, holding sit-ins and other assemblies in front of their homes and workplaces, and punching known Nazis become a nonverbal language of resistance when words no longer suffice.

Works Cited

@donswaynos. "I made one of those Richard Spencer videos." *Twitter*, 21 Jan. 2017, 9:02 a.m.
@dunndunndunn. "the sync at the end isn't perfect sorry." *Twitter*, 21 Jan. 2017, 8:27 p.m.
@PunchedToMusic. "4'33"—John Cage." *Twitter*, 22 Jan. 2017, 11:11 a.m.
@PunchedToMusic. "Just—Radiohead." *Twitter*, 24 Jan. 2017, 2:22 p.m.
@PunchedToMusic. "Song 2—Blur." *Twitter*, 23 Jan. 2017, 12:04 a.m.
Ahmed, Sara. "Happy Objects." In *The Affect Theory Reader*, edited by Melissa Gregg and Gregory J. Seigworth, Duke University Press, 2010, pp. 29–51.
Behlil, Melis. "*The Act of Killing*: An Interview with Joshua Oppenheimer." *Cineaste*, Summer 2013, pp. 26–31.
Charland, Maurice. "Constitutive Rhetoric: The Case of *Peuple Québécois*." *Quarterly Journal of Speech*, vol. 73, 1987, pp. 133–150.
Gaines, Jane. "Political Mimesis." In *Collecting Visible Evidence*, edited by Jane Gaines and Michael Renov, University of Minnesota Press, 1999, pp. 84–102.
Gerbaudo, Paolo. *Tweets and the Streets: Social Media and Contemporary Activism*. London: Pluto Press, 2012.
Greyson, John. "Still Searching." *The Perils of Pedagogy*, edited by Brenda Longfellow, Scott Mackenzie, and Thomas Waugh, McGill-Queen's University Press, 2013, pp. 258–267.
Manning, Erin. *Relationscapes: Movement, Art, Philosophy*. MIT Press, 2012.

Miller, Carolyn R. "Genre as Social Action." *Quarterly Journal of Speech*, vol. 70, no. 2, May 1984, pp. 151–67.

Rehding, Alexander. *Beethoven's Symphony No. 9*. Oxford University Press, 2018.

"Richard Spencer Punched to Paper Planes M.I.A. Mashup." *YouTube*, uploaded by killjoy, 21 Jan. 2017. https://www.youtube.com/watch?v=087xO5vl6gE.

"Richard Spencer Gets Punched in the Air Tonight." *YouTube*, uploaded by J L, 21 Jan. 2017. https://www.youtube.com/watch?v=nl_FzrzGnUg.

Stack, Liam. "Attack on Alt-Right Leader Has Internet Asking: Is It O.K. to Punch a Nazi?" The *New York Times*, 21 Jan. 2017. https://www.nytimes.com/2017/01/21/us/politics/richard-spencer-punched-attack.html.

"A society on the verge of a nervous breakdown"

The Death of Stalin, *Historical Film and Resistance to Trump's America*

SABRINA MITTERMEIER

Moscow, 1953. Director Andreyew at Radio Moscow is listening to the live performance of a Mozart concerto, as he gets a phone call. It comes directly from Joseph Stalin's office, sending the director into a frenzy. Awkwardly, like a teenager calling their crush, he disappears into the next room with the phone, now speaking to the man himself. Stalin wants a recording of the concerto that has just concluded. Yet, there is no such recording, and so everyone scrambles to put together another performance in a hurry, setting off a comedic routine à la *Monty Python* in which an ersatz conductor is pulled out of his home in his nightgown, while NKVD (the state's secret police) head Lavrentiy Beria's men are raiding the apartments next to the one he lives in. The conductor momentarily fears for his life, before he realizes that he will not end up in a gulag tonight—all they need him for is a "musical emergency."

Within the first 15 minutes of the opening scene of Armando Iannucci's 2017 *The Death of Stalin*, the film masterfully conveys an atmosphere of paranoia, a world in which just one wrong word or misstep can cost everything. The humor emerges from people's behavior; from circumstance, rather than an overdrawn parody of historical events. The absurdity of it all is simultaneously hilarious and sickening. Most shocking is that the events depicted are largely true. In fact, as Iannucci, the film's writer and director, has related, real life was even more absurd than fiction: the conductor actually brought in to replace the one that had passed out had been drunk, and so it took a third man to do the recording (see Tobias). The film takes more liberties with the past: it compresses time (the events in the concert hall happened years before Stalin's death and not on the same night) and the pianist, seemingly the only character with any moral backbone, is completely fictional. Such historical inaccuracies however do not hinder the powerful message the film conveys: that totalitarianism is as timeless as the megalomania of the men that feed it. And with this, the film could not have been released at a more fitting moment than in late 2017. *The Death of Stalin* masterfully blends the genres of historical film and satire and it is precisely this satiric outlook that drives home its message and elevates it when compared to other historical films. The urgency of its morale, and its reception with an international audience, has also turned it into a resistance narrative, I argue, as it exposes frightening parallels between the Stalinist regime and the current U.S. government (and beyond).

Masha Gessen, a Russian academic and journalist, has praised the film's opening scene as "the most accurate picture of life under Soviet terror that anyone has ever committed to film." Iannucci achieves this precisely because he was aiming for "an accuracy of atmosphere" (qtd. in Tobias) rather than the mere factual portrayal of events, and this is what makes the scene (and the whole movie) so powerful: it conveys a feeling, and atmosphere of what it was like to live in Stalin's Russia. Historian Jan B. Behrends has argued that the satirical elements the film uses to portray Stalinism succeed in coming close to conveying this political order and that the film is thus superior to the classic historical film that often only retells, or worse, (re)creates myths. Too often historical film falls into the trap of using the past merely cosmetically—recreating, in painstaking detail, locations, costumes, people's looks, and manners of speaking (think Steven Spielberg's *Lincoln,* 2012), but still failing to communicate the importance of the depicted events for the present. One might be able to immerse oneself into such a world but re-emerge from it none the wiser.

Historian Alison Landsberg argues that moments of shock and disruption in film can lead to a level of "alienation that goes beyond simple 'immersive identification'" in the viewer (36). However, the "ability to speak politically is partly a matter of genre—of what the conventions allow you to say, of what the audience expects" (Street 304). This is what often hinders historical film from achieving the effects Landsberg describes. Part of *The Death of Stalin's* strategy is to break with genre traditions: one example is the choice to have the actors speak in their (largely) natural and varied British and American accents, rather than in Russian inflections. This creates the famed Brechtian alienation or distancing effect (*Verfremdungseffekt*) that breaks the filmic illusion, surprises the audience, and thus allows them to take a step back and reflect on the events unfolding before them. Being able to laugh about the grim events depicted on screen leads to the same results. Iannucci has cited Charlie Chaplin's *The Great Dictator* (1941) as an influence for the film ("Humorless Politicians"), and it is not hard to see its impact; *The Death of Stalin* similarly emerges as an archetype of satire that knows how to balance its dark tone with laugh-out-loud moments.

Satire has often been lauded as the only genre truly capable of tackling the atrocities of totalitarian regimes, and it has also been important as a form of resistance and/or coping mechanism within them. For example, people in Soviet Russia circulating joke books making fun of Stalin did so despite facing the risk of being imprisoned or killed if caught with them (see Slate). People in power (or particularly those who are desperate to keep it) perceive satire to be incredibly dangerous; this is made abundantly clear by the fact that *The Death of Stalin* has been banned in Russia. While originally being cleared for screenings and shown to the press, the film was pulled last minute by Vladimir Putin's Ministry of Culture (see Burr). Reasons for this ban were not given, but, and this is striking, it has been called "an act of subversion" (Iannucci qtd. in Tobias) as well as a "targeted provocation" by the Ministry's spokespeople (Busche). As the film does not actually depict the current Russian government, such a strong reaction has to be understood in light of the fact that Putin has rekindled the Stalin cult, and has made no secret of the fact that he sees his nationalistic politics in direct tradition of Stalin's regime (see Busche). As Gessen has pointed out, *The Death of Stalin* is the first filmic depiction of the times that dares to make "Stalin and his circle look absurd," and is thus potentially more dangerous to the status quo than other films that have depicted him in a menacing and negative light (such as 1992's *Stalin*).

The film's ban in Russia has, somewhat predictably, led to its immense popularity in the country; reports from the national press suggest that a majority of Russians are now interested in seeing the film (see Iannucci, "Back in the USSR"). Since modern-day technology makes seeing banned films a lot easier than it has been in the past, many Russians have taken matters into their own hands: there is, for example, a "brilliant photo of a guy watching it in the Red Square, on his laptop, right under Putin's window," according to actor Jason Isaacs (qtd. in Slate). The taking of such a photo, made public by the Russian in question via Twitter (Iannucci, "Russia Banned"), is—I argue—an act of resistance, and as such, highlights the relevance of the film for contemporary times. So while, as in any good satire, *The Death of Stalin*'s connection to real world events is part and parcel of its narrative, this connection is not only one extending back to the Soviet Union under Stalin, but also one embracing current events. Much like the joke books circulated under the Stalinist regime, watching this film is an act of defiance of Putin's politics, and because of its transnational circulation, also to that of right-wing populism in other countries, including the U.S. under Trump.

Iannucci, a Scotsman, has considerable expertise with satirical comedy, having made a name for himself with television shows *The Thick of It* (2005–2012) and *Veep* (2012–2019) in which he takes on British and American politics, respectively. Many of Iannucci's fans have thus expected him to directly tackle the absurdities of Brexit or the Trump administration next (see Iannucci, "How do you"). Yet, he had no interest in doing so, since he said it would be difficult to address such current events directly in fiction while they are still unfolding (Iannucci, "How do you"), and more importantly, he worried about contributing to "normalizing" Donald Trump and his actions (Iannucci, "Bittere Zeiten"). Ever since Trump began campaigning for the presidency, the massive attention devoted to him by not only the press, but also comedians and satirists in the U.S. and abroad, has let voices grow louder and his constant media presence (no matter of what nature) not only promotes him, but also normalizes his right-wing populist ideas and hate-speech, as it drags them from the margins into mainstream public discourse. Trump's appearance with late-night talk show host Jimmy Fallon in September 2016, for instance, in which Fallon playfully ruffled his hair, drew a lot of criticism for contributing to this normalization process—and Iannucci feared that by making fun of Trump outright, it would have the same adverse effect of giving him more exposure, rather than helping to dismantle him and his anti-democratic rhetoric and actions.

The Death of Stalin thus addresses the current political climate only through the backdoor. Besides its historic setting, it does everything to make itself seem contemporary, as its writer-director has confirmed: "I wanted people to feel this is happening now, *right now* [and] in front of you, rather than a long time ago and far, far away" (qtd. in Tobias, emphasis in original). This then makes it possible for the audience to read it as an allegory on contemporary times and opens it up to become a resistance narrative. Almost every review from major media outlets I looked at (sampling German, British, and American media), mentions seeing eerie parallels between Soviet-era Russia and current political events. The same is true for many of the Twitter users that have reviewed it online, as well as those viewers that the creators of the film have engaged with directly (see Iannucci, "Humorless Politicians").

Besides the fact that filming concluded before Donald Trump's election to office, the film has resonated massively with the zeitgeist. Iannucci however was not clairvoyant, even before these events unfolded, the writing was on the wall elsewhere: he intended it as a nod toward some of Europe's "strong leader[s]" like Putin, Italy's Silvio Berlusconi, and Hungary's Viktor Orbán ("Back in the USSR"), something that has been picked up on in reviews, particularly when it comes to the parallels with Putin's Russia (see Gessen). Yet, by the time the film was released to wider audiences in the Western hemisphere (in October 2017 in the UK, and in March 2018 in the U.S.), a majority found a comparison to Trump's U.S. (and post–Brexit Britain) much more obvious, and frightening. Frightening because politicians in these democratic nations seemed to act increasingly like those running the Stalinist regime, and especially comparisons to Trump and his administration were myriad in press reviews. Peter Travers, writing for *Rolling Stone*, likens Stalin's infamous murder lists to a "lethal version of Twitter"; and Christopher Orr from *The Atlantic* provides a laundry list of eerie parallels, including Stalin's cult of personality and revolving-door cabinet. Notable film critic Christopher Kompanek simply concludes: "By implication, 'The Death of Stalin' is about all power-hungry leaders with shifting ideology and demands of absolute loyalty. Anyone … sound familiar?" Jeff Slate (*NBC News*) drives home what becomes apparent in all of these press echoes: "In the context of Trump's chaotic first 14 months in office … the film has taken on new meaning, especially in America." The depiction of Stalin's cabinet as a group of locker-room talking, back-stabbing schemers that ultimately only care for themselves, inevitably hits too close to home.

Iannucci himself however does not believe his work to have an impact on people's political opinion ("Humorless Politicians"). The film's ban by the Kremlin prompted him to write an op-ed for the *New York Times* in which he stated that Russia's decision did not make him proud or happy about the popularity, but rather sad that the government would resort to censorship; he said that for him, "the overwhelming emotion has been one of sad disappointment that in the world of instant communication, and the anarchic dissemination of information, people still think it's O.K. to ban stuff they don't like" ("Russia Banned My Movie"). Yet, the marketing department for the film seems to have caught on to its resonance and underlying potential for what political scientists James Brassett and Alex Sutton have described as "citizen satire," the active participation of citizens in political satire (260).

The official press kit for the film, for instance, included a set of matryoshkas with likenesses of the cast, modeled on similar satirical versions of the famous nesting dolls that often depict Russian heads of state. In mid–March 2018, several Twitter accounts connected to the film (the official handle @Death_of_Stalin, Iannucci's own, @Aiannucci, and that of IFC Films, @IFC-Films) tweeted pictures of the dolls placed at locations associated with Donald Trump or his government in Washington, D.C.—in front of Trump's hotel, at the Capitol, and near the White House—with captions reading "lobbying in D.C." or "There was no collusion!" taking jabs at the persistent rumors of a collusion between Russia and the U.S. government.

Other users made their own connections. Following Michelle Wolf's speech at the U.S. White House correspondents' dinner on April 29, 2018, for instance, a user named Craig Tuohy remarked, "We're in the Death of Stalin timeline!" (@kerraig_uk). Even novelist Joyce Carol Oates joined in the contemporary readings of the film, posting: "Seeing the harrowing 'Death of Stalin' in the era of our deeply corrupt, yearning-to-imprison journalists & over-all would-be dictator in the mode of Putin / Stalin T***p [*sic*] renders the acidic comedy more terrifying than funny. No—not 'funny'—not much. Not right now" (@JoyceCarolOates). But what does it mean for the film that it does dare make fun of such harrowing events in the first place, and that contemporary context now makes many a viewer gag on his/her own laughter? What are the political implications of all of this?

Resistance "is widely defined as opposition with a social and political purpose" (Knight Abowitz). Which works become part of, or even spark, a resistance movement, is arguably left to their audience more than their creators, as political scientist John Street points out: "[T]he 'meaning' of a ... film is not confined to the intentions and ideology of its maker. Meaning ... is contingent; it depends upon the context and conditions in which culture is consumed" (304). So, while Iannucci had not specifically intended it as such ("Humorless Politicians"), his film has emerged for many of its viewers as a satirical look on Trump's America (and beyond), and so its historical context and audience reception has turned into a narrative of resistance for many.

Addressing an ongoing public debate about the role of comedy for British politics, Brassett and Sutton have argued that political comedy, such as Iannucci's work on *The Thick of It*, gives audiences a chance at "everyday agency for reflection and critique," and have concluded that comedy is neither "'good' nor 'bad' for politics," but that "comedy *is* politics" (246, emphasis in original). The above-mentioned citizen satire, then, that also extends to the creation of memes, writing tweets, and other ways of engaging with public discourse, particularly online, has taken on an increasingly important role for the relevance of comedy in politics (Brassett and Sutton 260). The film's marketing department has further engaged with this idea by regularly retweeting users' positive reactions to the film, as well as posting exclusive satirical cartoons and inviting users to come up with witty captions. One of these cartoons, posted by the official handle on March 13, 2018, also directly draws a connection between the two heads of state, depicting Stalin lifting up a tiny Trump. The account also frequently uses satirical language, addressing users as "Comrades," and generally parodies Stalinist propaganda and modes of speech. Some of the produced promotional videos, for example, have emulated propaganda videos from the Stalinist era (@Death_of_Stalin, "We interrupt"). This active engagement with the film's audience via social media has strengthened the film's reading as a resistance narrative beyond academic and press circles. It is a more tongue-in-cheek way of resistance to the Trump administration than attending demonstrations or donating money to human rights' causes, but such engagement with popular culture plays an increasingly important role in mobilizing particularly a millennial audience. There is unmistakable power in recognizing actions and events taking place in your own country, a democratic nation, reflected in those upholding a totalitarian regime—something that may not be as apparent if presented in a dry history lecture.

The Death of Stalin is thus a prime example of what historical film, or historical fiction in general, can and should do. The affective nature of film, i.e., its power to grip audiences emotionally, is both its strength and weakness and is at the core of this discussion (Landsberg 25–27). The most prolific academic author on the genre, historian Robert A. Rosenstone, has concluded that written and visual media each have their own unique modes of portraying history that come with their own benefits and disadvantages (1179). I argue that such an affective portrayal of history, done by the means of popular culture, is particularly helpful when it comes to trying to convey the most harrowing chapters of our past. While critical distance is important for academic work, a certain degree of emotional investment is however vital for stopping history from repeating itself—we need to understand both the mechanisms behind, and the full depth of the atrocities of totalitarian regimes if we want to prevent them from happening again. Without emotional involvement in the subject, the suffering of people is too easily reduced to dates and numbers. *The Death of Stalin*'s satire, the fact that it can make us both laugh (and choke on our laughter in other moments), is thus part and parcel to it successfully conveying its message. As Landsberg has so aptly put it: "History is made productive and meaningful if, despite its difference from the present, it informs how people think about their world. Certain kinds of affective engagements fostered by a historical film might function to produce new knowledge that is useful in the present and that raises political consciousness" (30).

The Death of Stalin is more than just a narrativization of the past: it is a cautionary tale. Manohla Dargis, writing for the *New York Times*, sees further "political resonance" in the fact that the actors speak in British and American accents, as it suggests "that totalitarianism knows no borders," or for that matter, time frame. The film thus emerges as a universal tale on the famous dictum of "the banality of evil," reminding us that everyone, including ourselves, could become either victims or perpetrators of it. By not resorting to the often depicted and discussed Nazi Germany to make this point, but instead using the much lesser known atrocities of Stalinism, the film's message becomes arguably even more poignant. It drives home the idea that yes, it has happened before, and more than once, and if we are not careful, it will most certainly happen again. This is where the film's potential for resistance lies. It wakes us up to this sad truth. It alerts us to the fact that this is happening again, right here, and right now. As a historian, it has become abundantly clear to me that the writing is on the wall. And as a German, where the atrocities of Hitler's regime still loom large (and yet, in a sickening development, right wing populism is equally rearing its ugly head), we have to react before it is too late.

The Death of Stalin's ending suggests that there will always be someone else just waiting in the wings to seize power at the moment an opportunity presents itself. Yet it provides us with one solace: that we can learn from history. That by knowing, by being reminded that all of this has happened before, we can prevent it from happening again. Audiences of the film have seemingly not only understood its message, but also detected the frightening parallels to the events unfolding around them at the time of its release in 2017 and 2018. The next step would be to take the lesson learned from art and turn it into action. Maybe it is not a coincidence, then, that Maria Yudina, the film's only visible resistance fighter and its moral compass, is an artist.

Works Cited

@Aiannucci (Armando Iannucci). "Lobbying in Washington, D.C. #TheDeathofStalin" Twitter, March 16, 2018, 05:40 a.m.
_____. "There was no collusion!" #TheDeathofStalin" Twitter, March 15, 2018, 05:17 a.m.
@Death_of_Stalin (The Death of Stalin). "Citizens, send in your captions! The best entry shall be awarded Ministry employment." Twitter, March 13, 2018, 10:22 a.m.
_____. "We interrupt your vigorous toil to bring you an important message from the leadership.
#TheDeathOfStalin http://bit.ly/TDOSJVID" Twitter, October 19, 2017, 10:00 p.m.
@JoyceCarolOates (Joyce Carol Oates). "Seeing the harrowing "Death of Stalin" in the era of our deeply corrupt, yearning-to-imprison journalists & over-all would-be dictator in the mode of Putin / Stalin T***p renders the acidic comedy more terrifying than funny. No—not "funny"—not much. Not right now." Twitter, April 21, 2018, 7:26 a.m.
@kerraig_uk (Craig Tuohy). "At 15:55 in this vid of Michelle Wolff at the WHCD you can see a guy tell the woman sitting next to him not to laugh at the joke. We're in the Death of Stalin timeline." Twitter, April 29, 2018, 6:16 a.m.
Behrends, Jan C. "The Death of Stalin … oder Diktatur als Komödie." Zeitgeschichte Online, 9 Apr. 2018. https://zeitgeschichte-online.de/film/death-stalin.
Brassett, James and Alex Sutton. "British Satire, everyday politics: Chris Morris, Armando Iannucci and Charlie Brooker." The British Journal of Politics and International Relations, vol. 19, no.2, 2017, pp. 245–262.
Burr, Ty. "'The Death of Stalin' Is Brilliant Satire." The Boston Globe, 14 Mar. 2018. https://www.bostonglobe.com/arts/movies/2018/03/14/the-death-stalin-brilliant-satire/baqC6S8nnVmTxpjpbZtXrM/story.html.
Busche, Andreas. "Warum "The Death of Stalin" in Russland nicht gezeigt werden darf." Der Tagesspiegel, 29 March 2018. https://www.tagesspiegel.de/kultur/politische-satire-im-kino-warum-the-death-of-stalin-in-russland-nicht-gezeigt-werden-darf/21120362.html.
Dargis, Manohla. "Review: The Slapstick Horror of 'The Death of Stalin.'" The New York Times, 8 Mar. 2018. https://www.nytimes.com/2018/03/08/movies/the-death-of-stalin-armando-iannucci-steve-buscemi.html.
Gessen, Masha. "'The Death of Stalin' Captures the Terrifying Absurdity of a Tyrant." The New Yorker, 6 Mar. 2018. https://www.newyorker.com/news/our-columnists/the-death-of-stalin-captures-the-terrifying-absurdity-of-a-tyrant.
Iannucci, Armando. "How do you write political satire when politics are a farce?" The Washington Post, 29 Mar. 2018. https://www.washingtonpost.com/outlook/how-do-you-write-

political-satire-when-politics-are-a-farce/2018/03/29/76897978-3206-11e8-94fa-32d484
60b955_story.html?noredirect=on.
_____. Interview by Julia Ioffe. "Humorless Politicians Are the Most Dangerous." *The Atlantic*,
March 2018. https://www.theatlantic.com/magazine/archive/2018/03/the-death-of-
stalin-armando-iannucci/550937/.
_____. Interview by Neil Minow. "Back in the USSR: Armando Iannucci on 'The Death of
Stalin.'"
_____. Interview by Patrick Heidmann. "Bittere Zeiten haben Immer Humor hervorgebracht."
Spiegel Online, 3 Apr. 2018. https://www.spiegel.de/kultur/kino/the-death-of-stalin-polit-
satiriker-armando-iannucci-im-interview-a-1200390.html.
_____. "Russia Banned My Movie. Hold Your Applause." *The New York Times*, 9 March 2018.
https://www.nytimes.com/2018/03/09/opinion/death-stalin-banned-russia.html.
Knight Abowitz, Kathleen. "A Pragmatist Revisioning of Resistance Theory." *American Edu-
cational Research Journal*, vol. 37, no. 4, 2000, pp. 877–907.
Kompanek, Christopher. "'The Death of Stalin' deploys the satirical stings of 'Veep,' even
more pointedly." *The Washington Post*, March 12, 2018.
Landsberg, Alison. *Engaging the Past. Mass Culture and the Production of Historical Knowledge*. New York, Columbia University Press, 2015.
Orr, Christopher. "The Death of Stalin Is a Wicked Farce." *The Atlantic*, March 16, 2018.
RogerEbert.com, 14 March 2018. https://www.rogerebert.com/interviews/back-in-the-ussr-
armando-iannucci-on-the-death-of-stalin.
Rosenstone, Robert A. "History in Images/History in Words: Reflections on the Possibility
of Really Putting History onto Film." *The American Historical Review*, vol. 93, no. 5,
1988, pp. 1173–1185.
Slate, Jeff. "Armando Iannucci's 'The Death of Stalin' is a darkly perfect satire for a reality
that feels stranger than fiction." NBCNews.com, March 27, 2018.
Street, John. "The Politics of Popular Culture." *The Blackwell Companion to Political Sociology*,
edited by Kate Nash and Alan Scott, Blackwell, Malden, MA, 2001, pp. 302–311.
Tobias, Scott. "Armando Iannucci on 'Death of Stalin,' Political Satire and Trump's Funeral."
Rolling Stone, March 10, 2018.
Travers, Peter. "'The Death of Stalin' Review: Political Satire on Dictators, Corruption Draws
Blood." *Rolling Stone*, March 7, 2018.

Section II

"The only way to support a revolution is to make your own"

Amanda Firestone

The quotation that begins Section Two is by Abbie Hoffman and appears in his book *Revolution for the Hell of It* (1968) (188). One of the most enduring icons of the 1960s, Hoffman's flair for the dramatic and reportedly magnetic personality rallied young people across the country into political activism. He co-founded the Youth International Party—otherwise known as Yippies—in 1968 with Jerry Rubin ("Independent Lens"). The public protests that Yippies staged employed radical tactics that frequently garnered high media attention. And the more coverage that Hoffman and the Yippies accumulated, the more other people became invested in the causes that they backed.

Hoffman's voice captured that of a generation, and it was a voice that firmly rebelled against the conformity of the 1950s, against government oppression and against social injustice. Throughout the 1960s, he participated in Civil Rights, Anti–Vietnam War, Free Speech, and Anti-Capitalist protests, which led to numerous arrests, as well as a turn in front of the House Un-American Activities Committee in 1967 and 1968 (Cook). By the time he co-founded the Yippies, his acts of civil disobedience transformed into nothing short of protest theater. On August 24, 1967, Hoffman, along with Bruce Dancis and about 20 other Yippies, went to the balcony of the New York Stock Exchange and tossed money down onto the trading floor (Wiener). Brokers initially were confused, and then some made a dash for the cash, while others angrily insulted the group. They made a hasty retreat, miraculously avoided arrest, and met with the press.

While it's clear that shock-tactics were an important part of Hoffman's protest persona, he was also savvy about media and exploited the benefits of being a nationally recognized public figure. In Hoffman's own words: "We have often been accused of being media-oriented. As with all criticism, it is both true and not true. The Mobilization had five times the number of press conferences that we did but we received five times the amount of coverage. The impression that we are media freaks is created by our ability to make news. *MEDIA Is Communication.* The concept of getting it all out there applies whether you are speaking to one person or two hundred million" (186–187, emphasis in original). His ability to provoke people was undoubtedly bolstered by his use of multiple media platforms to channel his messages.

The 1960s—the Swinging Sixties—sharply contrast to the historic memory that enfolds the 1950s. At first thoughts, the decade appears in full color, a riotous jumble of hues that saturate photos, TV programs, and movies. There's a high-energy feeling that comes with thinking about the '60s, one that draws from the rock music that imbues many of the events of the era. With hindsight, it appears as a time of incredible optimism as groups publicly and en masse demanded social justice and inexorable changes to deep cultural mores. It is the decade of Civil Rights, Free Love, Women's Liberation, the Sexual Revolution, the Chicano Movement, Gay Liberation, and Black Power. For all of the rigidity that appears to characterize the 1950s, it is flexibility and resilience that seems indelible to the 1960s.

In its own way, this era is also one that is deeply idealized. There is something uplifting about remembering this decade as one of great potential energy with an aura of positivity and opportunity. Yet, the incredible number of media artifacts available from that time tell a much more complex and darker story. Television once again becomes a driving force in how people relate to each other in the wake of national events, both those that are highly divisive and those that bring folks together. As newscaster David Brinkley said, "Television showed the American people TO the American people" (qtd. in McLaughlin, emphasis in original). And, while entertainment TV focuses on sitcoms, Westerns, science fiction shows, and variety shows, it is the news that skyrockets in its importance to everyday life.

On November 22, 1963, President John F. Kennedy was shot while touring Dallas, Texas, in an open-car motorcade. The ABC radio commentator initially notes the numbers of people surrounding the route, but as the president slumps forward and the second fatal shot lands, he shouts, "It appears as though something has happened in the motorcade route. Something, I repeat, has happened in the motorcade route" ("ABC News"). Within minutes, ABC, CBS, and NBC broadcast to television sets across the nation that the president had been shot. It is Ed Silverman of ABC network who makes the first announcement—with only audio and the ABC news bulletin placard ("Kennedy"). Looking back on the broadcasts, Silverman says: "We were trained—make sure you get the story right. What you say today becomes engraved in stone, and when people go to the video tapes, or to the clips, or to the library, what you say becomes history, and if you repeat it long enough, it becomes fact. So get it right the first time" ("Kennedy"). Indeed, the broadcasts of that infamous event live on in perpetuity in easily accessible spaces, and it is our ability to access those, and other recordings of important occurrences, that provides a fuller perspective of the era.

Television was the conduit through which the death of President Kennedy met the public. And, as a result, it cemented TV news as the primary medium from which to receive information about the world. "When something major happened on TV, it affected the whole country at the same time" (McLaughlin). We mourned together as we watched the funeral procession and Kennedy's three-year-old son salute the hearse as it carried the president to his final resting place. We raged and debated with each other as we, for the first time, saw firsthand footage of combat during the Vietnam War, now often referred to as the Living Room War. CBS reporter Morley Safer's report from Cam Ne village showed American Marines using flame throwers to burn the thatched huts of rural farmers. This coverage, and other daily broadcasts like it, galvanized a portion of the populace to public protests, putting their own bodies on the line as they faced police brandishing batons and riot gear.

Abbie Hoffman was just one person who was disillusioned and angry with the state of things in the 1960s. Undoubtedly, he watched media that spurred him to action. His desire to make revolution, and his recognition that it should begin in himself, compelled him to use unusual tactics, which in turn gained him media notoriety that helped him make his messages more widely visible. "Media is communication" (Hoffman 187). Our authors in Section Two are well aware of this, and each takes a personal stake in the subjects that they analyze. Every essay in this section looks to both individuals and small communities as having the power to make irrevocable change in the world.

Kwasu David Tembo's essay examines the character of Erik Killmonger and his positionality as a Third Culture Kid (TCK), a person who comes of age outside of their family's home origin. Killmonger uses common colonialist/imperialist strategies as he seeks to overrule Wakanda, though those strategies are directly at odds with his mission to "free" all black people the world over from white, systemic oppressions. Ultimately, his uncontrollable rage at being resigned to live "out of place" is his downfall, yet the havoc he has wrought to Wakanda has immutable impact on the nation going forward.

While Killmonger is intent on destroying a nation-state, sometimes the destruction of a corrupt power system hinges on the possibility of saving a single person. Through the fairy tale trope of the voiceless heroine, Jeana Jorgensen analyzes Elisa, the main character of *The Shape of Water*, as a feminist and queer protagonist. Elisa's disability—her muteness—doesn't preclude her from forming a strong and loving community of friends, nor does it render her incapable of achieving sexual pleasure. Elisa, as a holistic representation of a disabled person, works to rescue her lover and defy the cruel antagonist Strickland. She may not be able to speak, but Elisa is far from voiceless.

The inclusion of a variety of voices is crucial to achieving a well-rounded understanding of experiences. Amanda K. LeBlanc interrogates how the hit Broadway show *Hamilton: An American Musical* contests the historical record by placing people of color in the lacuna of the story of America's founding. Lin-Manuel Miranda's remixed vision of historical figure Alexander Hamilton asks audiences and fans to envision how the resistance narratives crucial to American history are transformed when centering seemingly contemporary issues like immigration, identity politics, and intersectionality.

There is an important restorative power in the opportunity and ability to see marginalized people working together. While *Hamilton* re-centers people of color as the nation's architects, recent Disney films *Frozen* and *Moana* privilege women's relationships as key in overcoming obstacles, particularly those related to trauma. Jessica Stanley examines how the women in these two films—primarily Elsa, Anna, and Moana—embark on resistance journeys, striking out against the patriarchal order. The traumas these characters face are connected with the #MeToo Movement, and Neterer reveals the importance of seeing a major media producer like Disney tackle such subjects, even subtextually, as a way to potentially help viewers process their own experiences.

Our last essay in Section Two attends to the abilities of physical bodies to perform as sites of resistance in the public sphere. S. Katherine Cooper, Brittany M. Harder, and Corinne E. Fanta analyze the ways in which bodies are regulated based on weight and public perceptions of healthiness, productivity, and aesthetic beauty. There appears to be an extant moral panic about fatness, fat women in particular, as supported by reality TV shows like *The Biggest Loser*. However, it is through the lens of comedy that fatness can be reappraised and renegotiated as a normative identity. Famous comedians like Melissa McCarthy and Amy Schumer forefront the discussion as they break stereotypes and expectations heaped onto fat women.

The subjects in these five essays speak to Abbie Hoffman's sentiment that, effectively, revolution needs to begin inside the self. Our authors have chosen subjects that center on the ability of one person, or that of a few people, to make marked and long-lasting change through their actions. The events and characters analyzed here embody the spirit of the 1960s. In a decade embroiled in so much rebellion and friction between a generation of people swept up in a countercultural revolution and generations of others who looked to the comfort of well-trod beliefs and values, it was perhaps inevitable that Americans would clash, sometimes violently, against the sea change. Each of the people who participated in picket lines and sit ins, rock concerts and walk outs, letter campaigns and riots, all said to themselves at some point, "this is not the world I want to live in and I want to *do* something to make a change." While major events of the decade united people, like President Kennedy's death or the 1969 moon landing, it is the conflict that is best remembered. And every movement begins with a single step.

WORKS CITED

"ABC News Coverage of The Assassination of President Kennedy (1:30 P.M. 4:28 P.M. E.T.). *YouTube*, uploaded by JFK1963NEWSVIDEOS. 19 Nov. 2015, https://www.youtube.com/watch?v=qe_p2_4oasQ.

Cook, Dana. "Where Have You Gone Abbie Hoffman?" *Counter Punch*. 5 April 2019. https://www.counterpunch.org/2019/04/05/where-have-you-gone-abbie-hoffman/.

Hoffman, Abbie. *Revolution for the Hell of It*. 1968. Thunder's Mouth Press, 2005.

"Independent Lens. CHICAGO 10. The Yippies | PBS." *Independent Lens*, Independent Television Service, 2017. https://www.pbs.org/independentlens/chicago10/yippies.html.

"Kennedy assassination remembered by ABC News anchor." *ABC News*, 18 Nov. 2013. https://abcnews.go.com/US/video/kennedy-assassination-remembered-abc-news-anchor-20926278.

McLaughlin, Katie. "5 Surprising Things That 1960s TV Changed." *CNN*, 25 Aug. 2014, https://www.cnn.com/2014/05/29/showbiz/tv/sixties-five-things-television/index.html.

Wiener, Jon. "When Abbie Hoffman Threw Money at the New York Stock Exchange." *The Nation*. 24 Aug. 2017. https://www.thenation.com/article/it-was-50-years-ago-today-abbie-hoffman-threw-money-at-the-new-york-stock-exchange/.

The Trial of King Killmonger

Theorizing the Rage of a Third Culture Kid as Resistance

KWASU DAVID TEMBO

When I was 14 years old, I was given a Discman for my birthday, which I excitedly took with me to the dormitories of the boarding school I attended. I kept it secret for as long as I could as so many minor electronics, from cell phones to electric toothbrushes, had the tendency to vanish in our House. I was willing to risk theft and heartbreak because music was, and still is, the only thing in my life that has never let me down. However, a Discman without CDs is like an *assegai*[1] without a blade. I solicited, traded, begged, and borrowed music that moved me. Inevitably, Jeffrey, the dorm bully, found both my Discman and my then two favorite CDs—*Defenders of the Underworld* (1999) and *Nevermind* (1991)—and quickly, loudly, and cruelly made their disapproval known. It was one of many experiences of its kind whereby I was labeled "too white for the black kids" based on my interest in art deemed by my black peers to be quintessentially white. To my surprise, the white boys in the dorm stood in solidarity with Jeffrey, sharing his displeasure at my "eclectic" tastes. It was an instance of also being "too black for the whites" and as such, a common enemy, target, or Other for the short-sightedness of both groups. At that age, being of a "third kind" in that way filled me with rage as it was clear to me that my allegiance was to no flag or shade but to sound and feeling; an allegiance to art that we all seemingly shared. This was the first thought I had after exiting a theatrical screening of *Black Panther* (2018).

In this essay, I contend that to me and other people with similar shared experiences that Killmonger, the antagonist of *Black Panther* (hereon *BP*), is important because he embodies the rage we share of being out-of-place.

Through a combination of black writer/director Ryan Coogler's vision and Michael B. Jordan's performance, Killmonger's character and motivations act as important vehicles for several postcolonial ideas and critiques. These include: the struggle for identity in the African American diaspora and the identarian limitations of Pan African movements and/or ideologies; the issues of self-esteem and cultural connection across the dialectical divide between "African" and "American"; the figure of the Third Culture Kid (TCK) as rebel; the place and/or necessity of violence in revolutionary acts; and criticisms of the radical inconsistencies of African leadership. Using Killmonger as a case study, and also referencing the postcolonial theories of Said, Fanon, and Bhabha, this essay will examine how Killmonger embodies the aforesaid issues through two main lines of thought: First, Killmonger's positionality as a TCK and, second, the interesting complex that results from his tactics being both imperialist/colonialist but also ostensibly appearing as radical decolonization.

Are we drawn to revolutionary figures because we identify with their struggle, their pain? Do we secretly want their revolution to fail for fear that its success will morph into that which it sought to overthrow in the first place? These and other questions orbit broader issues and debates that the film's morally ambiguous antagonist embodies. Ostensibly, the rage that informs Killmonger's mission and motivations is predicated on a revolutionary ideal: to use Wakanda's Vibranium reserves and vast technological resources to fulfill his father's plan of the radical social, economic, and cultural empowerment of all people of African descent. Upon closer inspection, however, the character's motivations are based on an ardent desire for revenge at having been disowned by those he thought to be his "people." I emphasize the word "people" here as a way of drawing attention to the fact that concepts including but not limited to community, identity, race, and self-hood are interrogated in the film. I argue that Killmonger's desire to liberate all African peoples is a macroscopic goal for a microscopic problem—his own pervasive and traumatic sense of lack of identity, agency, culture, and pride. The braggadocio, charm, and focus with which the character pursues his goal seemingly muddies its unavoidable primary moral problem; namely, Killmonger has no compunctions about using violence in achieving said goal. In other words, such an emancipatory goal invites the viewer to overlook or permit the issues associated with the character's unresolved and vehement hatred, vengefulness, propensity for violence and, most troublingly of all, Killmonger's latently imperialist thinking.

It perhaps is difficult to reconcile the hurt lost child, the idealistic revolutionary, and the murderer encapsulated in Killmonger. However, the seemingly irresolvable tension between his goals and his actions are shown to be inherited from his father. Zuri tells T'Challa about the circumstances of

N'Jobu's placement in Oakland, California: "Your uncle took a War Dog assignment in America. [...] The hardships he saw there radicalized your uncle" (*BP*). While in Oakland, N'Jobu formed plans to forcibly end Wakanda's isolationist policies, and when confronted by King T'Chaka and Zuri for his treason, N'Jobu is killed in a skirmish. It is Erik, the child Killmonger, who finds his father's body. So, begins the sensibility of displacement and rage that consumes Killmonger's life. T'Challa refers to Killmonger as "a monster of our own making..." and it is particularly apropos (*BP*). While watching the film, my initial support of Killmonger and my personal identification with his abundant rage and desire for self and cultural acceptance was troubled by the sense that his entire goal can also be viewed as a corruption of his father's mission of revolution and emancipation.

Coogler's script characterizes Killmonger as an individual whose experiences of hardship and strife make any belief in a society verging on utopian repellent. It is an internal conflict further stoked by the fact that Coogler shows Wakanda to indeed be in possession of the techno-militaristic ability to liberate all oppressed black people across the world. I acknowledge that the sociopolitical issues and debates concerning the idea of "liberation" are complex here. Coogler's narrative draws attention to the problem of liberation alongside the question of who it is that gets to decide who it is that gets liberated, as well as other ancillary conundrums. These include questions like the manner, execution, and/or appearance of liberation itself, as well as those individuals who reject said liberation. The shimmering audio-visual spectacle framing the presentation of Wakanda to Killmonger, and by extension the audience, portrays the nation exactly as the character expects. Killmonger's father raised him on tales of Wakanda's beauty, might, culture, and seemingly inexhaustible fecundity: a utopia of black excellence built on a confluence of traditional African religious beliefs and practices, and sci-fi futurity. However, N'Jobu also taught his son about the reality of Wakanda's global isolationist practices, deceptiveness, and secrecy. It is a practice that he frames in terms of abandonment and cowardice as opposed to adroit global political strategy.

Perhaps the film's most sweeping claims are that from the perspective of the countless oppressed peoples of African descent all over the world, a place like Wakanda would represent *both* a type of mythical black Camelot, as well as a place of sociopolitical, economic, and cultural reprieve to which they have no access. On the one hand, Wakanda represents a non-place, a figment, a dream, a bedtime story, and a fantasy of "home." On the other hand, it represents an apposite means to achieve his global Pan African liberation goal in a way that requires the very real resources of Wakanda but is not limited to its borders. This is made clear in some of the character's most memorable pieces of dialogue: "y'all sitting up here all comfortable. Must feel good. Meanwhile, there's about two billion people all over the world that look like us, but their lives are a lot harder … all over the planet our people suffer because they do not have the tools to fight back" and "you know, where I'm from, when black folks started revolutions, they didn't have the firepower to fight their oppressors" (*BP*).

Dichotomously is the fact that his ostensible mission of reconciliation, revolution, and empowerment ultimately devolves into imperialist international arms dealing and the promotion of in-fighting between the very individuals, and by extension the very empire, he claims to seek to unify and establish. This problem evokes George Orwell's comment about the dangers inherent to the true nature of the relationship between revolution and power: "one does not establish a dictatorship in order to safeguard a revolution; one makes the revolution in order to establish the dictatorship" (220). This same danger is latently implied in Killmonger's goals and the behaviors he sees as necessary to bring them about. They are riddled with an inescapable sense of hypocrisy. Not unlike certain real-world scenarios, such as Robert Mugabe's half century vendetta against the English crown, Killmonger uses the guise of an altruistic ideology of large-scale liberation for all Africans as a vehicle for his personal revenge.

The paradox of Killmonger's ideology and his practices is by no means surreptitious. The character repeatedly annunciates it. For example, in one scene, Killmonger says to T'Challa, "the world took everything away from me! Everything I ever loved! But I'mma make sure we're even. I'mma track down anyone who would even think about being loyal to you and I'mma put their ass in the dirt, right next to Zuri!" (*BP*). In a very real sense, Killmonger's methods of revolution are in no way dissimilar to certain tools and techniques employed by the colonialists, monarchists, and imperialists he so despises. From his own scholarship of colonialist methods and tools and their continued ramifications in America (informed by actor Jordan's preparatory research into the work of Huey P. Newton, Fred Hampton, Marcus Garvey, and Malcolm X), coupled with his special forces training in destabilizing governments at moments of transition, Killmonger's plan to distribute Vibranium-based technology throughout the world and provide weapons to oppressed peoples are the same stratagems employed by colonial and imperial white Western powers in their oppressive global regimes. In this sense, his ostensible pride in and understanding of Wakandan customs, traditions, his own name and title, and the protocols and procedures of kingship are secondary to his maintenance of absolute power. This can be noted in his violent desecration of Wakandan holy sites, such as burning the City of the Dead and the Herb Garden to ensure no new Panther kings would follow and challenge his sovereignty.

However, I contend that his methods of authority and control are themselves secondary to Killmonger's desire for identity and revenge. In this sense, while seemingly essential to his machinations of global domination, these imperialist tactics do not stand as true markers of the *origin* of his plan. Killmonger concedes in his final moments at the end of the film that his entire plan was predicated on the dreams of a young boy chasing a black utopia his father told him about. This moment of self-awareness is summed up in the line "can you believe that? A kid from Oakland walking around believing in fairy-tales" (*BP*). The implication here is that Killmonger's belief in Wakanda ultimately has tragic consequences when met with the realities of its ideology of isolationism. To him, Wakanda will always remain inaccessible partly due to his own actions, but also due to the iniquitous history of his forebears, and the fact that the nation itself has expressed no reconciliatory desire to re-unite Africans with African Americans. Here, already certain inescapable problems with Killmonger's worldview emerge. Firstly, he assumes that all, if not most, African Americans have a desire, great or small, to reunite with Africa in any form. Secondly, though Killmonger is portrayed as a well-traveled soldier of fortune who has plied his trade across the continent and beyond, his approach to Africa as an undifferentiated landmass problematically overlooks its 54 individual nations, their geopolitics and customs. Such an approach bespeaks a radical sense of short-sightedness. As I will argue, the reason for this short-sightedness is, in a significant way, predicated on Killmonger's own psychological and emotional turmoil.

I contend that the film now inhabits a space of hope as a milestone of black representation in contemporary mainstream media. I speculate that there are two overarching outcomes that have and will emerge as a result. First, the film inspires thousands of disenfranchised black American youths to (re)research, (re)discover, and (re)endeavor toward an understanding of their African heritage. Second, that the cultural, economic, and political resonances of the film have been so broad and palpable in America and across the global centers of the African diaspora that many black—and within the context of the film—black American teenagers will see the film as a goal in itself, as opposed to a tool in a greater struggle for cultural identity and political agency. Here, the film risks becoming another fairy tale of black achievement as opposed to a clarion call for its continued growth and evolution, leaving said youths' feelings of being culturally unidentifiable and politically ineffective circumscribed in a powerful illusion in the form of a successful black superhero film.

It would seem that those most susceptible to this danger are those who experience pervasive feelings of sociopolitical and cultural displacement. In the context of this essay, these individuals are represented by the idea of the Third Culture Kid (TCK). Researcher Ruth Hill Useem describes a TCK as "a person who has spent a significant part of his or her developmental years outside their parents' culture. The third culture kid builds relationships to all the cultures, while not having full ownership in any. Although elements from each culture are assimilated into the third culture kid's life experience, the sense of belonging is in relationship to others of the same background, other TCKs." The word "kid" here refers to the condition of the TCK being raised as such for a significant portion of their developmental years. The latent implication of this definition is that TCKs' development is in some way disrupted; that is, the processes involved in an individual's development of a personal and cultural identity as sequestered to a single culture or society (Moore and Barker 553). The word "third" implies a personal and cultural triad. The individual's first culture refers to the TCK's parents' culture of origin. The second refers to the culture of where the TCK currently resides, and the third a fusion of the two, to varying degrees and in various ways (Melles and Schwartz 260).

One question here is: what advantages does Killmonger have over T'Challa as a TCK? While traditionally TCKs are deft at fostering various types of relationships with a broad spectrum of individuals hailing from a variety of cultures, their own culturalessness/hybridity/nomadism in terms of both membership in and cultural practices of a specific culture that facilitates this adaptability, is a phenomenon both affirmed and undermined by Killmonger. TCKs typically possess a broad worldview through which they are able to deal with the various experiences they encounter without reverting to limited purviews of socio-cultural essentialism(s); in other words, the world is multifaceted both conceptually and experientially to a TCK.

TCKs are also imbued with a particular cultural intelligence that can be thought of as a type of worldliness that allows them to function successfully in various ethnic, cultural, and national milieus. With skills first developed as a TCK, Killmonger adapts, strategizes, and executes what is tantamount to a coup all but single-handedly. It is this lateral, critical, and creative thinking born of his political and cultural status as a TCK that allows Killmonger to exploit the sociopolitical and cultural stagnancy he identifies as Wakanda's primary weakness. Bound to tradition, the authority of the throne, and its state-cult founded on the royally-controlled access to the supernatural powers of the Black Panther it oversees, to Killmonger, the ubiquity of Vibranium—not only as a resource, but as the literal foundation of their culture and way of life—stands out starkly from homogeneity of the Wakandan world view. However, his own personal anger and desire for identity makes him equally complicit in his own psycho-emotional stagnation; that is, the continuation of his unresolved traumas. The irony here is that while Killmonger's status as a TCK would seemingly make him more pragmatically adaptable and versatile than T'Challa, the trauma of being as such makes him also as homogenous about his own *personal* outlook, one predicated on the singularity of his mission, as much as T'Challa is to the views of his ancestors and royal kin.

In *Black Panther*, Coogler co-establishes a diegesis where Wakanda has similar attributes/sociopolitical and theoretical status as the real-world Orient as theorized and discussed by Edward Said in his seminal text *Orientalism* (1978). Like Said's deconstruction of the idea of the Orient, the *idea* of Wakanda can similarly be described as "a place of romance, exotic beings, haunting memories and landscapes, remarkable experiences" (Said 1). In terms of the so-called "black experience," which I do not hold as a static, homogenous, monolithic construction, Wakanda stands as a paradoxical bright shadow of the African American black experience in the same way that "the Orient has helped to define Europe (or the West) as its contrasting image, idea, personality, experience" (Said 2). While the origin, existence, and nature of Wakanda remains fragmentary in the conscience of the wider world in Coogler's narrative, Wakanda acts as a fictional conceptual space in which to place notions of "blackness" under review. The most notable of these pertain to the way that Coogler questions, undermines, and in some instances reaffirms quintessential audio-visual constructions of so-called "blackness." The implication here is that much in the same way Said argues that the West defined itself in contradistinction to the East, Coogler sets up Wakanda in contradistinction to *all* other types of non–African "blackness." This highlights the way in which Africans and African Americans define themselves in contradistinction to one another, as well as the material, social, political, economic, and cultural consequences that result from this conflict.

The concept of a place beyond colonial machinations, practices, and legacy defined by black sociopolitical, economic, and cultural cohesion, technological innovation, and military strength would seem a dream for many descendants of slaves. However, Africans populate Wakanda, and it was Africans who were absconded to the West.[2] Here, Killmonger is an example of the paradox of Wakanda in terms of its relationship to the black non–African diaspora and all the attended sociopolitical, cultural, judicial, and economic issues and debates that circumscribe that identity, performance, heritage, tradition(s), and so on. Killmonger is the black son of a black prince living in a "white" country built by black slaves. His existence as a Wakandan-American makes him the embodiment of the dream *in* the nightmare, a prince of a supra–Colonial superpower abandoned in and made to fight for a failing colonial superpower. The rage and turmoil this paradox creates in someone in this position is highlighted when Killmonger states that it is better to die than live in bondage of this kind (*BP*).

When Wakanda is finally presented to the rest of the world, there is no preceding history upon which to build a frame of reference for prior encounters with the "invisible" nation. Due to Wakanda's concerted efforts to remain clandestine, the world only knows of it as quintessentially "African" from a Western perspective: traditional and poor; in essence, not a threat, not minerally rich, and therefore not worth knowing. Such views frame how Western peoples typically speak about and approach Africa in general; how they make statements about it and rule over it by "dominating, restructuring, and having authority over" it (Said 3). It is, again, a dialectic of mastery Killmonger indeed seeks to break by using the tools of the master against him: a house Negro waking up in the middle of the night to burn the master's house to cinders while he sleeps therein.

Referring to Homi K. Bhabha's *The Location of Culture* (1994), I argue that Coogler characterizes Killmonger as what I call a *beyonder*. The term denotes a thirdspace that "provides the terrain for elaborating strategies of selfhood—singular or communal—that initiate new signs of identity, and innovative sites of collaboration, and contestation, in the act of defining the idea of society itself," Wakandan or otherwise (Bhabha 1–2). The covert implication here is that this space exists within but also as distinct from the dominant sociopolitical, economic, and cultural space it occupies. Examples of such specifically ethnic spaces in nations other than those of their origin, could be Little Ethiopia in central Los Angeles or Chinatown in San Francisco. These communities have to navigate the mores and practices of their host nations and their communities but in so doing, necessarily revalue, adapt, and critique their own. In this way, understanding the relationship between Killmonger and T'Challa, the rage of a TCK and the shock this brings to the heir of a quasi-utopian enclave, there is a "need to understand cultural difference as the production of minority identities that 'split'—are estranged unto themselves—in the act of being articulated into a collective body" (Bhabha 3). In being beyond a singular cultural identity or monolithic conception of "black," Killmonger occupies the interstice of foreignness and familiarity, black self and black Other in both sociopolitical, economic, and cultural settings of America and Wakanda. However, along with Coogler highlighting his emancipatory agenda, coupled with Jordan's menacing and volatile performance influenced by the equally complex message of late Californian rapper 2Pac, the film also latently problematizes the idea of Killmonger as a beyonder as defined above (Kyles). This can be noted in the fact that the character's position is far from neutral, detached, or altruistic. Killmonger occupies the fissure between cultural and racial familiarity and difference but he does so transgressively and violently.

When speaking to a museum curator of an African exhibit in London who tells him the artifacts themselves are not for sale, Killmonger responds by asking, "how do you think your ancestors got these? Did they pay a fair price, or did they take them, like they took everything else?" (*BP*). Replete with the attendant violence of murdering the curator, Killmonger's contention here is not unlike the issues of violence and decolonization as described by Fritz Fanon in *Wretched of the Earth* (1963). In the meeting of the highly hierarchic Wakandan state-cult and the guerrilla tactics employed by Killmonger, the latter's methods in relation to the rigidity of the former resembles Fanon's description of the underlying nature of decolonization: "decolonization, which sets out to change the order of the world, is, obviously, a program of complete disorder. But it cannot come as a result of magical practices, nor of a natural shock, nor of a friendly understanding [....] Decolonization is the meeting of two forces, opposed to each other by their very nature" (35). In this sense, Killmonger's entire mission can be read as analogous to decolonization as

> a process which never takes place unnoticed, for it influences individuals and modifies them fundamentally. It transforms spectators crushed with their inessentiality into privileged actors, with the grandiose glare of history's floodlights upon them. It brings a natural rhythm into existence, introduced by new men, and with it a new language and a new humanity. Decolonization is the veritable creation of new men. But this creation owes nothing of its legitimacy to any supernatural power; the "thing" which has been colonized becomes man during the same process by which it frees itself [Fanon 35–36].

In *Black Panther*, this ethic of decolonization truly begins in a scene where Killmonger reveals himself dramatically to the council of Wakandan elders in a pageant that functions as a declaration of war against "the old way" enshrined by Wakandan traditionalism. Here, the character presents himself as a new *black* man; one neither the descendent of an American slave, nor the cowering heir to a Wakandan prince. The presentation of his positionality in this way portrays Killmonger as a new threat or influence that seeks to not only modify the core infrastructures of Wakanda, but these elements within the broader scope of the entire balance of global power itself. As an individual who could only spectate in the play of power and agency in America, and indeed speculate about the same in a pseudo-mythic Wakanda, Killmonger turns his position of double abjection into one of privilege. Combining tactics syncretically, he seemingly is able to fashion a new language, discourse, and practices of "blackness"—African or non–African. Moreover, this privilege of abjection that allows Killmonger to painstakingly plan and execute his coup does not initially or totally depend on the intercession of supernatural aids like the Heart Shaped Herb and its associated Panther powers.

This is precisely what makes Killmonger's personal situation so antagonistic with that of T'Challa. T'Challa is not only the monarch, but the living embodiment of the comparatively extreme privilege of one *type* of "blackness" over, above, and away from *all* others. Wakandan isolationist philosophy and sociopolitical practices ensures that it remains a monolithic fixed community of blackness while paradoxically being essentially *distinct* from all other non–

Wakandan types of blackness. In contrast, as a Wakandan *beyond* said structures—one who negotiates culture and identity in America and, more broadly, the thirdspace of global sociopolitics—Killmonger represents flux, change, negotiation, and tactics of global multiplicity. Remember, for everything and everywhere outside of Wakanda, the horrors of war, genocide, colonialism, and their individual and collective repercussions witnessed and practiced in and by the West are intractably real and cannot be refracted or ameliorated by royal privilege or national isolationism. In view of these aforementioned horrors, it initially seemed to me that what Killmonger represents is a demand for "an encounter with 'newness' that is not part of the continuum of past and present," one that "creates a sense of the new as an insurgent act of cultural or aesthetic precedent; it renews the past, refiguring it as a contingent 'in-between' space, that innovates and interrupts the performance of the present. The 'past-present' becomes part of the necessity, not the nostalgia, of living" (Bhabha 7). That is to say, that his radical ideology and methods of achieving it all point to the exigency of reclaiming the past be it the land, beliefs, or practices of one's country of origin. The goal here is revaluing and interrupting the sociopolitical, economic, and cultural issues and debates that result from identifying with this past. Being that Killmonger is a beyonder, a TCK who exists and operates in the in-between spaces of African American cultures and conceptions of blackness, I thought Killmonger's revolution had a higher chance of success by *not* being practically encumbered by the beliefs and cultural codes of either side, America or Africa.

The notion of newness here—ideological, technological, epistemic, and/or cultural—is bound up with the character's self-identification with the figure of the revolutionary. He sees himself as "serving justice to a man who stole [Wakanda's] Vibranium and murdered [her] people. Justice [her] king couldn't deliver" (*BP*). Moreover, Killmonger's stance as a radical revolutionary can be summarized by, ironically, his last line: "just bury me in the ocean with my ancestors who jumped from the ships because they knew death was better than bondage" (*BP*). Similarly, several lines ostensibly confirm his discipline, obsessiveness, and revolutionary focus. For example: "I lived my entire life waiting for this moment. I trained, I lied. I killed in America, Afghanistan, Iraq…. I took life for my own brothers and sisters right here on this continent! And all this death just so I could kill you!," which he utters during his duel with T'Challa for the mantles of king and Black Panther (*BP*).

This question of what newness Killmonger brings to both Africa and America is made exigent because while Coogler sets up the antagonism between Wakanda and Killmonger as one of isolationist traditionalism and radical socialism, the encounter between the two parties does not guarantee that anything new (in terms of ideologies, government, and technology) will emerge as a result. Killmonger brings the following reason to this encounter:

"two billion people all over the world that look like us, but their lives are a lot harder ... all over the planet our people suffer because they do not have the tools to fight back," claiming that his purpose is to forcibly seize Wakandan resources to offer the globally black oppressed the means to combat their oppressors (*BP*). As the figurehead of the hoarding and obfuscation of this wealth, T'Challa counters with the sentiment that Wakanda cannot be involved in such a conflict at the expense of the dissolution of the secrecy of its own border. Here, Killmonger's plan for radical redistribution of Wakandan wealth resembles a former colony's demand of its former colonizer to reimburse the resources it forcibly seized in the form of reparations. However, from Killmonger's perspective, latent within this demand is a desire for power and personal restitution of deep familial psycho-emotional traumas. In other words, while potent and vociferously posed, the reality of Killmonger's plan is couched in very *old* psycho-emotional and sociopolitical concerns: a will to power and revenge, two goals that, on closer inspection, increasingly resemble as that which minorities and the oppressed decry so ardently, namely global imperialism. Thus, while it may appear that Killmonger indeed uses the master's tools to dismantle his house, he ultimately behaves like the master in his use thereof.

It would be easy enough to conclude from the above analysis that Killmonger is a colonist in a revolutionary's livery. On the one hand, he could rightly be called a hurt kid angrily and violently looking for both home and himself. For Killmonger, the death of his father ensures that "violence makes its way forward, and [he] identifies his enemy and recognizes all his misfortunes, throwing all the exacerbated might of his hate and anger into this new channel. But how do we pass from the atmosphere of violence to violence in action? What makes the lid blow off?" (Fanon 70). It is Killmonger who sees his desire for identity, culture, home, and purpose as inextricable from violence. In this sense, Killmonger as "the colonized man finds his freedom in and through violence. This rule of conduct enlightens the agent because it indicates to him the means and the end" (Fanon 86). In the last instance, Killmonger's justification for his actions, the image he would like others to see, the Rebel, noble and scarred, ultimately refer to this ethic of violence and begets more of the same.

Violence is so central to Killmonger's attempt at identity because "at the level of individuals, violence is a cleansing force. It frees [him] from his inferiority complex and from his despair and inaction; it makes him fearless and restores his self-respect" (Fanon 93). If, indeed, the systematic negation of self, identity, culture, history, and love Killmonger experiences doubly as a result of the colonialist legacy of America and his seeming abandonment by Wakanda, this double abjection forces him to constantly ask himself who he is, where he came from, and why he cannot go back there to find himself.

For Killmonger, the only way toward identity, purpose, revenge, and/or psychological and emotional relief from the traumas of being a TCK is, to borrow a phrase from Fanon, "illuminated by violence" (Fanon 94).

For both T'Challa and Killmonger, the fight for the kingdom of Wakanda is a fight for their identities in their respective ways, the King against the Rebel. The former's identity is predicated on the rigid and unchanging ideology of cultural and historical legacy, regardless of how rich it is perceived to be. The latter, in contrast, experiences life, let alone his own identity as a black man, as being in a state of constant flux. His status as a TCK in this way makes his experience of being completely contrary to the stability of concepts of "home" and/or "nation" embodied by Wakanda. In my personal experience of being a beyonder/thirdspacer, there was no will to violence despite there being vast amounts of anger and confusion I carried and still carry with me. In being too white for the blacks and too black for the whites, the value and adroitness of my thinking, creativity, perspectives, humor, and so on often felt valueless and overlooked. Unlike Killmonger, however, I had no desire to return home and establish myself, neither cooperatively nor antagonistically. I had no desire of revenging myself on "my" people or my "hosts" in the diaspora, even in view of my own father's lived experience of the twilight of colonialism in what was once known as North Rhodesia (modern day Zambia), or my mother's struggle to keep both her fight and her love alive in the saturnine milieu fashioned by Botha and his apartheid. This is due to the fact that throughout my personal experience of psycho-emotional and cultural hybridity, I have realized that I have no people in a framed or static sense, nor do I feel an exigent desire to identify as such-and-such, nor stand under a flag, as it were. While indeed painful, awkward, isolating, and difficult to explain, my experiences as a beyonder/thirdspacer have revealed the fact that despite humanity's pretensions at dominance and power, being is intractably myriad, and that its complexity is inherently combinatory.

In the last instance, Killmonger's greatest strength is ultimately his greatest weakness, one that acts as a tragic flaw, ensuring his failure as a revolutionary. The character's violent attempts to assuage the rage of feeling out of place only engenders more violence. It fails to illuminate a place wherein such feelings can be ameliorated because his brand of violence is shown to be totally destructive. There is no indication in Jordan's performance or Coogler's screenplay that suggests that such a space of redemption and peace exists for Killmonger to put down the *assegai*, as it were, and seek to rebuild a truly new type of blackness, neither African nor non–African. The film concludes by suggesting that his trauma is too penetrating for him to see the opportunity of turning the out-of-place into an outer-our-space: a truly radical space that undoes the dialectical divide between "African" and "American" and makes redundant the struggle for identity in the African American diaspora as it has historically attempted to navigate the identarian limitations of Pan African movements/ideologies; a space in which the issues of pride, self-esteem, personal and cultural connection are not holdovers of the past but goals around which to orient courageous sociopolitical, economic, and cultural play; a space in which the figure of the TCK is neither rebel nor tyrant but an artist; a space whose existence, dissolution, and reestablishment is not necessarily constituted by violence; a space not beholden to a throne, king, god, herb, technology, or weapon but only the myriad possibilities afforded those of fluid cultural identities. Ultimately, this is what the trials, successes, and failures of Killmonger represented for me and my positionality as a TCK.

NOTES

1. A short broad-bladed spear designed by the famous Zulu warlord and king Shaka for close quarters combat.

2. I acknowledge here the fact that in many cases, groups of Africans traded and/or sold other Africans into the European system of slavery.

WORKS CITED

Bhabha, Homi K. *The Location of Culture.* Routledge, 1994

Black Panther. Directed by Ryan Coogler, Walt Disney Studios, 2018.

Fanon, Fritz. *Wretched of the Earth.* Grove Weidenfeld, 1963.

Kyles, Yohance. "Michael B. Jordan Talks Listening to 2Pac for 'Black Panther' Role." *Allhiphop*, 15 Feb, 2018. https://allhiphop.com/news/michael-b-jordan-talks-listening-to-2pac-for-black-panther-role-_9G_ckmmPkOEwwcl4QtKjA/.

Melles, Elizabeth A., and Schwartz, Jonathan. "Does the Third Culture Kid Experience Predict Levels of Prejudice?" *International Journal of Intercultural Relations.* Vol. 37, No. 2, 2013, pp. 260–267.

Moore, Andrea M., and Gina G. Barker. "Confused or Multicultural: Third Culture Individuals' Cultural Identity." *International Journal of Intercultural Relations.* Vol. 36, No. 4, 2012, pp. 553–562.

Orwell, George. *Nineteen-Eighty-Four.* 1949. Penguin Books. 2000.

Said, Edward. *Orientalism.* Pantheon Books, 1978.

Useem, Ruth. "What Is a Third Culture Kid?" *TCK World: The Official Home of Third Culture Kids (TCKs),* http://www.tckworld.com/useem/art1.html.

Voiceless Yet Vocal

Speaking Desire in The Shape of Water

Jeana Jorgensen

Sometimes cursed, and sometimes silent of their own choosing, voiceless heroines populate fairy tales and fairy-tale-influenced media.[1] For example, the protagonist in the Grimms' tales "The Six Swans" and "The Twelve Brothers" is faced with an impossible choice: to be a good sister (to her brothers who have been turned into birds), or to be a good wife and mother. In choosing to be a good sister by remaining silent in order to disenchant her brothers, she inevitably condemns her marriage to fail, and her children to die. This story has a happy ending when her children are magically restored to her at the moment when her brothers are disenchanted, but in Hans Christian Andersen's "The Little Mermaid," the voiceless protagonist fails to win the heart of the prince, and she dies, transforming into a spirit of the air that may yet find redemption in a few centuries.

In previous work on these kinds of characters I argued for interpreting voiceless heroines, particularly those in the Grimms' tales, as expressing a coded protest against the impossible demands made on women (Jorgensen, "Queering Kinship" and "Strategic Silences"). Here, I bring this feminist and queer reading of silent fairy-tale heroines to the 2017 film *The Shape of Water* and expand on it. In the film, mute protagonist Elisa both recreates and inverts traditional fairy-tale structures by rescuing her beastly bridegroom and silently protesting patriarchal authority. Elisa's voiceless resistance to hegemonic gender, sexual, and able-bodied norms situates her among both fairy-tale and pop culture characters who resist dominant ideologies. Additionally, I incorporate a disability studies perspective by interrogating the medicalization of disabled bodies and the normalization of speaking bodies in the film. One of the main tenets of academic disability studies is that disabled or differently abled bodies are not necessarily lesser, inferior, or monstrous

(Davis). In *The Shape of Water*, Elisa's community of human friends accept and support her as she is, even as the film's antagonist fetishizes her differences. But it is only with her nonhuman lover that Elisa finds the complete acceptance and sexual satisfaction that she has been lacking. Indeed, the depiction of Elisa as a sexual being makes the film remarkably sex-positive, and provides a basis for reading the film as supporting the power of the erotic (not simply in terms of sensual content, but also in terms of an affirming connection to life and community).

As someone who is primarily a folklorist and fairy-tale scholar, I define terms from my disciplinary home base where they are relevant, both to aid readers and in the hopes that more people will come to understand the important contributions of folklore and fairy-tale studies. As a cisgender queer woman who is a feminist, I weave in terms and theories from feminism and queer theory, in the belief that gender and sexuality norms impact all of our lives, daily, even when these concepts go unnoticed, due to privilege or other factors. Finally, I wish to note that I am not disabled, and thus I do not speak for people or communities who are disabled. However, I am hoping that in learning and teaching about disability studies from a social justice and intersectional perspective, ideally, I am able to promote representation of marginalized voices and experiences. My opinion on disability issues is not a replacement for the opinions of those more directly impacted by disability, but rather a complementary outlook. The merging of fairy-tale studies with disability studies is a fairly new point of overlap (see Schmiesing), and that is yet another contribution I am hoping to make in this essay. Initially, though I will summarize the plot of *The Shape of Water* and draw attention to its connections to fairy tales.

In *The Shape of Water*, we follow Elisa, a mute woman, who works the night shift cleaning in a government facility. When she meets a captive non-human and teaches him sign language, the two form a bond and a romantic attachment, leading to Elisa's collaboration with her friends to free him. The film's antagonist, Strickland, is a federal agent who not only wants to kill the non-human but also fetishizes Elisa's voicelessness as a sexual trait contributing to her appeal as a sexual object in his eyes. With elements of romance, Cold War period piece, spy thriller, and, of course, fairy tale, the film ends on an ambiguous note, with the non-human romantic lead killing Strickland and being set free in the water, carrying Elisa's dying body with him. Whether we interpret Elisa's coming back to life in his arms underwater as wish fulfillment while she in reality dies, or as the actual ending, may depend in part on understanding the role of fairy tale in the film. The film incorporates many fairy-tale intertexts, in its use of tropes or motifs, plot structures, and framing devices. Thus, utilizing an analytical lens informed by fairy-tale studies provides a distinct advantage when studying this film.

Elisa fulfills multiple fairy-tale roles in *The Shape of Water*. To start, the film's framing introduces her as a princess. We hear a male narrator, who turns out to be Elisa's older gay friend Giles, speaking about Elisa and her life using allegorical language: "If I spoke about it—if I did—what would I tell you? I wonder. Would I tell you about the time? It happened a long time ago, it seems. In the last days of a fair prince's reign. Or would I tell you about the place? A small city near the coast, but far from everything else. Or [...] Would I tell you about her? The princess without voice. Or perhaps I would just warn you, about the truth of these facts. And the tale of love and loss. And the monster, who tried to destroy it all" (*SoW*).

The language of "long ago" and "far away" invokes the world of fairy tales, as does the reference to Elisa as a princess. The use of frame tales (or a story within a story) is itself a fairy-tale convention. As Christine A. Jones and Jennifer Shacker, among others, have demonstrated, fairy tales were not published as stand-alone texts (as they tend to be in illustrated storybooks today) in their earliest print renditions. Indeed, the word "fairy tale" itself "now conjures the expectation of relatively brief self-contained stories, which we tend to approach as though they speak for themselves" (Jones and Shacker 494). Rather, many fairy tales appeared within overarching frame narratives, as with *The Thousand and One Nights* and *The Pentamerone*. Alternately, fairy tales were anthologized. Either way, tales did not appear in isolation, and this is worth noting in the conflation of fairy tale plots in *The Shape of Water* as well as the use of the frame tale introduction voiceover. This device appears in many pop culture fairy tales, such as Disney's animated *Beauty and the Beast*, which is another important influence on *The Shape of Water*. Related to the understanding of fairy-tale texts as discrete plots is the scholarly innovation of the tale type system, whereby folklorists assign numbers to folktale and fairy-tale plots, in order to better trace their historic and geographic distribution. Henceforth in this essay I will refer to tale type numbers, prefaced by the letters ATU (standing for Aarne, Thompson, and Uther, the three scholars who have successively created and updated the tale type system) to indicate which traditional tale plot is under discussion.

The film also shares the fairy tale's stylistic conventions. As Max Lüthi notes in *The European Folktale*, fairy-tale characters tend to be one-dimensional in how they relate to supernatural elements (accepting as normal the numinous) and depthless and abstract in their representation. Lüthi articulates that fairy-tale protagonists are often isolated in fairy tales: "the hero is not embedded in a family structure" (17), which we see in Elisa's lonely life. She also does not hesitate when encountering the supernatural, which Lüthi notes is common: "All fear of the numinous is absent" (7). This can be seen in Elisa's first encounters with her romantic interest. Other characters fear and torment him, while Elisa calmly eats her lunch of hard-boiled eggs next to his pool. Egg as symbol is also reminiscent of "Bluebeard" and "Fitcher's Bird" (ATU 312 and 311 respectively), tales where murderous men test (prospective) brides with eggs and keys that, if the test is passed, will remain unblemished by the blood of the earlier murdered wives.

Further, as a human woman paired with a monstrous lover, Elisa is involved in retelling "Beauty and the Beast" (ATU 425C). However, the "monster" referenced in the introductory frame is not, in the end, the nonhuman lover, but rather the human antagonist Strickland. Her rescue of her nonhuman lover is consistent with the broader "Search for the Lost Husband" tale type (ATU 425), which includes "Cupid and Psyche" and "East of the Sun and West of the Moon." Notably, Elisa occupies the roles of both beauty (as human woman) and beast (as disabled, Othered person). In depicting a human paired with a piscine being, this film also retells "The Little Mermaid," though with a gender role inversion. As one of Hans Christian Andersen's original authored tales, "The Little Mermaid" does not have a tale type number, though it incorporates numerous motifs from oral tradition such as mercreatures, transformation across species lines, doomed love, and voicelessness.

Lucy Fraser notes that "the mermaid's movement and metamorphosis are tied to her gendered body in ways that have fascinated retellers of the tale in many different languages" (5). Indeed, as a retelling of "The Little Mermaid," *The Shape of Water* both reinforces and transforms some of the elements of Andersen's original tale. In line with Fraser's analysis, Elisa is an Othered protagonist: "The story is told from the mermaid's perspective, a female 'other' in the male, human world" (5). Due to her muteness, her gender, and her marginalized social role as an orphan, Elisa does not have privileged status in the world of the film. From an intersectional perspective—being attuned to how various forms of oppression intersect to create unique experiences—Elisa is one of the most marginalized characters in the film. However, Elisa's desires diverge from those of Andersen's protagonist: "She is portrayed as a desiring, active female agent whose willing abnegation for a man brings her a great deal of suffering" (Fraser 5). Elisa is certainly desiring and active: she masturbates in the film, and engineers the plan to free the Amphibian Man. However, unlike the protagonist of "The Little Mermaid," there is little abnegation about her. Elisa rejects Strickland's advances at every turn and silently mouths off to him, only barely reigning in her contempt for him in the workplace.

Finally, multiple fairy tales depict silenced women. *The Shape of Water* interacts with these existing traditional tales, perhaps carrying forward their subversion of gender and sexual norms. As I have noted elsewhere, many folktale and fairy-tale plots reinforce connections between women, silence, and disempowerment (Jorgensen, "Strategic Silences" 21–23). The pattern that emerges across European folk narrative is that "silence tends to be imposed on women more than on men…. When men choose silence it is not automatically disempowering" (Jorgensen, "Strategic Silences" 23). Silence is often a curse that strikes women, but in other tales, women may choose to be silent in order to cooperate with a scheme or a spell to disenchant someone, whether a prince or a set of brothers (as in ATU 451, "The Maiden Who Seeks Her Brothers"). Versions of ATU 451 such as "The Six Swans" and "The Twelve Brothers" in the Grimms' collection follow a young woman whose brothers have been turned into birds, and she must take a vow of silence in order to save them. She does, at great personal cost to herself. Notably, in a majority of these tales where women are silent by choice or silenced by magic, they are coerced into marriage, into giving up children, and into enduring hardship before the inevitable happy ending. Taken at face value, silenced women in fairy tales suffer, with silence the cause of the suffering.

Attention to gender roles, and the uneven distribution of power they dictate, is one of the key traits of feminist interpretations of fairy tales. Adding in queer theory complicates and nuances this approach. As Kay Turner and Pauline Greenhill elucidate in the first book-length marriage of queer theory with fairy-tale studies, the defining principles of queer theory "problematize sex, gender, and sexuality" and can thus "refigure the possibilities along relationality along lines that challenge fixed or normative categories but also address concerns about marginalization, oddity, and not fitting into society generally" (11). While a feminist reading might hone in on Elisa's silence as a reflection of the compliant feminist being projected onto her, a queer reading focuses on the disjunctures between Elisa's gender, sex, and sexuality—such as her attraction to the Amphibian Man—as well as her generally odd and outside-the-box demeanor.

Viewed from a feminist and queer lens, silence in fairy tales can have more than one meaning. When I analyzed ATU 451 in previous work ("Queering Kinship"; "Strategic Silences") I utilized the concept of coding to posit that the protagonist of these tales—a sister who undertook a vow of silence to free her brothers who were turned into birds, and in doing so, was a bad wife and mother—was not simply punitively silenced, but was also conveying a subtle social message about the impossibility of the demands placed upon her gender and sexuality. Coding "is a concept developed by feminist folklorists to describe the ways in which subaltern populations disguise their communicative messages so that dominant populations will not understand those messages" (Jorgensen, "Strategic Silences" 23–24). I posited that in fairy tales featuring silenced women, such as "The Maiden Who Seeks Her Brothers," the tales could present an implicitly coded message on behalf of female taletellers and audiences: a hidden warning about the dangers of marriage and the marital household for women, and pessimism that women can fulfill all the social roles that tug at them and force them to mute or mutilate themselves. The concept of coding also applies to *The Shape of Water,* as we see explicit coding (or, a code that is recognizable as such by outsiders, even if not easily deciphered), as when Elisa's sign language can only be understood by those close to her. I observed of the silent protagonist in "The Maiden Who Seeks Her Brother": "Substituting silence for speech, her story is a coded protest of the social conditions that condemn her to illegibility" (Jorgensen, "Strategic Silences" 29). This also applies to Elisa, whose silence can have the symbolic effect of resisting categorization by the patriarchal conditions that condemn her to a second-class citizen.

One element missing from the previous analysis, however, is a disability-inflected lens. In a world where speech is the norm, speechlessness is a disability. Losing sight of disability as meaning itself, not only being a metaphor or a code for another deeper meaning, can be deeply problematic. As Ann Schmiesing points out: "Reading disability merely as a metaphor for something else is in itself a form of erasure, because it abstracts the disabled individual and his or her impaired body" (13). Thus, I turn next to disability studies to help interpret resistance in *The Shape of Water.*

Key concepts in disability studies include the idea that disability is an unstable, socially constructed category; the notion of ableism, or "the centering and dominance of nondisabled views and the marginalizing of disability" (Schmiesing 5); a critique of the equation of normalcy with physical fitness and abnormality with criminality and deviance; drawing out distinctions between and the effects of medical and social models of disability; and arriving at an understanding of complex embodiment that does not erase the very real impacts of various impairments while also trying to comprehend the intersection of those impairments with the socially constructed lenses that impact the lives of disabled people (Schmiesing 4–6; Davis 1–12; Mitchell and Snyder 2–6).

While not an obvious connection at first glance, disability studies can provide a complementary perspective to fairy-tale studies. As Schmiesing points out, "it is not surprising that a genre so often associated with magical or extraordinary abilities portrays disability with such great frequency" (1). In depicting ogres, dwarves, hunchbacks, blind characters, children as tall as a thumb, maidens with their hands chopped off, and—of course—mute characters, fairy tales deal with disability on a frequent basis. Potential ramifications of these representations hinge on the frequent Othering of disabled characters, in how they are often made out to be villains or victims, with little in-between to map to the actual lives of disabled people.

Interpreting *The Shape of Water* from a disability studies perspective, then, requires attention to Elisa's complex embodiment as a mute woman in a society that values speech and assigns worth accordingly. It requires that viewers not medicalize or fetishize her difference (as Strickland does). One common ableist assumption is that disabled people are asexual, non-sexual, or non-procreative (Shuttleworth). Elisa's active sexual desire, seen in how she masturbates while alone, and eventually partners with the Amphibian Man, refutes that ableist assumption. Rather than being sexually inactive in compliance with social norms (ones that would govern her body as both a disabled person and as a non-married woman), Elisa is sexually active and agentic.

From a disability-centric perspective, however, the film was not without its flaws. Online commenters have focused on how Elisa never gains acceptance from the mainstream world on the border of which she has hovered for a lifetime, and how Elisa's death and ambiguous resurrection constitute yet another unhappy ending for disabled characters (Sjunneson-Henry). Others criticize her character (and many of the others) as flat (Crippledscholar). Another line of critique notes that this is yet another instance of a disabled character being played by a non-disabled actor, which is problematic in terms of representation (Borg; Sjunneson-Henry). All of these issues foreground the experiences and bodies of non-disabled people, continuing to mark disabled bodies as Other.

Thus, *The Shape of Water* is not necessarily a triumphant disability narrative to be embraced uncritically. However, I would suggest two mitigating factors that might help recuperate the film somewhat. First, as fairy tale retelling, the film accesses some of the stylistic qualities of the fairy-tale genre discussed above such as depthlessness and isolation. Characters in a fairy tale are often not well rounded as a matter of style in this genre, and while many fairy-tale retellings address this flatness by giving characters expanded backstories and motives, it is thus a reasonable expectation that Elisa and her fellow characters might not be the deepest characters. Additionally, queer readings of fairy tales have brought in the notion of transbiology, an outgrowth of queer theory that "demonstrates the awkward knottiness/naughtiness of the boundary between human and non-human" (Turner and Greenhill, 12). *The Shape of Water* engages with transbiology by featuring a cross-species romantic and sexual attraction, queering the lines between human and non-human. By "queering" I mean that the theoretically firm divide between human and non-human becomes playfully muddled, with the very categories themselves called into question. Indeed, the boundaries between human and divine are also queered in the film, as when Strickland refers at first skeptically, and then with his dying breath, to the Amphibian Man as a "god." While there is certainly room for a pessimistic reading of the film's ending as the human community rejecting—to the point of murdering—Elisa, reading the film as fairy tale with transbiological underpinnings helps contextualize the cross-species love match as part of the genre's expectation.

Second, I believe the concept of narrative prosthesis applies here in a positive way, precisely because it is lacking. Briefly, narrative prosthesis is the idea that much narrative relies on disability as a plot device, and that perhaps "all narratives operate out of a desire to compensate for a limitation or reign in excess," concepts which are often pictured in terms of disability (Mitchell and Snyder 53). In this model, disability serves as an "opportunistic narrative device" (Mitchell and Snyder 47) rather than an actual depiction of disabled people's experiences. In other words, many stories use disability as a convenient plot device rather than an accurate exploration of disabled people's lived experiences. Narrative prosthesis accounts for a pattern that many plots follow, moving "from disequilibrium to equilibrium, from enchantment to disenchantment, and from disability to ability and bodily perfection" (Schmiesing 2). One example Schmiesing gives of narrative prosthesis in fairy tales is when in the Grimms' tale "The Maiden Without Hands" (ATU 706), the story's ending makes the titular character "once again 'complete' in body and soul at the end" suggesting "that completeness, for her, involves restored bodily wholeness and marriage" (94). The maiden whose hands have been chopped off has her hands magically restored, erasing the marks of her disability and experiences. This is not a pattern that *The Shape of Water* fully follows, however. Elisa is not magically cured at the end of the film; she does not get to joyfully join the speaking world as one of its fully invested citizens. Instead, she goes to a place where the spoken word is irrelevant, either because she dies, or because the Amphibian Man resurrects her and gives her the ability to breathe underwater. The scars on her neck that she has had since childhood, instead of being seen as a freakish attribute, open at the Amphibian Man's healing touch, becoming gills to let her breathe. Thus, the markings that make her different and (to some) undesirable on land contribute to her health and vitality underwater. In this way, at least, the film resists the tug of narrative prosthesis, and situates Elisa's wholeness as a person in her body from the start. Resistance features in the film as a major theme in how the characters form community and connect to the erotic.

The characters in *The Shape of Water* demonstrate resistance through two main means: members of marginalized groups banding together, and the uses of the erotic. The quest to rescue the Amphibian Man before Strickland's orders to vivisect him are carried out is one that must be accomplished cooperatively if it is to succeed. In early scenes of the film, we see Elisa's gay friend Giles turning off the television when it shows news clips about the Civil Rights movement, saying he doesn't want to watch "that," negatively inflected. It is not until Giles sees the up-close ugliness of a restaurant server turning away an African American couple, before rejecting Giles for being gay, that Giles seems to recognize the importance of solidarity among marginalized groups. Elisa's African American co-worker friend, Zelda, is initially reluctant to join Elisa's rescue mission, asking, "Are you out of your mind?!" However, Zelda's compassion for Elisa and concern for her well-being compel her to help. Later in the film, Zelda's recriminations against her husband, Brewster, include accusations that he never spoke up and never helped her with anything, which again indicates that communal action and solidarity are key in uplifting marginalized groups. In addition to Giles and Zelda, Elisa also finds an ally in Dr. Robert Hoffstetler, a scientist, immigrant, and undercover spy for the Soviets. Dr. Hoffstetler aids in the rescue attempt, using a chemical to kill a guard so that Elisa can escape with the Amphibian Man in a van that Giles drives.

Strickland mistakes Elisa's voicelessness for passivity and subservience, reinforcing one of the film's major messages about resistance: that being quiet, silent, or silenced is not synonymous with being complicit. The agency of Elisa and her friends in *The Shape of Water* is beneath the notice of important men like Strickland, and Elisa and company benefit from this triviality barrier as their role in the rescue and its aftermath goes unnoticed. In folklore studies, the term "triviality barrier" was first coined by Brian Sutton-Smith to refer to how children's folklore is perceived as a trivial or unimportant subject, and thereby seems beneath the notice of "serious" scholars (4–5). In the film, a group of socially powerless people join together to make a difference, getting away with it largely because of the triviality barrier, while the facility's manager speculates in conversation with Strickland that "we're looking at a highly trained group, sir … special forces … highly efficient, ruthless, clockwork precision … my conservative estimate is that this was a strike force of at least ten men." The irony of Elisa being the one to engineer the escape, with a handful of marginalized friends, highlights the importance of community. Strickland clears Elisa and Zelda of any wrongdoing, muttering to himself: "What am I doing, interviewing the fucking help?" (*SoW*).

The Shape of Water also resists trivialization of sensuality and interpersonal connections, sometimes glossed as the "erotic." African American queer feminist Audre Lorde defines the erotic as a resource, a sense of internal pleasure, fulfillment, and empowerment. Lorde writes: "But when we begin to live … in touch with the power of the erotic within ourselves … then we begin to be responsible to ourselves in the deepest sense. For as we begin to recognize our deepest feelings, we begin to give up, of necessity, being satisfied with suffering and self-negation, and with the numbness which so often seems like their only alternative in our society. Our acts against oppression become integral with self, motivated and empowered from within" (58). From this sense of the erotic, Elisa's joy in sensual pleasure is contiguous with her desire not only to communicate with but also save the life of the Amphibian Man.

Elisa's engagement with the erotic not only propels her and the other human characters towards a greater consciousness of the oppressive forces in all their lives, but it also reflects an overall sex-positive attitude in the film. It is significant that Elisa keeps the Amphibian Man in her bathtub after rescuing him from the lab: this is the same place where she masturbates on a daily basis. And when he sickens and nearly dies, the tub is also where she revives him. Thus, the place where Elisa pursues what might be euphemistically called her "little death" is the site where she averts *his* death, giving the erotic the symbolic power to revive and renew (Mills). Resurrection through love also features in many versions of ATU 425C, where Beauty's declaration of love brings the Beast back from the brink of death. Elisa's erotic awareness is also intersectional, in that she recognizes the multiple forms of oppression impacting her and those around her; she knows that the same prejudices against her as a non-speaking person also are used to dehumanize the Amphibian Man and her human friends. And she refuses to be compliant in the face of such oppression.

Though voiceless, Elisa is shown as a whole person who still has sexual desires and moves to fulfill those desires, both by masturbating and by connecting with a partner who views her as whole. This is a remarkably sex-positive assertion about the rights of all humans—disabled or not—to attain sexual fulfillment regardless of its reproductive value. Because this film is also a fairy-tale retelling, Elisa's character talks back to silenced and subservient female characters: she rescues her lover, defies authoritarian figures, and demonstrates to those around her the power of the erotic and of community cooperation. Viewed through the lenses of intersectional feminist, queer, and disability studies concepts, we see Elisa as resisting patriarchal norms that dictate her value based on her voice. Vocal about her own worth, the worth of her oppressed human friends (African American and gay), and the worth of her non-human companion, Elisa subverts mainstream stereotypes about marginalized groups and recuperates the values of those often viewed as less-than-human.

NOTE

1. As per conventions in current fairy-tale studies, the noun reference is "fairy tale," while the adjective reference is "fairy-tale." This is the accepted standard in major fairy-tale studies journals such as *Marvels & Tales* as well as in academic books.

WORKS CITED

Borg, Kurt. "'The Shape of Water' and Disability: A Breath of Fresh Air, a Repetition of Stereotypes or Something in Between?" *Isles of the Left*, 19 Mar. 2018. https://www.islesoftheleft.org/the-shape-of-water-and-disability/.

Crippledscholar. "The Shape of Water Is a Toxic Romantic Fantasy: The Issues with This Disability Romance Narrative." Crippledscholar.com, 24 Jan. 2018. https://crippled scholar.com/2018/01/24/the-shape-of-water-is-a-toxic-romantic-fantasy-the-issues-with-this-disability-romance-narrative/.

Davis, Lennard J. "Introduction: Normality, Power, and Culture." *The Disability Studies Reader*, edited by Lennard J. Davis, Routledge, 2016, pp. 1–14.

Fraser, Lucy. *The Pleasures of Metamorphosis: Japanese and English Fairy Tale Transformations of "The Little Mermaid."* Wayne State UP, 2017.

Jones, Christine A., and Jennifer Schacker. "On Fairy Tales and Their Anthologies." *Marvelous Transformations: An Anthology of Fairy Tales and Contemporary Critical Perspectives*, edited by Christine A. Jones and Jennifer Schacker, Broadview Press, 2013, pp. 493–498.

Jorgensen, Jeana. ""Queering Kinship in 'The Maiden Who Seeks Her Brothers."" *Transgressive Tales: Queering the Brothers Grimm*, edited by Kay Turner and Pauline Greenhill, Wayne State UP, 2012, pp. 69–89.

_____. Strategic Silences: Voiceless Heroes in Fairy Tales." *A Quest of Her Own: Essays on the Female Hero in Modern Fantasy*, edited by Lori M. Campbell, McFarland, 2014, pp. 15–34.

Lorde, Audre. "Uses of the Erotic: The Erotic as Power." *Sister Outsider: Essays and Speeches*, Crossing Press, 1984, pp. 53–59.

Lüthi, Max. *The European Folktale: Form and Nature*. Translated by John D. Niles. Indiana UP, 1982.

Mills, Keegan. "Do Try This at Home: Making Good Use of Media Narratives about Sexual Well-Being." The Positive Sexuality Conference, 19 May 2018, Burbank Airport Marriott, Burbank, CA. Conference paper.

Mitchell, David, and Sharon Snyder. *Narrative Prosthesis: Disability and the Dependencies of Discourse*. U of Michigan P, 2000.

Schmiesing, Ann. *Disability, Deformity, and Disease in the Grimms' Fairy Tales*. Wayne State UP, 2014.

The Shape of Water. Directed by Guillermo del Toro, Fox Searchlight Pictures, 2017.

Shuttleworth, Russell. "Sex and Disability." *Encyclopedia of Sex and Gender*, edited by Fedwa Malti-Douglas, vol 2, Macmillan Reference, 2007, pp. 298–400.

Sjunneson-Henry, Elsa. "I Belong Where the People Are: Disability and *The Shape of Water*." Tor.com, 16 January 2018. https://www.tor.com/2018/01/16/i-belong-where-the-people-are-disability-and-the-shape-of-water/.

Sutton-Smith, Brian. "Psychology of Childlore: The Triviality Barrier." *Western Folklore* vol. 29, no. 1, 1970, pp. 1–8.

Turner, Kay, and Pauline Greenhill. "Introduction: Once Upon a Queer Time." *Transgressive Tales: Queering the Grimms*, edited by Kay Turner and Pauline Greenhill, Wayne State UP, 2012, pp. 1–24.

"Who tells your story?"

The Power of Hamilton's Fantastic Re-Telling of American History

Amanda K. LeBlanc

In the summer of 2015, in one of our weekly phone chats, my father mentioned wanting to see a new musical he had heard about: a musical based on America's founding fathers. This struck me as strange for a few reasons, but mostly because my dad doesn't care about musicals! That same week, Kelly Ripa, on the *Live with Kelly and Michael* show, told the audience how she had been to a preview of the new Lin-Manuel Miranda musical about the founding fathers, and it was *good*. I was a fan of Miranda's previous two Broadway musicals, *In the Heights* and *Bring It On,* so my interest grew despite material that otherwise might have flown under my radar (the founding fathers?!). Turns out I—along with my dad and Kelly Ripa—was not the only one paying attention to the show that would become *Hamilton: An American Musical. Hamilton* debuted on Broadway in August of 2015. Word of mouth, Miranda's reputation as a former Tony-award winner, and rave reviews of the show's off–Broadway run led to sold-out shows well in advance of its official debut. *Playbill Magazine* speculated that *Hamilton* had grossed over $30,000,000 before opening night (Gans and Gioia). Although the illegal mass-purchasing and re-selling of theater, music, and concert tickets (a practice known as "scalping") certainly pre-dates *Hamilton,* demand for the musical's tickets necessitated the implementation of new ticket-buying technology in an attempt to ward off skyrocketing prices: patrons paid as much as $3,000 for a (scalped) seat to the show's New York performances (Paulson). *Hamilton* has been sold out for every performance in New York City for nearly four years (Snibbe). *Hamilton* is in its fourth year on Broadway, three years into a residency in Chicago, two years into a national tour, and two years into a residency in London, with no sign of slowing down.

Hamilton's story is about resistance that contests hegemonic politics of representation. The show recounts the U.S. colonies' struggle to shed the shackles of the British Empire, with the young protagonists embodying the "American Dream" of life, liberty, and the pursuit of happiness. *Hamilton* pushes on and against this principle by using a cast of actors of color to play the (white) founding fathers, inviting the audience to experience the resistance of people of color as avowedly American resistance. This essay examines *Hamilton* and its representation of those founding fathers as they work to build the kind of nation we are taught about in history books. *Hamilton* tells this tale of the American Dream as a re-invented, or perhaps more fittingly, a re-mixed, history. In this way, I consider *Hamilton* a piece of Speculative Fiction [specfic] that "changes the logic" (Mosely) about which bodies are brave, heroic, and worthy of reverence. A specfic lens reveals the ways that *Hamilton* plays with historical "fact," in essence (re)writing the past to comment on the present and the future. By casting actors of color in the roles of white historical figures, by explicitly spotlighting the contributions of immigrants, by drawing attention to the in-between-ness of the figures of the early American founders, and by challenging notions of Western, or linear, temporality, *Hamilton* encourages us to fantasize about how *else* things could have been in the past, and thus, how else they can be now. I argue that *Hamilton* envisions resistance as being not easily contained within particular bodies, identities, and moments. Rather, *Hamilton* revels in the ways that stories can be, and often are, re-mixed, leading toward the potential for imaginative and inclusive narratives.

Hamilton's tremendous success brings with it several contradictions. An important methodological conundrum for those who would like to examine the work critically is that the musical is still all but inaccessible to the average playgoer. Something so popular is mostly out of reach of the populace for the financial reasons noted above. Indeed, this author has never seen the whole musical on stage. So, for this analysis, I rely on the countless hours I have spent listening to the original cast recording, with the help of Genius-Lyrics.com for close analysis of lyrics that are difficult to understand (there are several rapid-paced raps). As well, I use some of the many interviews with writer, composer, and original cast member Lin-Manuel Miranda. One advantage that theater-lovers without tremendous amounts of money have in the 21st Century is access to social media; Miranda and several other creative personnel have posted "official" photographs from rehearsals and preview performances on their social media pages. I use these, as well as photographs published by theater critics reviewing performances, to discuss the casting of the main actors. Finally, there are sanctioned-recordings of some *Hamilton* performances, including the 2016 Tony Award performance of "History Has Its Eyes on You" and "Yorktown," as well as in the 2016 *PBS* documentary *Hamilton's America*. However, bootleg video and audio recordings do circulate on the internet. In some ways, the internet age has compromised the Broadway bootleg industry, a time-honored if illegal enterprise, since the illegal recordings violate mainstream outlets' copyright policies. I found partial cell-phone uploads on sites such as The Daily Motion and Vimeo. However, the poor quality and editing of these recordings makes analysis nearly impossible, and, further, there are several ethical and legal issues at play when using them for an academic analysis.

Certainly, these clips and still images do not replace the experience of being in the audience as I interrogate the politics of representation and resistance in *Hamilton*, but for so many fans, like myself, this cobbled-together knowledge of the musical is all we have. Given our enthusiasm for the music and themes, together with the cultural zeitgeist that *Hamilton* has become, I think it is still crucial for those who do not have access to the live performances, indeed maybe *especially* for those without access, that we interrogate the musical's characters, stories, and messages. Indeed, Henry Jenkins argues that "the flow of content across multiple media platforms, the cooperation between multiple media industries, and the migratory behavior of media audiences who would go almost anywhere in search of the kinds of entertainment experiences they wanted" (2) *is* what constitutes our relationship to media texts. I do still have access to some material despite not being able to experience the "whole" show, and, moreover, I connect with the community of *Hamilton* fans who similarly can't get a ticket, but share enthusiasm, musical knowledge, themes, and even jokes about the show. It certainly is ironic that a text about accessing the American Dream is blocked for much of its audience, yet we push back by soaking in what we can get. Like one of the themes of *Hamilton* itself, fans recognize and overcome systemic and individual barriers to experiencing the material. So, my analysis of this musical is impacted by the fact that I've never sat in the live audience, but also by my determination to keep listening and looking for engagement with *Hamilton*.

I write this essay as a Broadway fan generally and *Hamilton* fan specifically. One of the most compelling parts of *Hamilton* for me is the hip hop and R&B–based music. This is the kind of music that I listened to growing up, so I not only enjoy the genre, but, being roughly the same age as Miranda, I get the specific song references embedded in *Hamilton*. For instance, "Cabinet Battle #1" pays direct homage to Grandmaster Flash's "The Message" in a verse that uses the latter song's melody and re-mixed lyrics. Another contradiction to note, however, as I attend to the use of hip hop and R&B in *Hamilton*, is that I am white. Arguably white youth (primarily young men) consume the most hip hop in the U.S. currently. The genre emerged in New York City in the late 1970s from black MCs (now known as DJs) and musical artists who explicitly rapped about social and economic inequalities. Contemporary mainstream hip hop is often (sometimes justifiably so) critiqued as misogynist, materialistic, and violent, but there are, as there have always been, artists who have carried on the genre's roots as fundamentally black and social-justice oriented (Durham 12). This to say that hip hop is not *for* me: my enjoyment of the genre, and in particular its contributions to the music of *Hamilton*, comes from a very different place than it might for a black listener. But beyond my preference for this kind of music, the musical's mix of traditional showtunes with hip hop is an integral part of its imaginative resistance of theatrical norms and structures. In keeping with hip hop's resistive roots, *Hamilton* incorporates sounds and lyrics that flip the script, so to speak, on what we might expect from a musical about men in 1776 (indeed, there's a traditional musical called *1776*).

Speculative fiction is all about "flipping the script." Specfic is a literary, filmic, and entertainment genre that confronts, challenges, and subverts traditional logics—whether that logic is place, time, custom, or technological possibility (Thomas). Although science fiction is perhaps the more well-known subgenre of specfic, expanding its boundaries to include less-scientifically, or technologically-based, fantasies allows specfic to utilize the supernatural, magical realism, or any other imaginative device to tell a compelling story. Imagining cultural and technologic possibilities beyond anything that could "exist" in the modern world has produced some of the most groundbreaking and enduring literature since the mid-nineteenth century, which then found its ways to cinema, TV, video games, amusement parks, and the Broadway stage.

Hamilton tells the story of one of the United States' founding fathers: those high-profile men whose contributions (in war, politics, innovation, or writing) build the foundation of the United States. Several of these figures became early presidents, while others live larger-than-life in American mythology. Miranda, after reading Ron Chernow's 2004 biography of Alexander Hamilton, wrote a musical based on just *some* of Hamilton's struggles and accomplishments. The opening number of *Hamilton*, "Alexander Hamilton," introduces the main character as a Founding Father who did *not* go down in history like many of his contemporaries. The show begins as the American Revolution is imminent, with a young Hamilton eager to fight on the side of independence and liberation from British rule. The lyrics to "Alexander Hamilton" tell us that Hamilton emigrated to the U.S. from a tiny Caribbean island, penniless but brilliant. *Hamilton* follows its main character through the Revolutionary war, his marriage into a prominent New York family, his position as the first U.S. Secretary of the Treasury, his uneasy relationship with the other members of government, a scandalous extra-marital affair, and finally, and perhaps most (in)famously, his death in a duel with Aaron Burr.

In order to tell this story of Alexander Hamilton's rise and fall, *Hamilton* employs all actors of color in the main (speaking) roles of the founding fathers (as well as for the Schuyler sisters). The casting for *Hamilton* is color-conscious casting, as opposed to color-blind casting, wherein casting agents open a role to an actor of *any* color (including white actors). *Hamilton* on Broadway, in London, and on tour specifically and purposely casts men and women of color in the principal roles, creating an important disruption from historical accuracy. The origin story of the United States, of course, traditionally centers people of European descent overcoming the British monarchy and installing a system of government meant to provide maximum benefit to people of European descent. The black and brown men and women of color on *Hamilton*'s stage are incongruous to the cultural "image" American children are provided with in school, in books, in film, and other educational materials (remember that ruler that had all the presidents on it?). Of course, the founding fathers were white, so the actors in *Hamilton* are an important entre into the consideration of power of speculation in this musical.

I want to attend to three black actors in *Hamilton* that fill roles of white historical figures, as they rupture the ways that history in the U.S. typically gets told in history books. The first *Hamilton* character we see and hear is Aaron Burr, who opens the show with the tune "Alexander Hamilton." Black singer and actor Leslie Odom, Jr., originates the role of Burr on Broadway. The Burr character serves as *Hamilton*'s primary narrator, and unlike Hamilton, lives through to the end of the musical. In Act Two, black rapper, singer, and actor Daveed Diggs plays Hamilton's main adversary, Thomas Jefferson. Finally, black Broadway veteran Christopher Jackson plays George Washington, a (white) man with one of the most well-known profiles and portraits in United States history. These original Broadway cast members all participated in the 2016 Tony Award performance and have made various public appearances in character so, for *Hamilton* fans, their likenesses are well-known in conjunction with historical figures. More to the point, their *blackness* is known, despite their roles as men who were, in fact, white.

The only major role in *Hamilton* regularly filled by a white actor is that of Great Britain's King George III: he has only three appearances on stage, and he sings a variation of the same song each time. This song diverges widely from the hip hop style that dominates *Hamilton*, sounding more like a 1960s' pop tune. According to Miranda, King George's song, "You'll Be Back," purposely resembles the sound of British-invasion bands like The Beatles. King George, then, sounds out of touch (and tune?) from the other characters of the show, as is his attempt to control his (former) subjects. King George's casting is significant as he represents the only clear "villain" in *Hamilton*. He is larger than a singular figurehead, as he represents the global superpower that is Great Britain at the time, and he is white.

There have been many successful Broadway musicals with casts of mostly or all performers of color. Some are shows about the experiences of people of color (*Shuffle Along, Porgy and Bess, Ain't Misbehavin', The Color Purple,* and Miranda's *In the Heights,* for instance), while others are all-minority versions of traditionally all-white popular shows (1968's revival of *Hello Dolly* is notable). Actors of color occasionally step into well-known roles that are traditionally played by white actors (Taye Diggs as *Chicago's* Billy Flynn in 2002 and Audra McDonald as Lucy in *Sweeney Todd* in 2014, for instance). Yet, unsurprisingly, theater historically and presently under-represents minority and marginalized people in both content and casting (Gardner). *Hamilton* was one of a few recent prominent Broadway shows that employed a large cast of non-white actors. Another notable example is the 2015 revival of *The King and I,* this time with Asian actors in the Siamese roles (historically the roles of the King of Siam and his children had been played by white actors). But unlike *The King and I, Hamilton* is *about* white people, who are played by people of color. This is unique, and this is important. To borrow from the documentary about gender representation in the media, *Miss Representation,* "you can't be what you can't see" (Newsom). Although a bit of an oversimplification, the message stands that seeing people who look like you *matters,* particularly when we are young.

In the opening to her groundbreaking book on Afrofuturism, Ytasha Womack both celebrates the wondrous science fiction that she watched as a child, while lamenting that she saw no black and brown characters (save for *Star Wars'* Lando Calrissian): "…the quest to see myself or browner people … was important to me. Through the eyes of a child, the absence of such imagery didn't escape me" (5). Moreover, seeing people of color in a multitude of roles is important for white people. As a child, I never noticed the lack of characters of color. Everyone looked like me so I, like so many white children, internalized that whiteness was universal—normal. Casting actors of color will not "confuse" children into thinking the founding fathers were black and Latinx,[1] rather it serves to dislodge stubborn mythology that *only* white men can be heroes. In its color-conscious casting, *Hamilton* operates as a kind of fantasy. Moynagh notes: "…the idea of fantasy itself as simultaneously a political structure and a literary form mediates our relationship to a particular social world" (212). *Hamilton* messes with the social and political order of a traditional recounting of what our founding fathers looked like. A speculative framework (re)imagines the world and what we (think we) know from a different perspective. *Hamilton's* insertion of bodies of color into these historically-white figures invites a consideration of the ways that people of color have historically fought for freedom and representation—including slave revolts and the civil rights movement—but also the very contemporary movements, notably Black Lives Matter and immigration, a major theme of *Hamilton.*

Of note, *Hamilton* offers little in the way of direct engagement with the horrors of slavery, and there's been plenty of good and important critique of Miranda's artistic decision (cf. Reed, *The Haunting of Lin-Manuel Miranda*). Related to the above discussion about issues of accessibility to Broadway shows, this problematic characteristic of *Hamilton* may impede audiences' ability to enjoy the show or the music. Yet, we see that the show is doing *something* different. It asks the audience to imagine the founding fathers as men of color, which illustrates that resisting racist and xenophobic oppression and violence undergirds the very birth of our nation, even if the show ignores certain violences. Through color-conscious casting, *Hamilton* literally centers the idea that brown and black faces played prominent roles in the construction of the United States. Even for those of us who haven't seen these main characters take center stage for a live performance, their prominent roles in televised performances as well as on the cast album indicate that people of color are important to this story—one of struggle, triumph, and tragedy.

Hamilton presents our main characters as antiheros who are debating complicated issues that still haunt American politics today: immigration, taxation, representation, and foreign policy. That the colonists are also colonizers cannot be ignored in any critical analysis of *Hamilton*; the revolutionaries portrayed were both. They fought for liberation from what they viewed as tyranny and control from the British Monarchy, while at the same time violating and abusing the freedom of others, notably black and brown people. Hamilton is an appropriate character through which to explore this in-between-ness. In Act Two, then President of the United States, John Adams, fires Hamilton and calls him a Creole bastard, a line that refers to Hamilton's ignoble birth in the Caribbean ("The Adams Administration"). President Adams is accusing Hamilton of being both mixed-race *and* born out of wedlock. In the show, the Creole bastard putdown receives a sound effect, is slowed down, and distorted in a deep voice, emphasizing the racist slur. This line, and the sound effect, illustrate that Hamilton, although a former high-ranking government official, was also an outsider, someone not born in one of the thirteen colonies. Importantly, Hamilton was white, both of his parents being of European ancestry (Chernow 9). The power in the Creole bastard line comes from the accusation that Hamilton was less-than white by virtue of being born in the Caribbean. Hamilton's status as an immigrant becomes fundamentally tied into his ethnicity here, with the re-mixed sound effect accentuating the ways that his foreign birth to an unmarried woman made him unworthy of holding a high-ranking government position.

A critical plot element of *Hamilton* is that Hamilton was an immigrant to the United States. Regarding his reading of Chernow's book, Miranda tells *The Atlantic*: "And when [Hamilton] gets to New York, I was like, 'I know this guy.' I've met so many versions of this guy, and it's the guy who comes to this country and is like, 'I am going to work six jobs if you're only working one. I'm gonna make a life for myself here'" (qtd. in Delman). Later, to *CNBC*, Miranda notes that, "And it's uniquely an immigrant story and it's uniquely a story about writers," connecting his father's experience as an immigrant to Miranda's own experience as a writer (qtd. in Gibbs). Moreover, Miranda is Puerto Rican, and as a writer and a performer of color, creating from this space engages in a unique, and potentially resistive, kind of theater. *Hamilton* is Miranda's fantastic take on how we *might* tell the story of the founding of this country. His revisionist tale allows modern audiences to (re)imagine their own struggles, tragedies, and triumphs in these figures.

In 2019, discourse about immigration, including who is an immigrant, and who is a *good* immigrant, has taken center stage in the United States. As a nationalist sentiment swept in with the Trump administration's hardline on immigration, a discursive fissure erupted about the role of the Europeans who settled what is now the United States. Were the founding fathers colonists—brave revolutionaries who fought off the shackles of their oppressors to forge their own destiny—or were they *colonizers*—savages who robbed, raped, and killed to claim land where others had lived for centuries? *Hamilton*, as a speculative text, plays with the in-between-ness of the founding fathers primarily through the main character of Alexander Hamilton, as played by Miranda. Hamilton is white, but an immigrant—Miranda is Latino, but *not* an immigrant. This in-between-ness is a productive space in which we, the audience, may be inspired to (re)consider the impact of racism and xenophobia on the well-being of our (still young) nation. As well, in keeping with the critical lens of specfic, *Hamilton* invites consideration, if not critique, of the very foundation of the United States.

To be sure, *Hamilton* is overtly celebratory of the American Revolution and its liberal democratic goals. After all, *Hamilton* is about a group of people who are fighting from a marginal financial and social location (those under British rule and taxation) towards the center of their own living conditions (their own nation state). *Hamilton* is about men clamoring towards the ideals of the Enlightenment—progress, reason, liberty, and liberal-democratic government—and away from tradition, dogmatic religion, and superstition. In the Act One closing number, "Nonstop," Hamilton reminds Burr that the revolutionaries fought and sacrificed for the opportunity to construct a new nation. These founding fathers stand in-between worlds here (quite literally in the musical, where the Act One finale serves as a bridge from one portion of the story towards the next). Burr is a prominent figure throughout *Hamilton*, when he is often given a one-note treatment in history textbooks as the man who killed Hamilton. The musical revels in the complexity of both men: as friends, colleagues, soldiers, and political enemies. Their lives intertwined for over twenty years, often uneasily, and by the penultimate musical number, "The World Was Wide Enough," *Hamilton* paints neither man as wholly a hero or villain—both men are both things. *Hamilton's* two main characters' positions as heroes *and* villains fit with the musical's larger theme of in-between-ness. *Hamilton* engages several points of in-between-ness of identity for its main characters: including those of immigrant and citizen, colonizer and colonized, and past and future.

Hamilton forwards a complicated endorsement of representative democracy, wherein all persons in American territories are not represented. For example, in "Cabinet Battle #1," Hamilton accosts Jefferson about who is indeed laboring for Virginia's economy to thrive, referring, of course, to slaves. On the surface, *Hamilton* is about the struggle for state-recognition of a liberal subject, the very-modern concept that we are in charge of our own destinies. But such a pursuit of life, liberty, and happiness, was, of course, available only for the few. So, while *Hamilton's* first Act asks the audience to root for the Continental Army and the young, idealist soldiers, Act Two not-so-tacitly presents a critique of the American liberal democratic experiment. In "Washington on Your Side," Thomas Jefferson and Aaron Burr, among others, are looking to oust Hamilton from the President's cabinet, citing *both* personal and institutional reasons: Hamilton works around the clock to ascend the ranks in Washington, while also acting the part with expensive new clothing. They believe Hamilton to be corrupt; that he is more interested in his own lot in life than those of the American people. To Jefferson, the main performer on "Washington," Hamilton's (subjective) pursuit of happiness included the few with power, not the many without. *Hamilton* explicitly invites us to consider the division within Congress as the result of individual egos, yet implicitly points us towards flaws within the very system the founding fathers built. Embedded within an otherwise congratulatory musical about Hamilton's tenacity and accomplishments, such a critique is another example of the in-between-ness that *Hamilton* draws on to paint its picture of the founding of this country.

This critique is accomplished, in part, through the imaginative superimposition of past narratives over contemporary political tensions. The song "Washington on Your Side" explicitly comments on complicated origins of representational government, while also directing our attention to the ways that things have not changed much since the late 1700s. Later in the song, Jefferson laments that President Washington is particularly fond of Hamilton and his ideas, that Hamilton has the President in his "pocket." To have a politician in "your pocket" is a common contemporary refrain for government corruption. Further, the word "Washington" is now a stand-in for all of the federal government thanks to the government being physically located in Washington, D.C. (which, as *Hamilton* teaches us, is partially due to a compromise struck by Hamilton himself!). Here, *Hamilton* invites us to think about time as circular, rather than strictly linear and progressive. *Hamilton*'s lyrics simultaneously call to the specifics of the founding father's disagreements *and* today's political squabbling—that they are inherently related.

Hamilton, throughout its story and the musical composition, uses nonlinear temporality to emphasize uneven power dynamics for its characters. One way that *Hamilton* plays with time is through a re-mix effect. In the Act One song, "Satisfied," Hamilton's future sister-in-law, Angelica, imagines how her life would be different had she decided to date him, rather than set him up with her sister Eliza. The song before "Satisfied" is "Helpless," which chronicles Eliza and Alexander's brief courtship, from Eliza's point of view. "Satisfied" opens with Angelica singing a toast to Eliza and Hamilton on their wedding day. We then hear an effect that resembles the sound a vinyl record makes as it is "scratched" (that is, manually manipulated on a turntable). Scratching records was a crucial component in the development of hip hop music in the 1970s, producing a unique and repetitive sound associated with the genre today. The scratch effect in "Satisfied" precipitates two things: the song is about to shift musical genres, and *Hamilton* is about to "time travel"— that is, blend the past and the present. Specifically, the word "rewind" is repeated several times before Angelica, who had previously been singing, begins to rap about the night she met, and fell for, Hamilton. A few verses later, "Satisfied" incorporates portions of the song "Helpless" as the two sisters' memories converge. We learn that Angelica set up Hamilton and Eliza, despite her own feelings for him, because he did not have the appropriate social or financial standing to marry the oldest Schuyler sister. By remixing the song from traditional showtune-style to hip hop, "Satisfied" emphasizes the intensity with which Angelica longs for a different set of choices—she tells us she has a gendered and familial responsibility to marry into money. And by layering the past (both Angelica's *and* ours as audience, for if we are listening to the cast album in order, we have just heard "Helpless") with the present, *Hamilton* demonstrates the ways in which past, present, and future subjugation are fundamentally entangled with one another.

We also hear the scratch-effect prominently at the beginning of each of *Hamilton*'s three duels. In the last of these duels, between Hamilton and Burr, there is a sharp change in diegetic time. As Burr narrates the scene in "The World Was Wide Enough," his voice increases in speed and volume, and his reasons for wanting to (needing to) win this duel become crucial. Once the chorus of singers reaches the end of their countdown, indicating the men are to finally shoot at one another, the song suddenly stops. *Hamilton* set designer David Korins posted a picture to his Twitter account in July 2015 (when the musical was in previews off–Broadway) showing an actor, dressed in all white, playing the role of the bullet that leaves Burr's gun. According to Korins's caption, the actor makes her way "achingly slowly" across the stage, as Hamilton takes over the narration. There is no music now, only Hamilton performing a soliloquy about his legacy, his faults, and the idea that death has always been chasing him. "The World Was Wide Enough" is the third time in the musical that Hamilton tells us that for his whole life, he's imagined death closing in on him: this future "memory" is (finally) about to be his present reality. The collapsing of time here in *Hamilton* is significant; we see that the death that Hamilton escaped from in the Caribbean (whether from infectious disease, hurricane, or poverty) has finally caught up to him. Just as he's been looking death in the face, so to speak, for most of his life, Hamilton in this slowed down version of reality, has time to think about the ways he was able to leave the world a better place, as he stares at a bullet headed straight towards him. The slow-down-effect of time in this last dramatic song and scene of the musical carries the same message about the entanglement of the past, present, and future as in "Satisfied," although with the more optimistic ending that the world has been improved because of Hamilton's moment in it.

Hamilton is an example of a Speculative Fiction text that engages audiences in questions about power, resistance, defeat, and triumph through the power of imagination. *Hamilton* is, if imperfect, a politically fantastic endeavor. The hit musical uses a 300-year-old setting and story to not merely make a comment on today's political gains and struggles, but to encourage audiences to ask questions about what else *could be. Hamilton* (re)imagines a world where people of color were instrumental, not just included, in the construction of a better, more just and inclusive world.

Works Cited

"The Adams Administration." *Hamilton: An American Musical,* by Lin-Manuel Miranda. Atlantic, 2015.
"Cabinet Battle #1." *Hamilton: An American Musical,* by Lin-Manuel Miranda. Atlantic, 2015.
Chernow, Ron. *Alexander Hamilton.* Penguin Group. 2004.
Delman, Edward. "How Lin-Manuel Miranda Shapes History." *The Atlantic.* 26 Sept. 2015 https://www.theatlantic.com/entertainment/archive/2015/09/lin-manuel-miranda-hamilton/408019/.
Durham, Aisha. *Home with Hip Hop Feminism: Performances in Communication and Culture.* Peter Lang. 2014.
Gans, Andrew, and Gioia, Michael. "*Hamilton* Opens with a Multi-Million Dollar Advance." *Playbill.* 7 Aug. 2015 http://www.playbill.com/news/article/hamilton-opens-with-multi-million-dollar-advance-356635#.
Gardner, Lyn. "Theatre Is Coming to Terms with Its Diversity Problem; Real Progress Is Vital." *The Guardian.* 2 Jan. 2017. https://www.theguardian.com/stage/theatreblog/2017/jan/02/theatre-diversity-progress-in-the-depths-of-dead-love.
Gibbs, Alexandra. "Award-Winning 'Hamilton' Musical Was No 'Over-Night Success,' Says Creator Lin-Manuel Miranda," *CNBC,* 28 Dec. 2017. https://www.cnbc.com/2017/12/28/hamilton-creator-lin-manuel-miranda-on-the-making-of-the-musical.html.
Jenkins, Henry. *Convergence Culture: Where Old and New Media Collide.* New York University Press. 2006.

Mignolo, Walter. D. "Sylvia Wynter: What Does It Mean to Be Human?" *Sylvia Wynter: On Being Human as Praxis*, edited by Katherine McKittrick, Duke University Press. 2015. pp 106–124.

Mosely, Walter. "Black to the Future." *Dark Matter: A Century of Speculative Fiction from the African Diaspora*. Edited by Sheree Thomas. Time Warner Books. 2000, pp. 405–408.

Moynagh, Maureen. "Speculative Pasts and Afro-Futures: Nalo Hopkinson's Trans-American Imaginary." *African American Review*, vol. 51, no. 3, 2018, pp. 211–222.

Newsom, Jennifer. S. *Miss Representation*. Girl's Club Entertainment. 2011.

"Nonstop." *Hamilton: An American Musical*, by Lin-Manuel Miranda. Atlantic, 2015.

Paulson, Michael. "*Hamilton* Tries New Sales Method to Battle Bots and Scalpers." *The New York Times*. 15 Aug. 2017. https://www.nytimes.com/2017/08/15/theater/hamilton-ticket master-verified-fan-broadway.html.

"Satisfied." *Hamilton: An American Musical*, by Lin-Manuel Miranda. Atlantic, 2015.

Snibbe, Kurt. "How *Hamilton* Measures up to the Greatest Broadway Shows." *The Orange County Register*. 3 Aug. 2017. https://www.ocregister.com/2017/08/03/how-hamilton-measures-up-to-the-greatest-broadway-shows/.

Thomas, P.L. *Science Fiction and Speculative Fiction: Challenging Genres*. Sense Publishers. 2013.

"Washington on Your Side." *Hamilton: An American Musical*, by Lin-Manuel Miranda. Atlantic, 2015.

Womack, Ytasha. *Afrofuturism: The World of Black Sci-Fi and Fantasy Culture*. Chicago University Press. 2013.

"The World Was Wide Enough." *Hamilton: An American Musical*, by Lin-Manuel Miranda. Atlantic, 2015.

"Promise me we'll do this together"

Trauma and the Restorative Power of the Feminine in Frozen *and* Moana

JESSICA STANLEY

In the recent Disney film *Ralph Breaks the Internet*, protagonists Ralph and Vanellope take a trip to OhMyDisney.com, the online home of Disney characters. Vanellope finds her way to a room marked "Princesses" where she encounters both classic and contemporary Disney heroines, from Snow White to Moana. When Vanellope enters the room, the princesses attempt to discern whether she is a *real* princess. Their initial questions focus on characteristics such as magical abilities or friendship with animals, but they soon take a darker, more serious turn. Snow White asks, "Were you poisoned?" Cinderella and Tiana ask, "Cursed?" and Belle and Rapunzel quickly follow with, "Kidnapped or enslaved?" Though these criteria may not be surprising to the audience, Vanellope hears them and is horrified. She whispers: "Are you guys okay? Should I call the police?" (*Ralph Breaks the Internet*). In a world where the #MeToo movement has inspired both high-profile court cases where women demand justice from their assailants, and conversations between women where traumas are shared and discussed rather than locked away, Vanellope's response reflects changing attitudes about how women should interact and address trauma, while simultaneously challenging the problematic nature of the traditional princess narrative.

This may be why the trailer received significant attention online, with individuals and even major news outlets pointing out that the trailer marked the first time the princesses interacted with one another in the same space. More importantly, however, the trailer reflects the first time that the princesses openly acknowledge the abuse they endure as part of their narratives. Like the connectivity associated with the #MeToo movement, this acknowledgement happens when the princesses are together in a space where they can empathize with one another and connect over their shared traumas. While the trailer marks a blatant shift for Disney in terms of its willingness to confront some of the most problematic ideology ingrained in its films, I argue that Disney began that transition several years earlier with the release of *Frozen* and *Moana*. In both films, Disney shifts the role of the antagonist from a particular villain to the various forms of trauma imposed by patriarchal figures onto women. These films allow women and girls to witness positive interactions between women and illustrate the restorative power of working together to overcome trauma, which becomes even more important in light of the #MeToo movement's original goals.

While the Disney Princess brand—which encompasses many of Disney's most well-known female characters—has evolved throughout the years to depict the princesses not as damsels, but as role models exhibiting characteristics like kindness, bravery, and a love of adventure, the franchise is not without problems. The princesses are usually positioned against other women, both in their respective films and in Princess-branded merchandise. In *Cinderella Ate My Daughter: Dispatches from the Front Lines of the New Girlie-Girl Culture*, Peggy Orenstein argues that Disney Princesses are set apart from other characters as unique and special by being isolated from other women. According to Orenstein, "princesses may confide in a sympathetic mouse or teacup, but, at least among the best-known stories, they do not have girlfriends" (23). The Princess line, and the films on which it is based, have historically rejected female relationships, reducing them at best to petty rivalries, and at worst to violent antagonism. Often, princesses are set apart from other women and coded as desirable to male characters because they are different, either due to their intelligence, kindness, or tomboyish traits. Disney films marketed to young girls have been no exception and recreate the ideology of the exceptional woman. In *Beauty and the Beast*, Belle is considered odd by most of the villagers due to her love of reading. The other young women of marriageable age that make an appearance are often referred to as "The Bimbettes" or "The Silly Girls" in outside material because of their superficial desire for Gaston. Viewers are meant to understand that Belle finds her happily ever after because her personality is superior to the other women around her. This notion is furthered in *The Princess and the Frog*; Prince Naveen attempts to woo Tiana by explaining that she "could not be more different" than the "thousands of other women" he has. Even *Mulan*, which is often lauded by Disney fans for its portrayal of a strong female character, features a scene in which the Emperor mentions to Captain Shang that "you don't meet a girl like that every dynasty" (*Mulan*). These characters are all portrayed as different from the women around them, and these differences are what make them deserving of a happily ever after.

The tradition of primarily positioning women against one another in media flies directly in the face of research pointing to the psychological and physiological benefits of woman-centered friendships. Multiple studies have explored the benefits of female friendships and social interactions, including a portion of the 2005 Nurses' Health Study from Harvard Medical School, where researchers found that women with close friendships were better able to cope with traumatic losses and less likely to develop physical impairments as they aged (Colditz and Hankinson). Others, like a 2000 study by UCLA researchers on human stress responses, suggest that while the well-known "fight or flight response" may be the primary stress response for men, women often exhibit a "tend and befriend" response. According to the study, women are "more likely to mobilize social support, especially from other females, in times of stress," so close friendships between women are essential to effectively coping with trauma and stress (Taylor 21). Despite the research, however, healthy friendships between women have, historically, been underrepresented in media. Instead, the exceptional woman, *a character who is quirky or not like other girls*, remains a staple in film and television.

Indeed, out of all the princesses in the Disney Princess line-up, six are depicted in primarily antagonistic relationships with other women. Snow White, Cinderella, and Rapunzel all face threats from mother-figures, either physical or psychological. Ariel and Aurora are positioned against more powerful, older women who seek to take control of their kingdoms. Jasmine is not shown interacting with other women at all, nor is Belle (unless a talking teapot and wardrobe are counted). According to Bram Dijkstra, the film industry's Victorian roots often led to "wholesale appropriation of the essential gender dichotomies characteristic of late-nineteenth-century art" in many twentieth-century films (qtd. in Tóth 186). Many twentieth-century princess films reflect similar ideology—women are either the angel in the house or the fallen woman, naturally leading to conflict. Only Tiana and Merida, two of the more recent princesses, are shown having healthy, substantive relationships with other women.

While many of the more traditional princesses may not have the benefit of healthy relationships with other women, they certainly experience their share of trauma, as highlighted in *Ralph Breaks the Internet*. Some of these characters face threats from female figures, but others experience trauma at the hands of male forces. Ariel's most prized possessions (and the dreams they represent) fall victim to her father's explosive temper, Jasmine is enslaved by Jafar after being led to believe that he killed the man she loves, and Belle sees her father imprisoned and the Beast stabbed by Gaston after she shuns his multiple unwanted romantic advances. Even the princesses who suffer at the hands of other women, like Snow White and Cinderella, do so because of a patriarchal system. In "Snow White and her Wicked Stepmother," Sandra Gilbert and Susan Gubar argue that the unseen king in *Snow White* is actually "the voice of the looking glass, the patriarchal voice of judgement that rules the Queen's—and every woman's—self-evaluation" (293). The stepmothers are a product of a system that forces them to compete with the princesses for male approval as their primary source of agency. In each case, trauma is a byproduct of a patriarchal world.

Judith Herman writes that "traumatic events generally involve threats to life or bodily integrity, or a close personal encounter with violence and death" (33), and Cathy Caruth broadly defines trauma as "an overwhelming experience of sudden, or catastrophic events, in which the response to the event occurs in the often delayed, and uncontrolled repetitive occurrence of hallucinations and other intrusive phenomena" (11). In most of the princess films, women are confronted with sudden, traumatic experiences usually brought on by patriarchal figures that threaten both their physical and mental wellbeing. In the traditional princess narratives, trauma is quickly remedied with the removal of the villain and the promises of marriage to a benevolent prince. None of the princesses address the ordeals they have been through, focusing instead on their happily-ever-afters. *Frozen* and *Moana*, however, acknowledge and confront the trauma experienced by the princesses, making it an integral part of the narrative. In both films, women experience trauma and initially respond by isolating themselves or lashing out at others in an attempt to regain a sense of agency. Ultimately, these methods prove ineffective, and even damaging, as the characters' isolation leads to further pain. These films make clear that only by opening themselves up to the support of other women do these characters begin the healing process.

This ideology echoes the goals of #MeToo founder Tarana Burke, who began the movement after a conversation with a 13-year-old survivor of sexual assault. In an interview with the *Washington Post* in 2017, Burke described guilt over being unable to comfort and counsel the girl after she disclosed her abuse. Burke explains that she found herself wondering "why couldn't you just say 'me too'?" She continued: "When I started putting the pieces together of what helped me, it was having other survivors empathize with me" (qtd. in Ohlheiser). For Burke, the #MeToo movement is ultimately about creating a space where women can support and encourage one another as they deal with the trauma of sexual assault and other forms of patriarchal oppression. *Frozen* and *Moana* package this ideology for a younger audience, providing models of connectivity and encouragement for girls and women, particularly those who have experienced trauma or who love someone that has.

Frozen (2013) tells the story of two sisters, Anna and Elsa, and their quest to save their kingdom from an eternal winter, triggered by Elsa's ice powers. In the film, Elsa's powers are closely tied to intense emotions and trauma from childhood that must be overcome in order for her to grow as an individual and as a queen. In one of the film's first scenes, a young Anna and Elsa are seen playing; an accidental blast of ice from Elsa's hand strikes Anna, and she falls unconscious. Their father immediately blames Elsa for using her powers, shouting "What have you done? This is getting out of hand!" (*Frozen*). Later, in a misguided attempt to help Elsa gain control, her father forces her to wear gloves to contain her magic, a decision that ultimately leads Elsa to fear and revile her own body, and separates her from the rest of the kingdom in a plan that includes "closing the gates, limiting her contact with people, and keeping her powers hidden from everyone" (*Frozen*). While Anna comes out of the ordeal physically unscathed, the damage to Elsa's psyche is deep. Not only does she blame herself for her sister's injury, she is haunted by her father's mantra of "conceal, don't feel" (*Frozen*). Elsa grows up believing that she is a monster, and over time, internalizes her father's warnings. By the time she reaches adulthood, she has become too fearful to touch, or even interact, with others, despite the fact that she is the most powerful figure in Arendelle. Of course, this proves to be an unsustainable way of living, and when her ice magic unleashes a blizzard throughout the entire kingdom, Elsa flees, hoping to protect her subjects from herself.

Throughout the film, Elsa exhibits the three major signs of post-traumatic stress disorder, as outlined in the *Diagnostic and Statistical Manual of Mental Disorders, 5th Edition*: "re-experiencing, avoidance, and hyperarousal" (271). On more than one occasion, she experiences a flashback to the night Anna was injured or responds to an event or a stimulus in a way that is directly influenced by her memory of that night. She never speaks about the event or her powers, avoids reminders of the event (including Anna herself), expresses feelings of fear and hopelessness several times and telling Anna that she must remain isolated so she can "be who I am without hurting anybody" (*Frozen*). When she is forced to interact with others, she is skittish and jumpy, and experiences several angry outbursts as she attempts to contain her emotions and stress. With women being "approximately twice as likely as males to meet the criteria for PTSD" according to the article "Gender Issues in PTSD," Elsa's very visible response to trauma offers a mirror for women viewers to see their own struggles reflected (Kimerling 211). Unlike her royal predecessors, Elsa takes time to deal with her pain (although some methods are more productive than others), and her healing is a process. Further, the narrative seems to *encourage* that process through the song "Let It Go," where those viewers are called not to shame Elsa, but rather to celebrate her move from oppression to freedom.

"Let It Go" serves as a powerful resistance narrative for young women. In this sequence, Elsa not only experiments with her powers, but completely rejects her father's ideology. One of her first decisions upon leaving Arendelle is to throw away her remaining glove (the other was taken by Anna), which she continued to wear even after her father died. No longer ashamed of her body or its capabilities, Elsa changes her clothes from a restrictive, high neck dress to a sparkling, more revealing gown, demonstrating her new acceptance of her body and her power. As Elsa sings, she uses her powerful and previously suppressed ice magic to produce more and more intricate creations, and she becomes more at ease with herself and her abilities. Throughout the song, Elsa's facial expressions, body language, and tone all demonstrate growing relief at abandoning the rules her father set out for her, as well as pleasant surprise at what her magic allows her to create. By the end of the song, Elsa appears in complete control of her magic and her feelings, having constructed an elaborate ice palace. She struts confidently to the balcony, declaring that she will not return to the oppression she felt in Arendelle and instead, will remain on the mountain where she can freely enjoy the use of her power. It is worth noting that although this is a form of running away, this is not necessarily a bad thing. Elsa does not give much (if any) indication at the beginning of the film that she even wants to be queen. In fact, she almost seems resistant to the idea. Even though this scene depicts her giving up one kind of power, taking steps to remove herself from a situation that is causing her stress and anxiety can be seen as exercising power of a different kind.

While acceptance of her powers helps Elsa begin the healing process, the film is clear that Elsa needs relationships with others, notably her sister, in order to truly heal. When Anna extends an invitation for Elsa to return to home and begin mending their broken relationship, Elsa flashes back to the moment she injured her sister. The flashback causes Elsa to lash out, and in doing so, she injures Anna with another blast of ice, this time striking her heart. Elsa sees hurting her sister again as confirmation of her monstrosity and flees. She is unable to escape the pattern of trauma on her own, but ultimately, Anna's persistence and love enable Elsa to break her cycle of self-loathing by demonstrating to Elsa that she is worthy of love. In the climax of the film, Anna, who is slowly freezing, chooses to protect her sister rather than go to Kristoff, whose kiss should break her curse. As she throws herself between Elsa and Hans' sword, Anna turns fully to ice, an act of self-sacrificial love, which ultimately saves both women. After witnessing her sister's sacrifice, Elsa begins to understand that sisterly love will help her control her powers, making way for the restoration of the kingdom and the sisters' relationship.

Both Anna and Elsa benefit from their restored relationship, in a process that Burke calls "empowerment through empathy" (qtd. in Ohlheiser). Elsa discovers that a relationship with her sister built on shared trust and understanding can help calm the fear and anxiety that previously ruled her life. Anna, who has suffered from years of isolation and her sister's rejection, also benefits from the relationship. While on her own, Anna demonstrates a dangerous level of naiveté and desperation for human connection, which leads her to believe she has fallen instantly in love with the villainous Prince Hans. The film marks the first time that a Disney movie openly confronts the notion that love at first sight (or first duet) is unrealistic, with both Elsa and Kristoff warning Anna that she should not marry someone she just met. Their concerns for Anna are realized when Hans tells Anna that he never really loved her. Although this realization is heartbreaking, with Elsa's support, Anna has the confidence to reject Hans and move on. The sisters' repaired relationship demonstrates that both trauma survivors and those who support and encourage them can benefit from working together.

Moana (2016) continues the theme of overcoming trauma by depicting a metaphorical assault, in which the demigod Maui steals the heart of the mother goddess, Te Fiti, and attempts to give it to the humans to control. The heart, which takes the form of a small green gemstone, contains Te Fiti's life-giving powers. By stealing Te Fiti's heart, Maui takes a vital part of her body and identity without her consent. Devastated by this betrayal and overcome by hurt and anger, Te Fiti transforms into the lava monster Te Ka, who is driven by a desire to reclaim the piece of her body that was stolen. In the process, her life-giving powers are replaced by a blight that threatens to consume the world. Moana's grandmother tasks her with finding Maui and restoring Te Fiti's heart.

The film begins with women committing subtle acts of resistance against patriarchal forces. Moana's father, the village chief, has outlawed the exploration of waters beyond the reef that encircles their island. Moana, however, finds herself inexplicably drawn to the ocean. Her grandmother, Tala, shares and encourages Moana's love of the water, telling her to listen to her father but to also acknowledge the gut feelings that drive her toward adventure (*Moana*). In one of the earliest scenes, Tala tells Moana and the other village children the story of Te Fiti and Maui, and later, she shows Moana a cavern full of the boats her people once used to explore the region. In doing so, she subtly begins grooming Moana to take her journey and become a different type of leader than her father.

Unlike Elsa, Moana's father wants her to claim her power, but only on his terms. When the blight comes to their island, Moana suggests that the villagers take the boats hidden in the cavern to find unaffected islands; her father becomes enraged, telling her "I should have burned those boats a long time ago!" (*Moana*). While Moana's suggestion demonstrates the levelheadedness she will have as future chief, her father refuses to listen because it contradicts his worldview. Although his decision to forbid travel beyond the reef is partially justified in a flashback scene that reveals he almost died while sailing, he never communicates this information to Moana (she learns it secondhand from her mother). Instead, he angrily dismisses Moana's suggestions, and in doing so, threatens to doom his entire village. This scene illustrates the dangers of ignoring the feminine and relying solely on patriarchal forces too focused on maintaining tradition. Moana's mother seems to recognize this, and rejects her husband's decision in favor of helping her daughter pack food and water for her inevitable journey. Her subtle act of resistance enables Moana to successfully complete her journey and further illustrates the ways that women can work together at various levels to affect change. The film makes clear that women do not have to make grand gestures in order to support one another, and that sometimes, small actions can be the most meaningful.

When Moana and Maui arrive at the place where Te Fiti should be, they encounter Te Ka. Maui's first instinct is to attack the monster, which only enrages her more. Only Moana stops to really look at Te Ka. In doing so, she recognizes that Te Fiti and Te Ka are one in the same. Her willingness to look past Te Ka's exterior and see the pain beneath allows Moana to calmly approach her when Maui cannot even get close. Moana asks the ocean, which, by all accounts, is a character in the film, to make a path for Te Ka to come to her. The water parts, leaving a literal path to healing for Te Ka to cross. As the women approach one another, Moana sings a reprise of a song she previously sang with her grandmother, in which she tells Te Ka that she does not have to let the actions of others define who she is (*Moana*). Once Te Ka realizes that Moana recognizes her, not as a monster but as a hurting woman, she is pacified, and Moana is able to restore her heart, allowing Te Fiti to transform back into her true self.

Multiple women have written in online platforms about their reactions to this scene; they recognize their own experiences with sexual assault manifested in Te Ka. Ana Mai Luckett describes watching the film and recognizing the pain and shame associated with the trauma of sexual assault reflected in the fire monster. She notes that in particular, the lyrics to "Know Who You Are" explain her feelings about a prior sexual assault, stating that "I am not just a rape victim. I am not just the leftovers of someone else's choices.... Just like Moana sings, it doesn't define who I am" (Luckett). Kimberly Poovey echoed these sentiments, noting, "I see my pain as a monster of fire. I am so afraid of it. I want to stay far, far away, but it is a part of me.... May I be as brave as Moana as I face what is part of me, but does not define me." For these women, watching Moana's acceptance of Te Fiti, pain and all, provided a much-desired metaphor for the process of confronting and working through their own trauma.

In the film, healing and restoration come from Te Fiti herself remembering who she is, however, she is only able to begin this process with Moana's help. This theme of women helping women repeats throughout the narrative, beginning with Tala and Moana's mother. In much the same way as she guides Te Fiti, earlier in the narrative Moana is guided by her grandmother and mother toward a fuller understanding of herself. Their support helps Moana understand her strengths and her role in protecting her people. While Moana initially believes that Maui should be the one to restore Te Fiti's heart (because he stole it in the first place), she ultimately is the only one who can do it, because her experiences—both with patriarchal oppression and supportive women—make her uniquely suited to understand Te Fiti. By positioning the women this way, the film illustrates, in no uncertain terms, the powerful effects of women working together to overcome trauma.

In both films, women characters are subjected to trauma inflicted by masculine power used without regard for the feminine. Elsa's father inadvertently inflicts deep psychological trauma that Elsa carries into adulthood, and the imposition of his views makes her believe that her power should be hidden rather than celebrated. Anna, while not directly traumatized by a male figure, indirectly suffers because of decisions made by her father and Hans. Te Fiti is robbed of a vital part of her identity by a male figure who feels entitled to possess it. In most cases, the women are unable to convince the patriarchal figures that they have caused any damage. Elsa's father dies before he can see the effects of the pain he has caused, and the other male antagonists are dragged out of Elsa's kingdom in chains, all the while protesting how *they* are being treated. These characters' reactions mirror those of real-world men who respond with outrage when women reject their advances. The internet is full of examples of men who accuse women of being crazy or revert to misogynistic name-calling when they don't respond enthusiastically to unsolicited pictures or requests for sex. In both cases, the men seem to have no concept that their behavior is inappropriate. Maui seems to show genuine remorse for the pain his actions have caused, however, this remorse is prompted by Moana who must remind him to apologize to Te Fiti. Like the men from *Frozen*, Maui spends much of the film concerned with his own needs and wants. Since the women cannot count on these patriarchal figures to recognize their trauma and provide pathways to healing, they must rely on one another instead. Much like the #MeToo Movement, these characters reject patriarchal power and subvert the popular narrative that women cannot and should not work together.

The films depict relationships between women and empowerment through empathy as the best way to overcome trauma. While neither film condemns women for their varied responses to trauma—though she flees, Elsa is promptly reinstated as queen upon her return, Anna is allowed a moment of revenge when she punches Hans, and rather than judging her actions as Te Ka, the people of Moana's village simply celebrate Te Fiti's return—they clearly present connectivity with other women as the *ideal* response. This message becomes even more meaningful in light of real-world statistics about assault and harassment. According to the Rape, Abuse & Incest National Network (RAINN), the majority of sexual assaults are not reported to the police, and an even fewer number of perpetrators of sexual violence will actually go to prison. In fact, the organization reports that, "out of every 1000 rapes, 994 perpetrators will walk free" ("The Criminal Justice"). Through characters like Anna and Moana, the films illustrate the kinds of responses that will support and encourage survivors of trauma outside of official reporting. In a world where women are often faced with painful decisions about reporting and seeking justice for their trauma, these films provide another option: there is healing to be found in connecting with other women.

WORKS CITED

Caruth, Cathy. *Unclaimed Experience: Trauma, Narrative and History.* Johns Hopkins UP, 1996.

Colditz, Graham A., and Susan E. Hankinson. "The Nurses' Health Study: Lifestyle and Health Among Women." *Nature Reviews Cancer,* vol. 5, May 2005, 388–396.

"The Criminal Justice System Statistics." *RAINN,* 2018. https://www.rainn.org/statistics/criminal-justice-system.

Diagnostic and Statistical Manual of Mental Disorders: DSM-5. 5th ed., American Psychiatric Association, 2013.

Frozen. Directed by Chris Buck and Jennifer Lee, Walt Disney Pictures, 2013.

Gilbert, Sandra, and Susan Gubar. "Snow White and Her Wicked Stepmother." *The Classic Fairy Tales,* edited by Maria Tatar. W.W. Norton & Company, 1999, pp. 291–297.

Herman, Judith. *Trauma and Recovery: The Aftermath of Violence—From Domestic Abuse to Political Terror,* Basic Books, 1992.

Kimerling, Rachel, Paige Ouimette, and Julie C. Weitlauf. "Gender Issues in PTSD." *Handbook in PTSD: Science and Practice,* edited by Matthew J. Friedman, et al. The Guilford Press, 2007, pp. 207–228.

Luckett, Ana Mai. "How Disney's 'Moana' Gave Me Hope After My Sexual Assault. *The Mighty,* Mighty Proud Media, 7 Mar. 2017, themighty.com/2017/03/moana-sexual-assault-doesnt-define-me/.

Moana. Directed by Ron Clements and John Musker, Walt Disney Studios Motion Pictures, 2016.

Ohlheiser, Abby. "The Woman Behind 'Me Too' Knew the Power of the Phrase When She Created It—10 Years Ago." *Washington Post,* 19 Oct. 2017, https://www.washingtonpost.com/news/the-intersect/wp/2017/10/19/the-woman-behind-me-too-knew-the-power-of-the-phrase-when-she-created-it-10-years-ago/?utm_term=.e367c813a892.

Orenstein, Peggy. *Cinderella Ate My Daughter: Dispatches from the Front Lines of the New Girlie-Girl Culture.* Harper, 2012.

Poovey, Kimberly. "What Moana Taught Me About Dealing with Trauma as an Adult." *Motherly.* https://www.mother.ly/life/moana-taught-trauma.

Ralph Breaks the Internet. Directed by Phil Johnston and Rich Moore, Walt Disney Animation Studios, 2018.

Taylor, Shelley E., Laura Cousino Klein, Brian P. Lewis, Tara L. Gruenewald, Regan A.R.

Gurung, and John A. Updegraff. "Biobehavioral Responses to Stress in Females: Tend-and-Befriend, Not Fight-or-Flight." *Psychological Review*, vol. 107, no. 3, 2000, pp. 411–429.

Tóth, Zsófia Anna. "Disney's Violent Women: In Quest of a 'Fully Real' Violent Woman in American Cinema." *Brno Studies in English*, vol. 43, no. 1, 2017, pp. 185–212.

Real Curves in the Revolution

Body Politics, Unruly Bodies
and Comedy as Resistance

S. KATHERINE COOPER,
BRITTANY M. HARDER *and* CORINNE E. FANTA

In the current U.S. political climate, the human body is in many ways at the center of various political battles; for example, bodies are racialized and stigmatized; controversial "bathroom bills" aim to restrict public bathroom use by trans bodies; and debates over abortion, reproductive rights, and women's bodily autonomy have been reignited. One way that bodies continue to be regulated in many Western societies like the United States is through our cultural preoccupation with body size and physical appearance. Public engagement with body size, health, and beauty ideals are being hashed out and negotiated. Dominant ideologies on bodies and body weight assert that (1) fat bodies are unhealthy, (2) fat bodies are unproductive, and (3) fat bodies are unsightly. Even though the majority of the U.S. population is now considered overweight or obese (thanks in part to changes in medical definitions of these very categories), fatness remains a marginalized social category, and research shows that fat people are discriminated against in a variety of social arenas such as employment, promotion, fashion, healthcare, public transportation, education, and cyber-space. Every *body* is not treated equally, but mass media and popular culture have become the primary vehicles for resisting cultural meanings of fatness, promoting body positivity, and challenging the bodily status quo.

Media hysteria over rising obesity rates has created a "moral panic" about fatness, where fatness and obesity are framed as an "epidemic" (Boero 42). News coverage of this issue has increased dramatically in recent decades and tends to frame "overweight" and "obesity" as problems of individual failure, rather than focusing on genetic factors or structural concerns (e.g., lack of nutritious foods in low-income neighborhoods). Obesity and fatness, therefore, are framed in the mainstream as a health crisis, where fat is suggested to be a measure of poor health caused by individual lifestyle choices. "Overweight" and "obese" are categories assigned based on one's Body Mass Index (BMI), or roughly the ratio of one's height to their weight. The American Medical Association declared obesity to be a "disease" in 2013, thereby labeling tens of millions of Americans as having defective bodies and marking many otherwise healthy bodies as "diseased." General public knowledge about America's "obesity problem" does not include the history of BMI and the various reclassifications of BMI categories that "created" millions of overweight Americans overnight (Boero 47; Fletcher 348), research that challenges the utility of BMI as an accurate measure of both fatness and health, or research that challenges a direct causal relationship between fat and health. Mainstream coverage thus tends to reflect wider cultural values, and this social problem stands in contrast to media representations of anorexia and bulimia, for instance, since thinness is highly valued in U.S. society.

In addition to news media, dominant ideologies of individualism and individual failure to maintain a healthy body weight are also frequently represented in entertainment media. Fat characters remain underrepresented in fictional television programming, but reality television puts bodies on display, both explicitly and implicitly. Popular reality shows like *The Biggest Loser* (2004–) and *My 600-lb Life* (2012–) depict the medicalized version of obesity and weight loss, where fatness is an urgent threat to health and is in desperate need of "fixing." Such television shows circulate narratives about fat people not only as unhealthy, but also as failing to abide by socio-cultural expectations of pleasant aesthetics and hygiene. "Do you have the will power?" This message aired within the first few minutes of the series opener of *The Biggest Loser,* which has led to numerous spin-offs and weight loss competition shows across the world. With millions of viewers tuning in each week, the show follows contestants as they take on diet and exercise regimens from professional chefs and trainers. Contestants vie for the most weight lost and ultimately, a $250,000 grand prize. *The Biggest Loser* draws on the assumption of society's rejection of the overweight body and sees this televised process of weight loss as motivation for overweight people to lose weight, implicitly associated with regaining their membership into society. Such representations of fatness reinforce the stigma of fat bodies, and further outcast millions of people whose bodies do not fit the glorified prototype. This show highlights how obese bodies are considered deviant bodies, compared with socially constructed perceptions of what a normative, healthy, and attractive body is supposed to look like.

However, there is growing resistance to these programs from contestants on the show, as well as from the viewers. Former contestants such as Kai Hibbard have been quite vocal about the show's deceptive approach to showing weight loss, claiming that while filming, contestants work out up to eight hours a day and are pressured to starve and dehydrate themselves to maximize perceived pounds shed before "weekly" weigh-ins—that actually occur on an alternate filming schedule—all to make it seem like rapid weight loss is purely the result of hard work and discipline. Increased public scrutiny concerning rumors that weigh-ins are rigged and allegations that contestants were given drugs to lose weight more rapidly spurred internal investigations from NBC (Gardner). *The Biggest Loser* was never formally canceled by the network, but new episodes have not aired since 2016; it was recently announced, however, that the show would be rebooted on USA Network beginning in 2020.

There has also been growing viewer and public resistance to the show. For example, Holland, Blood, and Thomas' study found that many people who were classified as either "obese" or "morbidly obese" were resistant to *The Biggest Loser*. Many expressed that the show was not an accurate representation of their own lived reality, and some were also concerned that the show perpetuates pejorative stereotypes about fat people, describing the program as "demeaning, humiliating, exploitative, disgusting, cruel, gimmicky, vile, lowest common denominator, commercialized, and degrading" (Holland et al. 21). Resistance in this case originates from contestants on the show as well as from some viewers. Criticism derives from the show's dismissal of individuals' personal stories and health biographies, as well as the show's ingrained focus on how an individual's weight loss can solve all of their problems.

Cultural associations of femininity as thinness have been historically prevalent in film and television, but some recent examples demonstrate instances of increased viewer resistance, such as the public dialogue surrounding Netflix's new dark comedy series *Insatiable* (2018–). As seen from the first episode, fatness is viewed negatively and is highly stigmatized, including the protagonist's nickname, Fatty Patty. However, early in the first season a broken bone forces her to have her jaw wired shut and adopt a liquid diet that allows her to lose significant weight. Discussions about weight are frequent throughout the series, such as when Patty's pageant coach suggests that her senior year of high school will be different by saying, "Trust me. Skinny is magic" ("Skinny Is Magic"). Patty begins to seek revenge on those who criticized her figure prior to her weight loss, and she frequently uses her new shape to seduce men for her own benefit. Patty feels rejected by her peers due to her weight prior to her transformation, and it isn't until she loses the weight that she becomes *fit* to train for pageants with her newly embraced beauty and charm. Charm, as an intangible quality, is tied to the societal constructions of beauty ideals and the moral imperatives connected to bodies, where bodies are seen as outward expressions of one's character.

Fat bodies presumably express qualities of laziness, gluttony, and sloppiness. Thin bodies, in contrast, are associated with societal assumptions of hard work, self-discipline, and pleasant aesthetics. Thinness and beauty represent ideal cultural standards of femininity, and pageantry has served as one of the main stages for the presentation and the speculation of bodies that evoke such standards. These qualities, in addition to a pleasant and likeable personality, enable pageant contestants to evoke the intangible, yet familiar characteristic of charm. As such, Patty learns from others' reactions to her that being thin has power. *Insatiable* quickly became one of Netflix's more controversial but also one of its most streamed series. Although *Insatiable* was well received by many, the themes throughout the series are triggering for some viewers, including eating disorder survivors, for its depiction of certain bodies as appropriate and others as intolerable. In an August 2018 op-ed published in *Teen Vogue*, for instance, eating disorder survivor Ellen Ricks observes, "The message I got from watching the show is that skinny equals strong, which is the mindset for many anorexics.... What they were hoping to position as dark comedy, felt only dark."

Insatiable sparked a great deal of public discussion, as well as public resistance. Prior to the show's release in August of 2018, a Change.org petition was established—ultimately receiving more than 235,000 signatures—with the intent to keep the series from airing on Netflix. Despite the backlash, however, the second season is currently scheduled to air later in 2019.[1] Although the petition was unsuccessful in its underlying goal, this instance of public action does successfully demonstrate a collective resistance to the series' representations of bodies, diet culture, and objectification of women. This adamant opposition to the show exposed the variation of what constitutes an ideal body and the means to achieving this standard. Body positivity has become more pervasive across society, and the resistance to television shows that use the body as a platform for plotlines, jokes, and the outcomes of a character's success or failure stems from a rejection of the common ideals glorifying thinness. While fatness was once rare in popular culture, usually relegated to the role of comic relief or derision, as the proportion of the population considered fat increases, so too does rhetoric of self-acceptance and confidence (Petersen 29). In contrast to the reception of *Insatiable*, Netflix's hit comedy film *Dumplin'* (2018) was widely praised for its messages of body positivity. *Dumplin'*, based on the popular Young Adult novel by Julie Murphy, revolves around a plus-size teenager who enters the small-town beauty pageant ran by her former-beauty-queen mother. The film's protagonist Willowdean counters dominant narratives on body image since she demonstrates no efforts or desires to lose weight, nor is it suggested that she is unhappy with her body. Instead, she mocks cultural beauty standards along the way. Body positivity resists standard cultural norms and dominant ideologies around defining a certain body as the ideal standard body, shown by Willowdean when she proclaims, "As far as I'm concerned, a swimsuit body is a body with a swimsuit on it" (*Dumplin'*).

Media are powerful tools in shaping public consciousness on a variety of issues, and comedy as a particular genre within popular culture is a unique arena for revealing taken-for-granted norms and exposing the social constructedness of social life. Women in comedy, in particular, have been breaking new ground in the historically "old boys' club," opening dialogue about a range of issues concerning gender, race, ethnicity, sex, bodies, and body image. An emphasis on women's physical appearance and bodies has historically been a central feature of their comedy (Rowe). Kathleen Rowe discusses the role of the "unruly woman" in popular culture who is "too fat, too funny, too noisy, too old, too rebellious" and consequently can disrupt social hierarchies (19). The spectacle of the unruly woman's excessiveness (both physically and figuratively), loose behavior, and vulgarity undermines dominant standards of femininity. More specifically, unruly women in popular culture often illuminate how idealized femininity is itself a performance, as well as how femininity is generally held to stricter standards than masculinity. For example, Rowe dissects two popular unruly women in the 1990s: Roseanne Barr and Miss Piggy. According to Rowe, "it is no accident that the most obviously gendered Muppet is a female, that the female is an animal, and that the animal is a pig" (26).

Roseanne initially aired in 1988, ran for nine seasons through the 1990s, and was later revived for another season in 2018. In the 1990s, *Roseanne* dominated network television and the series tackled a variety of feminist and working-class politics. Regarding body politics specifically, however, the very presence of a 200-plus-pound woman in a prime-time sitcom lead was indeed significant (Rowe 60). An emphasis on the physical body, particularly "grotesque" bodies, is central to cultural understandings of unruly women, highlighting our cultural uneasiness with "excessive" women's bodies in Western culture (Rowe 33). Rowe further identifies "the cult of thinness" as inextricably tied to "true femininity," which has become one of the "most insidious means of disciplining the female body" (62). The cult of thinness and the cultural stigmatization of fat people disproportionately affects heavy women more than heavy men, exemplified by the numerous fat jokes about Roseanne Barr (then Arnold) while her onscreen (and overweight) husband John Goodman was spared, because a woman's social status is largely dependent on her appearance. Despite her transgressive '90s primetime character, even Barr, however, is nonetheless impacted by external and internal pressures for weight loss. In 1998, Barr had gastric bypass surgery, and she has also undergone a tummy tuck and breast reduction surgery in past years. Barr has spoken publicly about her weight loss over the years, and it was even a punchline in the 2018 revival season. During the second episode, "Dress to Impress," Roseanne's daughter at one point claims she is going to throw away old photographs where her parents look "fat"; Roseanne responds, "Those were the only ones where we look happy!"

Whereas representations such as those in *My 600-lb Life* or *The Biggest Loser* maintain fatness to be a moral and medical dilemma, comedy often plays with taken-for-granted social meanings and may encourage the audience to question the very social constructedness of bodies and body image. *Roseanne* stands out in the 1990s because it was, at that time, rarer to see representations of fat women. Today, media representation is slowly starting to become more diverse. Contemporary comedians such as Leslie Jones, Queen Latifah, Melissa McCarthy, Rebel Wilson, Mindy Kaling, Amy Schumer, and Lena Dunham represent modern iterations of unruly women and have garnered widespread fame and celebrity status while resisting the "cult of thinness."

This is not to say, of course, that *all* comedy resists dominant discourses on body weight. Indeed, one could certainly choose from a range of circulating "fat jokes" in popular culture that disparage fat people and reinforce dominant fat narratives. However, a great deal of contemporary comedy does take a critical approach to its topic material, and therefore we focus specifically on comedy that challenges dominant portrayals of bodies and femininity. McCarthy and Schumer have each achieved celebrity status in the U.S., which also comes with widespread visibility and audience attention. Furthermore, they each write, perform, and produce comedy across multiple mediums, including television, films, and/or book authorship, and specifically they have both starred in several major comedy films in recent years. McCarthy and Schumer have also become known for their public engagement with body politics and messages of body positivity. Comedy is therefore a potential space in popular culture for challenging narratives pertaining to the hypermedicalization of fatness and definitions of feminine and healthy bodies as thin bodies.

Melissa McCarthy performs numerous comedic personas in her films that tend to be confident, independent, sexual, and stylish. Stukator notes that fat women have rarely been featured in film comedies, and, when present at all, are typically relegated to the role of sidekick or other stereotypical character (200). While this trend still largely holds true today, comedians like Melissa McCarthy are breaking the mold. McCarthy first rose to stardom for her portrayal of the quirky side-character Sookie St. James on the drama *Gilmore Girls* (2000–2007). She then later starred in the sitcom *Mike & Molly* (2010–2016), a comedy about a married couple that met at an Overeaters

Anonymous meeting. She won her first Emmy in 2011 for the role of Molly. More recently, however, McCarthy has become a prominent celebrity and a recurring box office hit. Her more transgressive roles include her Oscar-nominated performance of Megan in *Bridesmaids* (2011), self-assured Michelle Darnell in *The Boss* (2016), and the intelligent CIA analyst Susan Cooper in *Spy* (2015). Whereas her earlier TV roles were characterized by a certain brand of sweetness, her more recent major film characters are shameless, hilarious, unfiltered, sometimes bombastic, and empathetic.

When McCarthy dominates the big screen, not only does she provide an image for audience relatability that contrasts the historical trend of only featuring very thin women in leading roles, but she also acts in zany and out-rageous ways that women have rarely been allowed to do. Her character Megan from *Bridesmaids*, for instance, is confident, boastful, magnanimous, and shameless; Megan comically contrasts societal notions of traditional fem-ininity in both her dress and her decorum. Counter to frames of feminine behavior surrounding wedding planning, one of the most infamous scenes from the film is when the bride (played by Maya Rudolf) and her group of bridesmaids attend a dress fitting appointment, but after a bad bout of food poisoning, the scene concludes with the majority of the group physically ill and McCarthy's character shitting in the bathroom sink of a fancy bridal store, as she grunts, "Look away! Look away!" (*Bridesmaids*).

Offscreen, McCarthy maintains a more traditional middle-class respect-ability, and she uses her public platform to advocate for body positivity mes-saging. Not a stranger to sizeism in the fashion industry—during her early years of stardom, for example, McCarthy was notoriously unable to find a designer who would make a red-carpet dress in her size, sparking some public attention to the issue—the comic created the size-inclusive clothing line Seven7 that designs clothes for women's sizes 4 through 28. With her clothing line, McCarthy aims to eliminate categorical distinctions between "standard" and "plus" sizing. In a 2015 *Refinery29* interview, McCarthy states, "Women come in all sizes. Seventy percent of women in the United States are a size 14 or above, and that's technically 'plus-size,' so you're taking your biggest category of people and telling them, 'You're not really worthy'" (qtd. in Wang). Later in the interview, McCarthy also observes how these labels carry addi-tional symbolic meanings of difference: "I don't like the segregated plus size [in clothing stores]. You're saying, 'You don't get what everybody else gets. You have to go shop up by the tire section.'" Here, McCarthy uses humor to allude to another level of marginalization by illuminating the perception that fat women cannot share physical space with thin women. On one hand, most clothes do not come in plus sizes, and on the other hand, there is often a deliberate segregation of department store space, arguably to hide fat bodies away from the "normal" bodies.

Additionally, in a 2016 interview with *Redbook* magazine, McCarthy explains her concerns about the cultural scripts about bodies that young women like her daughters receive: "There's an epidemic in our country of girls and women feeling bad about themselves based on what .5% of the human race looks like. It starts very young. My message is that as long as everybody's healthy, enjoy and embrace whatever body type you have" (qtd. in Newman). McCarthy therefore adds a subtly subversive statement debunking a deeply ingrained cultural myth where, contrary to popular misconception, being healthy and being fat are not mutually exclusive identities. Fat bodies can be healthy bodies and thin bodies can be unhealthy. Or fat bodies can also be unhealthy, but not necessarily because of their weight. McCarthy's statement also raises a concern that these normative practices may be ironically creating new health problems, particularly those concerning mental health (e.g., depression, body dissatisfaction, and poor self-esteem). McCarthy's public persona, therefore, indirectly engages an alternative framework to understanding health and bodies that has gained increased attention in recent years: the Health at Every Size (HAES) approach. Many healthcare workers, health researchers, activists, and consumers argue that such an approach "emphasizes self-acceptance and healthy day-to-day practices, regardless of body weight" (Burgard 42). Rather than focusing on weight as defining one's health, a HAES approach defines health by the process of daily life (Burgard 42). Harder, for example, found that among 29 participants that were categorized as "obese" or "morbidly obese" by medical standards, 28 saw themselves as healthy and reported engaging in health-promoting behaviors such as regular exercise, eating healthy foods, and utilizing preventative and primary health care. In health care settings, however, these healthy day-to-day practices, other health outcomes (besides one's BMI), and patients' main complaints were less likely to be given proper attention during a clinical visit once the patient had been deemed as "obese" by BMI standards (Harder).

Despite these cases of demonstrated resistance against the medicalization and stigmatization of fatness, fat women comedians are not always wholeheartedly embraced in the public sphere, however. Public reactions to comedians like McCarthy are sometimes diverse and contradictory, and discourse equating fat as repulsive and unhealthy continues to persist. McCarthy has endured several public attacks based on her appearance, such as in 2010 when *Marie Claire* blogger Maura Kelly caused a stir for her commentary on *Mike & Molly*, where she claimed, "[I'd] be grossed out if I had to watch two characters with rolls and rolls of fat kissing each other.... To be brutally honest, even in real life, I find it aesthetically displeasing to watch a very, very fat person simply walk across a room" (qtd. in Previte and Gurrieri 340–341). Kelly later edited her post and apologized for her inflammatory words after

Marie Claire editor-in-chief Joanna Coles reported the magazine had received 28,000 email responses to the piece.

Additionally, film critic Rex Reed incited much public outrage for his reviews of McCarthy's films *Identity Thief* and *Tammy*. In his 2013 review of *Identity Thief*, Reed called her "tractor-sized," a "female hippo," and a "gimmick comedian who has devoted her short career to being obese and obnoxious with equal success." While there have been great strides in resistance in popular culture, comments like those by Reed demonstrate how deeply ingrained dominant narratives regarding weight, health, and beauty remain. Despite the uproar caused by his review, Reed never issued an apology and, in fact, doubled down on his stance. McCarthy did not publicly respond until a few months later in a *New York Times* article where she said, "I felt really bad for someone who is swimming in so much hate. I just thought, that's someone who's in a really bad spot, and I am in such a happy spot. I laugh my head off every day with my husband and my kids who are mooning me and singing me songs." Noting that she is raising two daughters in "a strange epidemic of body image and body dysmorphia," McCarthy adds that articles like Reed's review "just add to all those younger girls, that are not in a place in their life where they can say, 'that doesn't reflect on me'" (qtd. in Itzkoff).

Increased attention to the "obesity epidemic" in U.S. media culture has perpetuated a new medical justification for the practice of fat-shaming (Meeuf 138). Fat-shaming comments like those by Kelly and Reed are therefore couched in the common, though not well substantiated, rhetoric of "I'm just worried about your health." This also calls into question our general tendency to focus on the *visibility* of one's health. *Health* varies in people's personal experiences and is not something that is necessarily visible on the body (e.g., chronic pain, mental health), yet this strong cultural connotation continues to persist. Public health approaches tend to emphasize individualistic weight loss, though this approach has been largely ineffective and stigmatizing (Bombak e65). A Health at Every Size approach argues that weight and health are not synonymous and treating them as such may lead to an inaccurate understanding of one's health and potentially harmful outcomes via an obsession with weight-loss behaviors (see Campos et al.). In fact, a HAES approach to focusing on *health*, rather than on *weight*, may be most effective in addressing chronic disease (Bombak e65). Fat-shaming is not new. What *is* perhaps new, however, is the public outcry and condemnation of comments like those by Kelly and Reed. Social media in particular has greatly extended and democratized people's ability to engage in such public dialogue and express disapproval of those who publicly body-shame women.

McCarthy's resistance in public discourse may be seemingly subtle, but nonetheless impactful. As Petersen observes, "[S]he's attempting to reframe the conversation away from *her* body and toward representation *writ large*:

the importance of bodies, of any size, that don't attempt to convince viewers that there's only one manifestation of normal" (36, emphasis in original). Much of McCarthy's career and public persona therefore challenges and undermines dominant narratives about fatness by normalizing mainstream media representation of fat bodies, offering multidimensional characters in her films, and publicly addressing fatphobia, discrimination, and body positivity.

Amy Schumer is another celebrity comedian who frequently engages body politics in her humor. Schumer is well known for her stand-up specials, her comedy blockbusters *Trainwreck* (2015) and *I Feel Pretty* (2018), and her Emmy-winning sketch show *Inside Amy Schumer* (2013–) that airs on Comedy Central. Schumer's comedy centered on bodies differs from McCarthy's because, although she resists the cult of thinness, she doesn't really embody fatness or obesity. Nonetheless, she is still sometimes labeled and categorized as "heavy," such as when *Glamour* magazine featured her in their 2016 "plus-size" special issue aimed at women size 12 and up. Throughout much of her humor, Schumer uses her embodiment of hyperfemininity to deconstruct dominant frames of thinness as the model for femininity. Blonde-haired and "average-sized," Schumer is conventionally attractive, feminine, and seemingly innocent-looking, and she strategically uses her cuteness to undermine cultural beauty ideals and body weight expectations. More specifically, Schumer often plays up her "average" appearance, and especially men's reactions to her appearance, in order to ridicule cultural glorification of thinness for women. As she put it in her acceptance speech for the Trailblazer Award at *Glamour UK*'s 2015 Women of the Year Awards, "I'm probably like 160 pounds right now and I can catch a dick whenever I want."

In Schumer's stand-up humor, she ridicules body image standards for women. For example, in her debut *Mostly Sex Stuff* (2012), Schumer provides commentary on bodies like hers, which she characterizes as "not a twig," and rather would be "the base" of a "cheerleading pyramid." Given her hyperfeminine appearance, it is not a far stretch to imagine Schumer on a cheerleading squad; the coy punchline in this bit references how Schumer is not thin enough to be at the top of the pyramid but doesn't need to be. Moreover, she utilizes humor to suggest the cultural links between thin, feminine bodies and sex appeal. Later in the routine, Schumer claims that she "knows her body type" because men do not usually hit on her at the bars until last call, when they begin aggressively pacing around "like Predator" to find someone to take home: "But when I do get hit on, like, this guy just came up to me, and he was from, like, Texas or somewhere I'm not going.... And he comes over and he's like, [imitating a gruff, inebriated Texan] 'Hey, I like you. You're sturdy.' [shifts to a confused face] I'm like, 'I'm sorry?' He's like, 'You look like you could take a punch.' I'm like, 'Oh. Well don't I just feel like the belle of the ball?'" Some of Schumer's humor is self-deprecating on the surface, and the satire is subtly resistant in this context. As Schumer walks around on stage in heels, a short dress, and neatly styled long, blonde hair, her performance of femininity is incongruous with a man calling her "sturdy" and "like [she] could take a punch," thereby satirizing the ways people bluntly comment on women's bodies, but especially on non-thin women's bodies. Schumer's engagement with body politics in her humor embodies a feminine and attractive woman and she uses her "average" size to play up the perception that her body is excessive and subsequently ridicule cultural beauty norms and the regulation of women's bodies (Cooper).

Amy Schumer also specifically highlights the *gendered* processes of cultural production of body image standards for women. For example, the episode of *Inside Amy Schumer* titled "12 Angry Men Inside Amy Schumer" (S3E3) satirizes patriarchal constructions of beauty tied to thinness. In a parody remake of the 1957 film *12 Angry Men*, the episode features an all-male "jury" gathered to deliberate and decide whether Amy Schumer is "hot enough" to be featured in her own television series. In the same serious tone, one might imagine a jury deliberating a murder trial verdict, the 12 jury members debate: Is Amy Schumer hot enough to be on TV? Throughout the episode, the men openly discuss Schumer's physique, commenting that she is "built like a lineman" with a "potato face" and "cabbage-patchy" features. However, the jury eventually declares, albeit hesitantly, that since they would, in fact, "bang" her that they must therefore declare her hot enough for cable TV. Here, Schumer's comedy highlights how women's bodies are regulated and objectified; they are judged by their looks first before they even speak, and bodies that fall outside of typical mainstream expectations are subject to extra public scrutiny. Though the jurors' blatantly misogynistic commentary through parody of the 1957 film is consistent with Schumer's style of humor, it becomes clear to the audience that Schumer is actually targeting and ridiculing patriarchal culture itself. This episode culturally works to reveal how normative mainstream representations of bodies derive from (and subsequently perpetuate) patriarchal expectations. Therefore, although Schumer and McCarthy are known for differing styles of comedy, both are "unruly" for their resistance to and mockery of dominant cultural narratives about bodies; both onscreen and offscreen they demonstrate how "true femininity" and sex appeal are actually social constructions, and sometimes unhealthy ones.

Every *body* is not treated equally, but can you imagine a world where every*body* mattered? (see Allan). A world not categorized by visual markers of bodily differences? Not evaluated by the socially defined assumptions attached to those differences? It is these questions that beg us to challenge the dominant ideologies of bodily variation that shape legislation, practices, and interpersonal interactions that value certain bodies over others. Without efforts of resistance, the body remains a political site of control, scrutiny, regulation, surveillance, and violence, which becomes justified within the sociocultural parameters of its very existence. Regarding cultural ideals of body shape and size, resistance demonstrated by comedians and others throughout this essay reveals how fat bodies have also become sites of social resistance. Fat bodies are resisting as they are regulated and regulated as they are resisting.

Media representation of bodies are nuanced, often contradictory, and shifting. Overall, we consider media as spaces where popular representations and associated ideas of the fat unruly body are both maintained *and* increasingly resisted. This paradox is exemplified, for instance, through the differing audience reactions to Netflix's *Insatiable* and *Dumplin'*. We also see some examples where social media is embedded with this paradox, noted by contrasting hashtags #bodypositivity versus #obesityisadisease. Representations of fatness and bodies have traditionally been constraining, stereotypical, and stigmatizing. But, cultural spaces for resistance have begun to emerge. Film and television representations have begun to feature confident and healthy fat protagonists, and the general public has become more attuned to feminist critiques of unrealistic body image ideals.

Comedy can encourage "lightbulb moments" for the audience when taken-for-granted ideas and assumptions are exposed as socially constructed phenomena. This type of disruption can be effective in breaking commonplace ideologies of fat bodies that enable the degradation and shame of bodies and therefore, of people. Comedy's role in resisting social and cultural bodily norms remains important and serves as an example of how resistance to the fat unruly body can be used to reshape not fat bodies, but the dominant ideologies that maintain and justify their marginalization. Is it possible for bodies to be fat and healthy? Is it possible for bodies to be fat and attractive? Recent comedic representations emphasize such possibilities, which we see as both positive and progressive in a society where every *body* should matter.

NOTE

1. As of writing this essay, *Insatiable* Season 2 had yet to air; it is now available on Netflix.

WORKS CITED

Allan, Scott, writer. *EveryBody Matters*, directed by Roisin Clarke. Dathuil Canada Inc. and Dathuil Australia Pty Ltd & BC Production Office Inc., 2019.

Boero, Natalie. "All the News That's Fat to Print: The American 'Obesity Epidemic' and the Media." *Qualitative Sociology*, vol. 30, no. 1, 2007, pp. 41–60.

Bombak, Andrea. "Obesity, Health at Every Size, and Public Health Policy." *American Journal of Public Health*, vol. 104, no. 2, 2014, pp. e60–e67.

Bridesmaids. Directed by Paul Feig, performers Kristen Wiig, Maya Rudolph, and Melissa McCarthy. Universal Pictures, 2011.

Burgard, Deb. "What Is 'Health at Every Size'?" *The Fat Studies Reader*, edited by Esther Rothblum and Sondra Solovay, NYU Press, 2009, pp. 42–53.

Campos, Paul, Abigail Saguy, Paul Ernsberger, Eric Oliver, and Glenn Gaesser. "The Epidemiology of Overweight and Obesity: Public Health Crisis or Moral Panic?" *International Journal of Epidemiology*, vol. 35, no. 1, 2006, pp. 55–60.

Cooper, S. Katherine. "Breaking the Crass Ceiling? Performing Irony and White Femininity in Amy Schumer's Mostly Sex Stuff Stand-Up." *Sociological Focus*, vol. 52, no. 3, 2019, pp. 201–215.

"Dress to Impress." *Roseanne*, season 10, episode 2, ABC, 27 Mar. 2018. *Dailymotion*, https://www.dailymotion.com/video/x6h13kc.

Dumplin'. Directed by Anne Fletcher, performers Danielle Macdonald, Jennifer Aniston, and Odeya Rush. Netflix, 2008.

Fletcher, Isabel. "Defining an Epidemic: The Body Mass Index in British and US ObesityResearch 1960–2000." *Sociology of Health & Illness*, vol. 36, no. 3, 2014, pp. 338–353.

Gardner, Eriq. "NBC Internal Investigation Probed Whether 'Biggest Loser' Contestants Were Given Drugs." HollywoodReporter.com, 18 Jul. 2018, https://www.hollywoodreporter.com/thr-esq/nbc-undertook-investigation-biggest-loser-contestants-were-supplied-drugs-1128067.

Harder, Brittany M. "The American Medical Association's Designation of Obesity as a Disease and Its Influences on Experiences of Body Weight." *Open Access Dissertations*, 2017, pp. 49–98.

Holland, Kate, R. Warwick Blood, and Samantha Thomas. "Viewing *The Biggest Loser*: Modes of Reception and Reflexivity Among Obese People." *Social Semiotics*, vol. 25, no. 1, 2015, pp. 16–32.

Itzkoff, Dave. "Melissa McCarthy Goes Over the Top." NewYorkTimes.com, 13 June 2013, https://www.nytimes.com/2013/06/16/movies/melissa-mccarthy-goes-over-the-top.html.

Meeuf, Russell. "Class, Corpulence, and Neoliberal Citizenship: Melissa McCarthy on *Saturday Night Live*." *Celebrity Studies*, vol. 7, no. 2, 2016, pp. 137–153.

Newman, Judith. "Melissa McCarthy Shares Her Ultimate Secret to Happiness in Redbook's April Issue." *Redbook*, 8 March 2016, https://www.redbookmag.com/life/interviews/a42962/melissa-mccarthy-redbook-april-2016-cover-star/.

Petersen, Anne Helen. *Too Fat, Too Slutty, Too Loud: The Rise and Reign of the Unruly Woman*. Plume, 2017.

Previte, Josephine, and Lauren Gurrieri. "Who is the Biggest Loser? Fat News Coverage is a Barrier to Healthy Lifestyle Promotion." *Health Marketing Quarterly*, vol. 32, no. 4, 2015, pp. 330–349.

Reed, Rex. "Declined: In Identity Thief, Bateman's Bankable Billing Can't Lift This Flick Out of the Red." *Observer*, 5 Feb. 2013, https://observer.com/2013/02/declined-in-identity-thief-batemans-bankable-billing-cant-lift-this-flick-out-of-the-red/.

Ricks, Ellen. "Watching Netflix's *Insatiable* as an Eating Disorder Survivor Triggered Me." TeenVogue.com, 17 Aug. 2018, https://www.teenvogue.com/story/watching-insatiable-as-an-eating-disorder-survivor-triggered-me.

Rowe, Kathleen. *The Unruly Woman: Gender and the Genres of Laughter*. University of Texas Press, 1995.

Schumer, Amy, performer. *Amy Schumer: Mostly Sex Stuff*. Comedy Central, 2012.

"Skinny Is Magic." *Insatiable*, season 1, episode 2, Netflix, 10 Aug. 2018. *Netflix*, https://www.netflix.com/watch/80231643.

Stukator, Angela. "'It's Not Over Until the Fat Lady Sings': Comedy, the Carnivalesque, and Body Politics." *Bodies Out of Bounds: Fatness and Transgression*, edited by Jana Evans Braziel and Kathleen LeBesco, University of California Press, 2001, pp. 197–213.

"12 Angry Men Inside Amy Schumer." *Inside Amy Schumer*, season 3, episode 3, Comedy Central, 5 May 2015. *Hulu*, https://wwsw.hulu.com/watch/315c1129-b546-4413-be22-0a74f028a10e.

Wang, Connie. "Melissa McCarthy Is Not a Fan of the Term 'Plus-Size' for Some Very Legit Reasons." *Refinery 29*, 17 Aug. 2015, https://www.refinery29.com/en-us/2015/08/92450/melissa-mccarthy-plus-size.

Section III
"You celebrated the small victories, and you dreamed of the big ones to come"

AMANDA FIRESTONE

The final five essays in this edited collection ask us to look for the glimmers of optimism and shards of positivity that present themselves, even in dark times. The section's lead quotation from author Charlie Jane Anders' novel *All the Birds in the Sky* (2016) beautifully encapsulates this theme (31). The novel follows two people, Laurence and Patricia, who, after a brief time together in middle school, have a chance to reunite as adults under strained circumstances—either destroying or saving the world. The quote, part of Laurence's inner monologue when he's a tween, comes at a moment when he has, for the first time, found a group of people who recognize him as one of their own; the acknowledgment Laurence receives in their acceptance and his understanding that he is not alone bolsters him in ways nothing has before.

All the Birds in the Sky was Anders' first speculative fiction (specfic) novel, and it was celebrated by the science fiction and fantasy community, winning accolades like the Crawford Award, a Nebula Award for Best Fiction, and the Locus Award for Best Fantasy Novel ("Award Bibliography"). Anders has practiced her craft since the early 2000s, publishing more than one hundred short stories ("The City"). A self-described "weirdo," Anders told an audience at WisCon 2019—a feminist-oriented science fiction and fantasy convention—that "being a weirdo has made my life as a trans person so much better. I don't know where I'd be today, if I hadn't had the power of silliness and playfulness and small-time anarchy on my side. I decided a long time ago that reality is kind of intrinsically absurd, and the only way to deal with

135

it is to be more ludicrous than this ludicrous world" (Anders, "Here's My"). It is this spirit of positivity and hopefulness that imbues her writing, capturing the necessity to always look for the light in the dark.

We cannot yet know the magnitude of the events of the 2010s. At the time of this writing, it is late 2019, and while we are on the precipice of a new decade, it will not be for another 20 or 30 years that we will achieve the perspective and hindsight necessary to evaluate the impacts of the events and culture of this one. Even a cursory glimpse at the last 10 years seems to yield dim revelations about the state of the world. A quick look at the *Wikipedia* page for the decade of the 2010s lists events in this order: Politics and Wars, Assassinations and Attempts, Disasters (non-natural and natural), Economics, Cyber Security and Hacking, Health (epidemics), Science and Technology, Society, and Culture ("2010s"). The creators of *Wikipedia*, since its launch in 2001, have always extolled the site's existence as a collaborative space for knowledge. Anyone, typically, can contribute to and edit entries. What perhaps, then, is the significance of the ordering of the sections for the pages pertaining to decades?

Each decade on *Wikipedia*, from the 1810s forward, begins with Politics and Wars. To be sure, those subjects, usually intimately intertwined, are incredibly influential and important in people's daily lives. The decisions of government officials and the repercussions of those decisions affect everyone in large ways and small ones. Today, given the *miracle* of digital technologies, people have an unprecedented ability to consume information about, well, anything. A global Pew Research Poll concludes that 81 percent of adult Americans own a smartphone, while 13 percent have a mobile phone that does not classify as a smartphone (Taylor and Silver). Only 6 percent of adult Americans do not own a mobile phone at all (Taylor and Silver). We are inundated with information, and most people would have to make a concerted effort to avoid media pertaining to politics and wars.

Starting in the 1950s, TV brought politics into American homes in more tangible ways than the newspaper or the radio. Famously, people who tuned into the debate between John F. Kennedy and Richard M. Nixon in 1960 were divided about who won based on whether they listened to it or watched it (Botelho). Marshall McLuhan's assertion that "the medium is the message" certainly came to fruition in that moment (340). Through the 1960s and 1970s, a balancing act formed between print, radio, film, and TV as the primary sources of media engagement. Then another seismic shift occurred with the introduction of the desktop computer in the 1980s and the gateway to the world, the contemporary internet in the early 1990s.

By the late 1990s, cell phone manufacturers were working to put the connective power of the world wide web into mobile technology. At the turn of the millennium most mainstream cell phones were internet capable, even if in small capacities. Apple's launch of the iPhone in 2007 has been, perhaps, the most influential change in mobile phone technology, setting the precedence for nearly all contemporary hardware devices and software applications. In the iPhone unveiling speech, Steve Jobs tells the audience "today, we're launching three revolutionary products [...] An iPod, a phone, and an internet communicator. [...] These are not three separate devices, this is one device, and we are calling it iPhone" (qtd. in Wright).

Nearly 15 years on, our phones are as crucial to our everyday existence as the clothes and shoes we wear. The introduction of the iPhone irrevocably changed the ways that people fundamentally consume their media, and perhaps even more importantly, it changed how people *make* media. The possibility of instantaneous connection through smartphone technology means that in both times of crisis and times of joy, people can privately and publicly communicate about what is happening around them and how they feel. Rather than waiting for a news crew to arrive or a "lucky" passerby who happens to have a camera,[1] our phones give everyone the potential to become a citizen journalist.

Through the decade, this has intensified as events couched in terror, violence, and fear appear to occur more frequently than ever before. And, crucially, people caught in the midst of those experiences are choosing to share those events as they unfold around them. On February 14, 2018, Aidan Minoff made an eight-word tweet: "I am in a school shooting right now..." (qtd. in Griggs). Minoff, a freshman at the time, was hiding under his desk at Marjory Stoneman Douglas High School in Parkland, Florida. By the time he and his classmates were evacuated, 17 people were dead and more than a dozen others were wounded.

One of Minoff's tweets directly after the event read: "Love each other. You may never know when it may be the last day you meet someone" (qtd. in Griggs). His tweets join the ever-growing numbers of posts, videos, and texts aimed at making connectivity, especially in the face of danger or adversity. In times when people are scared or afraid, knowing there's someone else out there can be comforting. For Charlie Jane Anders:

> In my writing, I'm thinking more and more lately about how to show the power of community, and how to include everyone who's marginalized and pushed outside the lines of communal membership.
> Being a weirdo has helped me find communities over and over again. And I really believe that your imagination is your strongest defense against everyone who wants to dehumanize and control you, and make you smaller. Your imagination is HUGE. Your capacity for constructive nonsense owns no limits. The people who want to shove us into boxes always want everything to make sense and to be clear-cut and simple, and it's on us to complicate and confuse them ["Here's My," emphasis in original].

All of the essays in our final section of this edited collection have hope as their central theme. Whether the subject concerns a public event or person, a fictional universe or character, each essay looks to those instances when a moment of resistance becomes a sustaining memory to help keep the fight alive. After the march has ended, the protesters forced to go away, the election results have come in, the war has ended, and the villains seem more powerful than ever, it is then that imagination, the ability to look to a better future, is the most vital for survival.

The section begins with Elizabeth J. Dickhut's analysis of the #ICantKeepQuietChoir and its performances during the Women's March in January 2017. The song "Quiet" was composed by MILCK as a way for her to give voice to her personal struggles through sexual violence and depression. With the a cappella group, the song took on new meanings for the women singing it, as well as the protestors listening to it. Dickhut examines the intrinsically connective quality that music, and singing particularly, has, and she provides important observations about the song's ability to unite a diverse group of people assembled during a single event.

Chandra A. Maldonado focuses on the 2016 Standing Rock protests that sought to prevent the Dakota Access Pipeline from construction near the Standing Rock Reservation. Much of the protest was captured for the documentary *Awake: A Dream from Standing Rock* (2017), and Maldonado analyzes the rhetorical impacts that documentary films can have in terms of wider social change. Ultimately, the protest efforts failed and construction for the pipeline commenced, but the networks and resources that grew as a result of the documentary were invaluable. The film helped to make the general public aware of the oil industry's tactics and the different ways that people could get involved in protecting the environment, as well as supporting indigenous peoples' efforts in preserving their culture.

Documentaries like *Awake* bring people together in support of a cause. Julia Gillard's public fannish support of *Game of Thrones* gave Australians additional incentive to rally around her after she became prime minister in 2010. Ana Stevenson's essay explains the ways that the cut-throat and convoluted politics present in the show's narrative appeared to parallel and sometimes parody the struggles and inconsistencies in politicians in Australia's parliament. While news outlets sometimes aligned Gillard with power zealot Cersei Lannister, Gillard herself has expressed her affinity for Daenerys Targaryen, setting her up as the underdog in a corrupt system. Ultimately, Stevenson concludes that Gillard's adoption of *Game of Thrones* provides insightful commentary about the leadership roles of women in global politics.

Mary F. Pharr's essay also tackles a powerful woman battling a staunchly patriarchal political system: Wonder Woman. The 2017 eponymous film presents a naïve Diana Prince who wants to destroy the god Ares in order for humans to live peacefully. For Pharr, this conflict is really the perilous struggle to resist violent, hegemonic power while not being corrupted by those same tendencies. It is, in part, Gal Gadot's portrayal of Diana as compassionate and single-minded in her protection of others and her fierce rejection of Ares' power that renews Wonder Woman's cultural capital. While there is no real-life Wonder Woman to fight oppression, the character's prominent reappearance on screen provides a positive role model for other people wanting to rise above.

Finally, our last essay is Annika Gonnermann's analysis of *The Last Jedi* (2017). For her, the *Star Wars* franchise is intrinsically connected to the perpetual struggle of the ill-equipped but committed Rebellion against the Dark Side. Importantly, the defining hallmark of the space opera series is that of hope. *The Last Jedi* is read as a concrete dystopia, forcing audiences to engage with the desire to see a better, more positive outcome for the characters and story. The film's narrative privileges the "nobodys" of the galaxy as the people best equipped to defeat the Empire, rather than the pseudo-mythical Jedi. Giving that importance to everyday people has the possibility of sparking hope inside of audiences, offering the positive perspective that battling oppression requires micro acts of resistance as well as grand gestures.

Truly, we all have the capacity to resist—if we just find the courage to act.

NOTE

1. An example of this is the film footage taken by Abraham Zapruder, who was in the crowd in Dallas, Texas, to watch President Kennedy's motorcade drive through the city. His 8mm camera captured the assassination. It isn't the only footage of the event, but it is the most complete and clearest (particularly the gruesome frame 313). It is widely considered one of the United States' most important historic media texts.

WORKS CITED

Anders, Charlie Jane. *All the Birds in the Sky.* Tor Books, 2016.
Anders, Charlie Jane. "Here's My Wiscon Guest of Honor Speech!—The City in the Middle of the Night." 30 May 2019. https://www.cityinthemiddleofthenight.com/blog/2019/5/30/heres-my-wiscon-guest-of-honor-speech.
"Award Bibliography—Charlie Jane Anders." *The Internet Speculative Fiction Database.* 1995–2019. http://www.isfdb.org/cgi-bin/eaw.cgi?146327.
Botelho, Greg. "The Day Politics and TV Changed Forever." *CNN*, 14 Mar. 2016. https://www.cnn.com/2016/02/29/politics/jfk-nixon-debate/index.html.
"The City in the Middle of the Night." https://www.cityinthemiddleofthenight.com
Griggs, Brandon. "Hiding Under a Desk as a Gunman Roamed the Halls, a Terrified Student Live-Tweeted a School Shooting." *CNN*, 15 Feb. 2018, https://www.cnn.com/2018/02/15/us/student-live-tweeting-florida-school-shooting-trnd/index.html.
McLuhan, Marshall. "Myth and Mass Media." *Daedalus*, Vol. 88, No. 2, Spring 1959, pp. 339–348.
Taylor, Kyle, and Laura Silver. "Smartphone Ownership Is Growing Rapidly Around the World, but Not Always Equally." *Pew Research Center: Global Attitudes and Trends*, 5 Feb. 2019. https://www.pewresearch.org/global/wp-content/uploads/sites/2/2019/02/Pew-Research-Center_Global-Technology-Use-2018_2019-02-05.pdf.

"2010s—Wikipedia." *Wikipedia*, 9 Sept. 2019. https://en.wikipedia.org/wiki/2010s.

Wright, Mic. "The Original iPhone Announcement Annotated: Steve Jobs' Genius Meets Genius." *TNW: The Next Web*, 09 Sept. 2015. https://thenextweb.com/apple/2015/09/09/genius-annotated-with-genius/.

"A one woman riot"

The Voice of the #ICantKeepQuiet Choir

Elizabeth J. Dickhut

Music allows underrepresented voices a space in which to act in politically and socially significant ways, such as MILCK and the #ICantKeepQuiet Choir's performance of "Quiet" during the 2017 Women's March on Washington. On January 21, 2017, a single song was able to unite 26 diverse voices "from the out of state 18-year-old student to the local, working, mother of three" to professional a cappella singers[1] ("The Choir"). These protestors gathered to affirm the mission of the Women's March to "stand together in solidarity with our partners and children for the protection of our rights, our safety, our health, and our families—recognizing that our vibrant and diverse communities are the strength of our country" ("Mission").

An estimated 4.9 million people gathered in more than 600 Sister Marches around the world from January 21 to 22, 2017 ("Sisters"). Ultimately, participants of the Women's March assembled to celebrate diverse communities and make their voices heard. During the process, March organizer Carmen Perez found that "we can't continue to work in isolation. We can't continue to be one-dimensional … we have to make sure that we look up, that we begin to really coordinate our efforts" (qtd. in Wang). At the March, NPR reporter Pam Fessler found the demeanor of the crowd to be "more festive than [other] protests" (Dwyer). One woman marched in order to "make her voice heard" (Dwyer) while another protestor had a nationwide message for Donald Trump, the president inaugurated by a minority of the votes: "I just want him and his administration to know that no, you can't silence us, and we won't be silenced" (McCammon). Indeed, the final line of the mission of the Women's March ends with a call to "HEAR OUR VOICE" ("Mission," emphasis in original). Before and during the March, this common theme of being heard, as well as having a voice and what that signifies, played an important role in the reception and adoption of "Quiet" as the song of the movement.

Though Connie Lim, known as MILCK, wrote the song "Quiet" before the March to speak out about partner abuse, the music expanded through the March to protest other forms of violence and forced silence. The purpose of the #ICantKeepQuiet movement is summarized in the title and the hash tag, with the essence represented through the 26 women from diverse backgrounds, ethnicities, and cultures that convened to form the #ICantKeepQuite Choir. Through its strong message, I believe that this song questions the construction of "voice," realizes the paradoxical relationship of women with society as simultaneously actively present and forced silent, and creates a space to enable a countercultural protest voice. "Quiet" achieves this through the interplay of vocal production, musical texture, and lyrics. In singing "Quiet," both at the March and after, women and other minority groups are able to find a voice with which to force their way into the conversation and reclaim a space within their communities.

Lim and cowriter/producer AG publicly released the song "Quiet" on her website three days before the Women's March on Washington, linking the two irrevocably ("About"). Lim wrote the song as her personal anthem and her refusal to remain quiet about her own experience with abuse. She then approached the George Washington (GW) Sirens and other women to create an a cappella version to perform as a flash mob during the Women's March (Steinhardt). Through the lyrics of "Quiet," Lim narrates the struggle to be yourself while being oppressed by public pressures; this true self is at first represented, through fairytale language, as a "monster," but by the end of the song is transformed into "a one woman riot," and results in the response "let it out," pushing past those oppressing her voice and making private experiences public issues (MILCK). This original, non–a cappella recording of the song crescendos to mirror this narrative, starting with a repetitive piano introduction, layering in Lim's solo voice, and then building the sound with other percussive instruments and background vocals.

The a cappella, flash mob version of the song, then, was created for the Women's March, which developed as a response to the 2016 presidential election cycle. After the results of the presidential election were officially confirmed in November 2016, plans for a Women's March began. Ultimately, it was scheduled for January 21, 2017, the day after the swearing-in ceremony that would confirm Donald Trump as the 45th president of the United States. It was strategically placed to echo the first time women marched on Washington, in 1913, in order to demand the right to vote from the newly elected president Woodrow Wilson (women's suffrage was fully ratified in 1920). While the new president-elect was the impetus for the initial planning stages, the event morphed into a march about women and broadened to include a discussion of race, immigrant and minority rights, and healthcare, among other concerns (Wang). This tight, 10-week window to organize a nationwide protest forced organizers to address nationwide apprehensions about voice, image, and representation.

These fears were solidly grounded when, in October of 2016, a video segment of an *Access Hollywood* interview was recirculated with Trump making disparaging remarks towards women. These comments ranged from "I did try and fuck her. She was married.... I moved on her like a bitch. But I couldn't get there" to "I'm automatically attracted to beautiful—I just start kissing them. It's like a magnet. Just kiss. I don't even wait. And when you're a star, they let you do it. You can do anything.... Grab 'em by the pussy. You can do anything" (qtd. in Bullock). These remarks surged from concerning to alarming, as Trump became the future president of the United States, the supposed representative of the American people and a positive role model. Towards the end of her concession speech, Democratic nominee Hillary Clinton directly addresses this concern: "and to all the little girls who are watching this, never doubt that you are valuable and powerful and deserving of every chance and opportunity in the world to pursue and achieve your own dreams." In this speech, Clinton formally concedes but addresses her concerns about the future where girls may not have a role model.

This sexually and politically charged mess set the stage for a strong, new voice to emerge and give hope to future generations by addressing the current situation and providing an actionable solution. "Quiet," through both the lyrics and music, flows progressively by stating what women in society are currently prescribed as proper social activity: "put on your face/know your place," to "shut up and smile" and "don't spread your legs." The song and singer then question if she should be the countercultural voice against these norms by asking, "Would I be that monster, scare them all away/If I let theem hear what I have to say [*sic*]." The singer realizes that "no one ever" will know her "if I don't say something," even though, by speaking out, she might be perceived as a "monster." She comes to the realization "but I have to do this," facilitating the adoption of a woman's protest voice that needs to be heard. In doing so, she is able to "Let it out" and have her voice be heard, reinforced by the song's refrain "I can't keep quiet... A one woman riot" (MILCK).

The lyrics of "Quiet" represent the struggle that women and minorities face in society with a lack of voice, a challenge that is sometimes difficult to convey. This disparate group persona of the #ICantKeepQuiet Choir is shaped by their relative diversity of race, sexual orientation, and age, unified through their choice of headwear. Diversity is emphasized on both the MILCK and the Choir webpages, as the choir is meant to highlight women and minority struggles. Difference can be seen through clothing, hairstyles, and ethnicities of the singers. The Choir is also visually unified through their participation in "The Pussyhat Project," started by Krista Suh, which uses a pointed, square-shaped pink hat as a visual cue for resisting sexist culture. A friend of Lim's links the two projects: Suh's project provided hats for marchers across the nation and the #ICantKeepQuiet Choir served as ambassadors for the project by wearing and distributing the hats while singing (Ammann). This connection between two smaller initiatives within the larger protest reiterates the collective "one woman riot" resounding throughout the many voices that comprise the March.

As seen at the March, song can unite diverse people through a strong emotional bond and shape how concerns are raised. Voice "is a particular kind of speech phenomenon that pronounces the ethical problems and obligations incumbent in community building and arouses in persons and groups the frustrations, sufferings, and joys of such commitments" (Watts 185). These emotions that arise are incredibly important to both Eric King Watts and Sheila Whiteley who see voice as the result of shared emotions. Music, and particularly singing, is especially adept at drawing people together. When performing a song becomes a public ritual, such as singing the national anthem at a sporting event, it is performed by "citizen singers" (Watts 186–189). Therefore, voice as practiced by an individual or a group is about realizing emotions, and singing is a powerful form of expressive action that syncs people together in emotional and ideological harmony. The performance of "Quiet" at the Women's March can be acknowledged as a voice because of the shared emotions of the group singing the community-recognized anthem that represents a diverse understanding of citizenship and personhood.

Within society, subversive women's voices can be developed through music. The study of the relationship between women and music, as well as how the two are influenced by society, highlights how women's voices are found through music and have the opportunity to present an alternative, countercultural perspective. Music can reinforce societal behaviors and gender identities (such as the basic choral practice of dividing male and female voices) or function as a space to challenge and redefine expectations (Koskoff 9–10). "Quiet" creates room for an alternative perspective, depending on how the song is read. For Lim, "Quiet" started as a way to come to terms with sexual assault; her composition and reading is not inherent to the song, as it has been picked up as an anthem for minority oppression at large. More importantly, "Quiet" can be performed for free by other singers; the text adapts to communicate effectively through innumerable choruses to diverse communities.

There is also a further communal aspect to popular music; not only can we all understand it but music also has the potential to give voice and be spoken by other groups with diverse cultures. Popular music's multiplicity can be seen through "a dialogic relationship with various types of verbal, musical, visual as well as social and cultural elements" (Kaindl 259). This interplay creates a polysemous nature, or one with multiple meanings, that allows music to speak to groups not previously addressed by popular culture and society. In fact, "music seems to be saying something, something so intuitively obvious that it has at times been proclaimed a 'universal language' that transcends history and culture" (Tolbert 453). Applied to "Quiet," the song was able to be universally understood, but also create room for those sentiments to be voiced by non-dominant groups.

Through the multiplicity of music, intersecting with power and gender, song can potentially challenge social orders and promote a platform for inclusivity. The female voice encompasses contradictions "in which the distinctions between social personae and their material voices bleed into one another" (Tolbert 463). The social representations of women versus the actual materiality of their beings, are the enigma of womanhood. This complex system, which includes power dynamics, explains how protest music can use a "secret language" or exist as code (Koskoff 11). The perception of women by their audience mars their voices and what they are saying. This complication is addressed in the first part of "Quiet," detailing the ways that society dictates how women should act, such as "don't spread your legs."

If the female voice as subversive is complexly coded through social systems, a form of translation needs to occur to integrate it with the common, audience-driven understanding of voice. This is more accessible through protest music that desires to be cross-cultural, widespread, and popular, and can be done in two forms: *aural*, what would be heard at a shop or on the street, and *visualized*, or staged performances (Kaindl 235, emphasis added). "Quiet" takes both forms, as the song is both an aural recording and a visualized experience. However, the more important aspect is the visualized performance, as found on YouTube and other social media, paired with the aural experience of the #ICantKeepQuiet Choir at the March.

"Quiet" and the #ICantKeepQuiet movement developed from tumultuous social and political shifts and was enhanced through social media connectivity. Videos and hashtags helped to keep the song and community visible with easy sharing and searchability. Media, most notably Facebook and YouTube, played a role in the remediation of the song for a diverse audience, but also the reproduction of the experience, resulting in an amplification of both the voice and its reach. The song that gained the most traction was a truncated group a cappella version posted to Facebook via YouTube video by filmmaker Alma Har'el, published with the desire to make "Quiet" the official anthem of the Women's March (Har'el). This video was posted to YouTube and Facebook the same day as the March and, by the next day, had been viewed 2.5 million times, with 15 million views less than a month later (Har'el).

Har'el mediated her experience through Facebook, to users like me, and shared how the harmony created from diverse voices was representative of the March, allowing "Quiet" to unite others beyond those marching in Washington, D.C.

The message of "Quiet" reached a larger digital audience by the video being hosted on YouTube, facilitating further connectivity and inviting more diverse communities. Har'el's reaction, mirrored by some of those in the immediate, digital audiences (conveyed through the video comments), included crying while listening to the song (Har'el). Through singing as an a cappella group, the "Quiet" choir develops a countercultural female voice which radiates through the digital platforms, opening more traditional forms of communication to diverse groups. Transmission of "Quiet" on YouTube and Facebook highlights the song's ability to be easily repeated and shared, but also captures the true essence of the Women's March, or sincerity, frustration, and plurality.

"Quiet" is not limited to only Facebook and YouTube but has utilized other digital platforms. The digital component of the Choir's origins, over Skype and electronic communication, also played a significant role in recirculating the finished text. In fact, the Choir practiced the song via Skype, with only one face-to-face rehearsal, and some singers not meeting until the choir convened for the March (Har'el). Further limitations were removed when Lim opened the song to the public, removing paywalls and middlemen. The sheet music for "Quiet" and the version from the March are both available for free on the #ICantKeepQuiet webpage in an effort to create a global choir with a single message ("The Choir"). "Quiet" is made even more accessible through vocal tracks and step-by-step guides to assist with teaching and spreading the song, removing music reading barriers (MILCK). Choirs are then encouraged to share their progress and music through the #icantkeepquiet hashtag as a way to keep the voices resounding. Lim and the movement are effectively driving audience energy and participation in a positive direction. Their respective websites encourage users to interact with the singers on a variety of social media platforms, but also share their own experiences in relation to the movement. Through open access to the music of the March and intentionally removing barriers, the #ICantKeepQuiet movement invites those from all backgrounds to use a musical voice to connect with others through listening to or singing about emotionally-triggering subjects in a safe environment.

Immediately following the March, *GW Today*, an on-campus newspaper for George Washington University, extensively covered the song, as the school had 14 members of their GW Sirens with Lim. Madison Sherman, their musical director, recalled that "we saw women crying, men crying—people were so moved" (qtd. in Steinhardt). The song was also picked up by news sites like *Mashable* that made connections between Lim's history of abuse and the intimate, emotional reaction from other women with similar backgrounds (Wezke). Similarly, NPR found that "the performance is unadorned and profoundly moving, capturing at least part of the mood that settled on the march, with a balance of defiance and love" (Hilton). After the January 21 March ended, the Choir continued to share their voice by recording a professional version of their rendition, not yet available (Steinhardt). They also performed on *Full Frontal with Samantha Bee* on January 25, during her coverage of the Women's March, where Bee called "Quiet" a "protest anthem for the ages" ("Who March"). The coverage of the story by local, national, and popular news sources increased the network of impact and added to the importance of analyzing the piece as a significant cultural and rhetorical text.

The viral nature of "Quiet" cannot be overemphasized, but what I find even more important and compelling is the dissonance between word (lyric) and action created through the truncated nature of the music. By extension, the lyrics represent a search for self-authenticity to act to overpower social norms that can control the behavior of women both publicly and privately. Indeed, before even leaving the privacy of their space, women are told to "put on your face" in order to successfully enter into the public arena. Once there, further commands follow, dictating proper gendered behavior and morality. Promiscuity is celebrated among men, but where women are warned "don't spread your legs" (MILCK). This disconnect, however, is overshadowed by the fact that this partial video is only a fragmented entrance into the discourse, turning private personal actions of women to become public and political. The #ICantKeepQuiet Choir makes "public" actions (music) actually for everyone, and political, through disseminating the music and encouraging others to participate in the discourse, but also through the flash mob style of singing.

Starting in downtown Washington, D.C., Lim characterized the performances of her choir as "renegade style … plotting to surprise passerbys" ("About"). This ability of the choir to exist at one moment for a performance and disappear the next moment, almost instantaneously, further amplifies the importance of performance and how the voice exists and is mediated beyond music through flash mobs. Flash mobs exist as both aural and visualized performances, as viewers might experience either one element or both, enhancing the multifaceted nature of the text. Flash mobs mirror female and minority voices within society as they seemingly exist as part of the organization while silent and only gain a voice when participants come together as a group and call an audience into being. In the case of the #ICantKeepQuiet Choir at the March, they call to the audience to join in the protest and then disappear back into the crowd, removing the visual and musical element of their voice but leaving behind the emotions and concerns raised.

Voice in "Quiet" is illustrated through the performance and Lim's personal quest for voice. The song is rooted in the personal trial of Lim as "a survivor of abuse, anorexia, and depression" ("About"). The performance also centers on her as the conductor and soloist/improviser, which the Choir mimics in its formation of a semicircle around her. This way, every performer is more in tune with Lim, take cues from her, but also hears the other singers. Physical centrality and bodily performance shift the attitude of the individual singers to a unified experience. From this develops an incredible determination that "I have to do this, do it anyway" (MILCK). The Choir conveys this attitude through the buildup of sound with vocals and handclaps, which remains strong until Lim cuts off the Choir, an interesting contradiction to the standard flash mob, where the performers appear and disappear as a mass, with no apparent leader.

The performance also amplifies the voice through the embodied experience. In "Quiet," as well as other examples of protest, "protesters used synchronized, scripted behavior suggesting that individual limitations and obstacles can be overcome only by working together, an ethos that runs counter to the individualism of neoliberal ideologies" (Fuentes 34). An appropriate example of previous tactics of using music to unify protestors occurred during the Civil Rights Movement in which protestors relied heavily on carefully planned actions, which also helped their protests thrive in the early 1960s through singing modified spirituals taught at the Highlander Folk School, adopting "We Shall Overcome" as their initial anthem (McCollum). The #ICantKeepQuiet Choir, in a communal effort to counter societal norms, desires not only to have a voice, but also to be heard. Besides voices working in tandem in the song, the Choir utilizes shared action to enhance the meaning beyond the sound and lyrics. In using their bodies, protestors are "sharing the experience" and promoting inclusion (Fuentes 36). For the Choir, this is through the flash mob structure, encouraging viewers to feel like participants, but also through the use of #ICantKeepQuiet. In particular, for Lim, this is also through the free release of her arrangement of "Quiet" so long as others adhere to the common goals of the movement. This sharing is part of the alternative, artistic woman-centered voice that is then viewed and acknowledged by others that become the audience for the song.

A large portion of the disjuncture with voice and "Quiet" exists in the shared action, but also embodied experience of the Choir. Women have a voice in the song, singing that they will not be quiet, even while the political culture is pushing towards a deepening of hegemonic masculinity that will not listen. Popular images of women are the Madonna-whore binary and virgin-Other ideals, binaries that leave very little room for reimaging femininity. "Quiet" needs to address this disconnect and does so through the image and performance of the Choir, as well as the music of the song. By using a "simple, straightforward" voice and a "pure, clean tone," the Choir appears in a nonthreatening, familiar form while directly challenging stereotypes (Bernstein 168). To understand "Quiet," we cannot separate voice from music, the two need to be considered together as they are mutually constitutive: the music would not thrive without the voice and the voice would not be acknowledged by an audience without the music. While initially viewed as simply a song, "Quiet" exists as plurisemiotic, embodied text that codes a countercultural female voice as music in order to be heard and acknowledged by an audience.

Protest music, much like minority groups, often finds itself operating within the in-betweens of music. In the case of Lim, "Quiet," and the #ICantKeepQuiet Choir, the search for an authentic voice that then encourages action to challenge society is part of what makes this song as a text important. While the song may seem simplistic and repetitive, the lyrics masterfully extend Lim's emotional experience to both fellow performers and listener, giving voice to others through a shared experience and adaptable, plurisemiotic text. I believe a complex narrative is hidden behind the song's simplicity that is revealed through the impact on the audience of the Choir's performance of the song. Furthermore, Lim opened the song to those "all over the world" to "unite as one, harmonizing body of citizens" through their own performances of the text, even though the piece cannot be performed exactly the same, even by the original composer/performer/rhetor. Not only does every interpretation matter, but also every part of the sound, from conception to production. Understanding the musical makeup of the text allows for further, in-depth analyses of the text in order to illuminate its significance.

Through "Quiet" the #ICantKeepQuiet Choir has made private experiences accessible to a larger public sphere through the song and the visual performance. Special consideration should still be given to texts that may not resonate with the dominant culture. By expanding beyond the listener and reception, voice, especially as an act of protest, is able to retain its power and not simply be another form of discourse where the minority voice is suppressed. Likewise, reconsidering what constitutes a specific audience, and how certain audiences choose to listen or ignore the voice presented, can assist in redefining and figuring out the protest, voice, and accessibility dynamic. Music is also uniquely placed to expand on this understanding, especially in a digital era where dissemination of a piece can stretch and transcend audience boundaries. Furthermore, much like Lim and the push towards a global choir, the song "Quiet" offers minority and countercultural perspectives the opportunity to unite in a stronger, harmonious voice that will not remain quiet, whether they are heard by the hegemonic public sphere or not. The voices, now encompassing a global choir, continue to push the movement forward.

NOTE

1. An a cappella choir is comprised of only voices, with the singers providing all parts of the song, from the harmonies to percussion. Professional groups like Straight No Chaser and Pentatonix popularized the style through covering pop hits, while college-level a cappella was highlighted in the *Pitch Perfect* film series.

WORKS CITED

"#IcantKeepQuiet #Anthem in the Women's March on Washington." *YouTube*, uploaded by almaharel, 22 Jan. 2017, https://www.youtube.com/watch?v=zLvIw8J8sWE&feature= share.

"About." *MILCK*. http://www.milckmusic.com/about/.

Ammann, Ana. "Voices Carry: MILCK Launces #icantkeepquiet Protest Project." *Oregon Music News*, 18 Jan. 2017, http://www.oregonmusicnews.com/voices-carry-multicultural-artists-inspire-expression-participation-in-upcoming-march-on-washington.

Bernstein, Jane A. "'Thanks for My Weapons in Battle—My Voice and the Desire to Use It': Women and Protest Music in the Americas." *Women's Voices Across Musical Worlds*, edited by Jane A. Bernstein, Northeastern University Press, 2004, pp. 166–186.

Bullock, Penn. "Transcript: Donald Trump's Taped Comments About Women." *The New York Times*, 8 Oct. 2016, https://www.nytimes.com/2016/10/08/us/donald-trump-tape-transcript.html?_r=0. Text transcription.

"The Choir." *MILCK*. https://www.icantkeepquiet.org/the-choir/.

Clinton, Hillary. "Hillary Clinton's Concession Speech (Full Text)." 9 Nov. 2016. *CNN*, http://www.cnn.com/2016/11/09/politics/hillary-clinton-concession-speech/.

Dwyer, Colin. "Women's March Floods Washington, Sparking Rallies Worldwide." *NPR*, 21 Jan. 2017, http://www.npr.org/sections/thetwo-way/2017/01/21/510932265/demonstrators-gather-early-to-kick-off-womens-march-on-washington.

Fuentes, Marcela A. "Performance Constellations: Memory and Event in Digitally Enabled Protests in the Americas." *Text and Performance Quarterly*, vol. 35, no. 1, 2015, pp. 24–42.

Har'el, Alma. "These Women Are from Different States and Never Met Till Today. They Practiced This Song Online. I Was Crying..." *Facebook*, 21 Jan. 2017, 7:26 p.m., https://www.facebook.com/almah/posts/10154436649558720.

Hilton, Robin. "A Flash Mob Choir at the Women's March Turned This Unknown Song into an Anthem." *NPR*, 23, Jan. 2017, http://www.npr.org/sections/allsongs/2017/01/23/511186649/a-flash-mob-choir-at-the-womens-march-turned-this-unknown-song-into-an-anthem.

Hirschman, Albert O. "Voice." *Exit, Voice, and Loyalty: Responses to Decline in Firms, Organizations, and States*, Harvard University Press, 1970, pp. 30–43.

Kaindl, Klaus. "The Plurisemiotics of Pop Song Translation: Words, Music, Voice and Image." *Song and Significance: Virtues and Vices of Vocal Translation*, edited by Dinda L. Gorlée, Brill Academic Publishers, 2005, pp. 235–262.

Koskoff, Ellen. "An Introduction to Women, Music, and Culture." *Women and Music in Cross-Cultural Perspective*, edited by Ellen Koskoff, Greenwood Press, 1987, pp. 1–23.

McCammon, Sarah. "Mothers, Daughters, Sisters, and Men Unite to Protest Trump's Presidency." *NPR*, 21, Jan. 2017, http://www.npr.org/2017/01/21/510991284/mothers-daughters-sisters-and-men-unite-to-protest-trumps-presidency.

McCollum, Sean. "The Story Behind the Song: We Shall Overcome." *ArtsEdge*. Sponsored by The Kennedy Center, https://artsedge.kennedy-center.org/students/features/story-behind-the-song/we-shall-overcome.

"Mission." *Women's March on Washington*. Sponsored by Planned Parenthood, 2016, https://www.womensmarch.com/.

MILCK. "The Song." *I Can't Keep Quiet*. https://www.icantkeepquiet.org/thesong/.

"Sisters." *Women's March on Washington*. Sponsored by Planned Parenthood, 2016, https://www.womensmarch.com/sisters.

Steinhardt, Ruth. "A Cappella Singers Become Viral Voice of Women's March." *GW Today*,
30 Jan. 2017, https://gwtoday.gwu.edu/cappella-singers-become-viral-voice-women%
E2%80%99s-march.
Tolbert, Elizabeth. "The Enigma of Music, the Voice of Reason: 'Music,' 'Language,' and
Becoming Human." *New Literacy History*, vol. 32, no. 3, 2001, pp. 451–465.
Wang, Hansi Lo. "Protestors Prepare for Women's March After Trump's Inauguration." *NPR*,
20 Jan. 2017, http://www.npr.org/sections/thetwo-way/2017/01/20/510706246/protesters-
prepare-for-womens-march-after-trumps-inauguration.
Watts, Eric King. "'Voice' and 'Voicelessness' in Rhetorical Studies." *Quarterly Journal of
Speech*, vol. 87, no. 2, May 2001, pp. 179–196.
Whiteley, Sheila. "The Person Is Political: Women's Liberation, Sexuality, Gender, Freedom
and Repression." *Women and Popular Music: Sexuality, Identity and Subjectivity*, Rout-
ledge, 2000, pp. 44–50.
"Who March the World? Girls." *Full Frontal with Samantha Bee*, episode 37, act 2, TBS, 25
Jan. 2017, http://samanthabee.com/episode/37/clip/who-march-the-world-girls/.s

Documentary Agitation and Outreach

The Rhetorical Networks of Resistance in Popular Nonfiction Film

CHANDRA A. MALDONADO

Picture it. A petite woman shattering the skull of and then skinning a cute brown bunny to put on the dinner table. Rhonda Britton's infamous "Pets or Meat" scene became the longest, most disturbing, and most captivating two minutes of Michael Moore's *Roger and Me* (1989), and it sparked my love for documentary films in an undergraduate film class in the summer of 2009. A few years later, I would find myself in graduate school studying the rhetoric of documentary film, which would later become a central focus of my research. During that time, I had the opportunity to view *Gasland* (2010) and participate in a question and answer session with the film's director, Josh Fox, while he was "shopping" around his film on a college tour. It was not until after I saw *Gasland* and heard Fox speak about his mission that I realized that even the common everyday person could pick up a camera and connect with an audience in hopes to generate enough interest in a cause to be active in facilitating change.

As part of both an independent and commercial network, advocacy documentary has been used as a medium for activists who desire to enact social and political change. This has been even more apparent in the last 20 years or so with the success of films such as *Super Size Me* (2004), *Waiting for Superman* (2010), and *Blackfish* (2013). These films have generated significant outcomes related to changes in legislation and institutional reform. Some films have led to changes in their target's policies, such as *Super Size Me*, which associated McDonald's portion sizes with health concerns, leading the corporation to suspend its "supersize" menu options. David Guggenheim's *Waiting for Superman* helped spark a national dialogue on school choice and voucher systems, and it generated donations sufficient to provide assistance to 2.8 million students (Pazerski). While some research has indicated the inaccuracy of information in *Blackfish*, a film which documents Seaworld's poor treatment of orca whales, the film is frequently identified as the cause of the company's subsequent financial struggles resulting in a more than 80 percent loss in profits since the film's launch (Neate). Regardless of fact or fiction, the rhetorical potency of this genre does not come from the consequences of these films; instead, the rhetorical maneuvers emerge from the structural patterns and functions of the genre.

With a decline in production costs, expanded distribution possibilities, and the need to compete in a crowded and partisan media market, access to making nonfiction media has become a possibility for everyday activists. This is due in part to easy accessibility to on-scene mobile recording technology and quick video uploads to networks, which rapidly spread information. Increasingly, these efforts include expansive public outreach and education campaigns so that the actual cinematic product is only one component of a larger assemblage of elements designed to engage and mobilize audiences. Thus, these advocacy documentary campaigns offer both textual and out of theater engagement with audience members, directing and mobilizing them to action.

To illustrate how these networks function and their possibilities, I will examine *Awake: A Dream from Standing Rock* (2017), as a significant rhetorical text because of the film's successful efforts towards network expansion and collaboration—necessary functions for the creation and sustainability of a movement. *Awake* documents the peaceful resistance against the Dakota Access Pipeline on the Standing Rock Sioux Reservation in North Dakota, a movement that received national attention in 2016.

While these documentaries do engage in advocacy efforts through argumentative structures, as shown in *Awake,* the genre's principle rhetorical effect is not a change in policy (which assumes an outcome) because of the film, but instead a change in the nature of community, which results in the building of a coalition and change in public dialogue. To be clear, while it is important to look at outcomes associated with the film to illustrate their significance, the point of this essay is to identify the possible rhetorical maneuvers of these networks, so that critics can better understand the scope in which an advocacy film provides the basis for sustainability efforts to make change possible. Those scholars concerned with measuring the effect of film(s) will miss the possibilities offered through the scope in which the film functions as a catalyst for events, which exceed that narrow measure (one policy change).

In the case of *Awake*, there are multiple parts that are vital to the mechanics of the film and the movement's campaign. Throughout this essay, I identify a change in the contemporary advocacy documentary by listing three main characteristics as successful campaign networks. First, the importance of community collaboration and involvement is significant because it, to an extent, gives agency to the community with control of the narratives, instead of the singular (usually white) perspective of the filmmaker. In offering platforms for public deliberation and dialogue, advocates create the conditions for what Kellner has called the "essential element" of a citizen's active self-development (262), directing coalitions towards the sustainability of a movement. Moreover, this approach produces the activists necessary to take part in stabilizing the movement. Secondly, the production and circulation of extra-cinematic mechanisms for a campaign network can range from the standard movie promotional materials (flyers, posters, trailers, and social media blasts), to college tours and town hall meetings, and sometimes the establishment of online portals where audiences dialogue with one another, all of which are ways that viewers can learn about how they might become citizen activists. Lastly, I engage in a short exploration of other advocacy films in order to suggest that a change in trajectory of the advocacy genre has occurred in the last 20 years, and to suggest possible paths for future research.[1]

I also want to note that my perspective of *Awake* and its collaboration and networking efforts in developing the "Water Is Life" movement comes from one privileged position. As an American white woman, I want to comment on the extent to which the showcasing of this collaboration is significant for the authenticity of the film, the campaign, and the movement in general. I am not specifically laying claim to the label of "indigenous authenticity," but instead I am seeking to explain the extent to which identification takes place between indigenous and non-indigenous viewers when encountering firsthand accounts of Dakota Access Pipeline (hereafter, DAPL) protestors on the frontlines and the aftermath of their disorienting experiences with PTSD.

Awake opens with sequential images of running water, a fitting account of the natural wonders of our world and a tranquil reminder of our dependency on these resources. This peacefulness breaks with images of frightening, and what some would label catastrophic, natural disasters, such as cars being whisked away in highly populated areas by unimaginable roaring floods and deadly thick tar-like black smoke and fire emerging from what looks to be a busy oil drilling site. The film cuts to boots-on-the-ground footage of violent outbursts of a suited and heavily armed militarized police force spraying protestors with water cannons in close proximity, while some participants are beaten bloody with police batons. Between high-and low-end production, the footage juxtaposed against one another creates a mash-up of visual spectacle, one of violence and police brutality, with interviews of protest partic-ipants and self-proclaimed "Water Protectors," as well as a glimpse into every-day life on the campsite and the spirit of tribal members and supporters from multiple points of view.

Josh Fox, as a well-known national environmental and anti-fossil fuel activist, did not agree with mainstream media's representation of activists (Water Protectors) as violent, and he wanted to set the record straight. Thus, he collaborated with several indigenous people, leaving his on-screen pres-ence out of the film as he felt it was appropriate (Fox). Among those indige-nous voices, two are key collaborators that become a central rhetorical feature, setting the stage for the circulation of their narrative throughout the move-ment. Of those key collaborators, Myron Dewey noted the reasoning behind his documentation of the protests: there was a lack of reporting from an indigenous perspective. As Stephanie Merry notes, what makes *Awake* an important documentary in the genre is the collaboration of multiple per-spectives, and especially indigenous ones, at the forefront of Standing Rock's narrative. Merry explains, "The documentary stands out because there's a clear sense that Fox, who is white, didn't just parachute in and tell this story through his eyes. It's an example of how filmmakers are taking steps toward more-inclusive storytelling. Not only did Fox collaborate with Native Amer-icans on the film, he also incorporated footage from livestreams, which have become a democratizing force, helping marginalized groups to get their mes-sages seen." This move towards collaborative filmmaking is important because it rejects the hegemonic Eurocentric lens that has dominated contemporary nonfiction films through narrativizing and instead invites marginalized groups to tell their own stories with as little outsider mediation as possible.

This collaborative approach can give new perspective and value to the final product of the film. For example, Dewey—as part of his tactics as an investigative journalist—was responsible for drone footage of the protests and circulation via social media, giving viewers a "firsthand glimpse of what it was like to live under 24–7 police surveillance, in what looked and felt like a war zone, and during the tender moments of camp life, in the largest Indigenous-led protest in recent memory" (Estes 383). With a strong indige-nous presence, both on screen and in the making of *Awake*, indigenous col-laborators like Dewey are able to collectively identify with those in their tribe and other indigenous groups to circulate narratives about the issues in which they are advocating, and in this process create and take ownership of their story. The film identifies the need to protect home and resources to survive and also reminds non-indigenous viewers of their own privilege in society— one that can be used in a way which does not speak for indigenous commu-nities but works alongside them to create change. Indeed, *Awake* acts as a lesson by reminding non-indigenous viewers of the continual pattern of brutality that colonial practices have maintained and supported throughout American history.

The networking feature of collective identity does not stop with the creative endeavors of Dewey and other indigenous people in the film. The nation-wide and international screenings of *Awake* have kept the conversation going about environmental and climate change movements at various colleges and universities, indigenous centers, and peace and justice centers, sometimes with the coupling of Q & A sessions directly after the screening of the film. For example, in November 2017 the Simon Ortiz and Labriola Center Lecture on Indigenous Land, Culture, and Community at Arizona State University hosted a public lecture series in which Dewey was invited to speak about his work on the film and in general on the struggles associated with indigenous issues and activism in America. During that same month, the Native American Cultural Center at Colorado State University featured keynote speakers Floris White Bull and Doug Good Feather, other indigenous contributors on the film, to continue the film's conversation.

While the Dakota Access Pipeline ultimately (and despite the protests) began its construction shortly after President Trump took office, those involved with *Awake* and the protests on Standing Rock continue to organize social actions on an array of environmental concerns. There has been an emergence of multiple coalitions across the country and world battling the same issues regarding access to and preservation of clean water in nearby communities. For example, Nancy Shomin, a member of the Grand Traverse Band of Ottawa and Chippewa Indians moved from protesting the Dakota Access Pipeline in 2016 to the current involvement of the Canadian oil transport company (Enbridge, Inc.) because of safety concerns regarding petroleum products that run through Line 5 in the Great Lakes. Shomin exclaims, "the goal is to shut it down" (qtd. in Kaufman and Allen).

While anti-pipeline coalition building and activism across the nation have become more prominent because of the Standing Rock protests, there are real-world ramifications associated with the activist endeavors of the movement. Marcus Mitchell, a 21-year-old indigenous Standing Rock activist, has experienced extensive medical injury because of the Standing Rock protests, including the permanent loss of vision in his left eye with partial hearing loss in his left ear. He also suffers from cervical spine damage, a result of "police officers kneel[ing] atop him, torquing his arms behind his back to place him in handcuffs," leaving Mitchell to feel as if he were "drowning in his own blood" (Parrish). In November 2018, Mitchell faced class A misdemeanor charges for criminal trespass with a maximum sentencing of two years in prison and a fine of $6,000. However, according to the "Solidarity with Marcus Mitchell" Go Fund Me campaign used to help with Mitchell's medical expenses, all charges have been dropped (Rouge).

Another leg of the movement has recently emerged in Louisiana where indigenous and non-indigenous people disrupted the construction of the Bayou Bridge Pipeline in September 2018. Protestors now face felony charges with up to five years in prison due to the state's recent reclassification of oil and gas pipelines as "critical infrastructures." Bill Quigley, a Loyola University law professor in New Orleans, notes that these new regulations are unconstitutional and a "ridiculous over-criminalization of people who protest" (qtd. in National Public Radio). Quigley plans on challenging this new law in court in hopes that other states will reconsider their own laws.

Advocacy campaigns provide numerous opportunities for audiences to take action at various levels. For example, the use of the internet and social media have become vital ways the genre uses technology to spread information and mobilize a disengaged public (Palczewski). The website for *Awake* is an example of the ways in which the advocacy genre works on multiple levels to connect and engage with audiences. Through the film's website users are able to donate to the cause where 100 percent of proceeds go toward supporting pipeline battles and the work of indigenous journalists. Young indigenous people interested in journalism and activist media can also find information on the film's website about Awake Media's newly established fellowship where seven scholarship recipients will get the opportunity to receive hands-on-training in filming, editing, cinematography, etc., so that they are equipped to tell stories about the lives of indigenous people.

The website also provides additional resources to help users become active citizens. For example, users are invited to join "The Action Network" where visitors can start their own campaign by creating petitions, campaign letters, and other means such as fundraising to spread information, or continue to support anti-pipeline movements and other climate resistance efforts that are popping up across America by joining the #ClimateRevolution. Beyond the downloadable screening package provided on the website to help direct groups who are interested in screening *Awake* for their communities, what users will also find is a call-to-action guide which educates readers about the "Water Is Life" movement and provides them with practical steps to resistance in support of other environmental causes.

What is important to remember about the protests that took place at Standing Rock is not if the protests were successful in stopping the pipeline, because on many accounts the protests failed. Instead, we should take stock of the actions that took place *after* the protests in order to understand the extent to which outreach efforts and suggested courses of action traveled beyond Standing Rock protests as the rhetorical situation.[2] While simple, this includes wide-scale movements toward the divestment of big banks that funded pipeline activities (#DefundDAPL). Other actions include the utilization of popular publications as venues for indigenous voices to educate the public about how they too can continue the action. An example of this can be found in a recent article written by 23-year-old Jackie Fielder, a Mnicoujou Lakota, Mandan, and Hidatsa organizer, which appears in *Teen Vogue* (March 2018) about the importance of divestment from big banks, which fund pipeline activities, and calls for the public to move their money into credit unions and local banks. In this case, we can look at the Standing Rock protests as a starting point, one which put into practice the "after-protests" of Water/Environment Protectors. To date, the results of the divestment movement totals $4.3 billion ("Stop the Dakota").

The continual coverage of pipeline activists as they face criminal charges for those months protesting at Standing Rock, too, acts as an accelerator for keeping the movement alive. As for Marcus Mitchell, before what *The Guardian* calls a turning point in police violence, Mitchell was a student at Northern Arizona University. After he saw live stream coverage of protesters getting shot with rubber bullets and sprayed with water hoses in freezing temperatures, he dropped out of school and hitchhiked to North Dakota the next day. At the beginning, he was hesitant to draw attention to his experience, but because of the growing and continual indigenous-led nationwide battle for the preservation of natural resources, Mitchell states, "People in the movement need to know what happened to me" (qtd. in Parrish). Indeed, transformations such as these are just the types of results that demonstrate the "after effects" of communication networks that facilitate change in private/public roles, which are vital to sustaining a movement. In Mitchell's case, the movement transformed his role as a student and private citizen into a public activist.

Of course, the campaigns associated with Standing Rock are not the only cases where films have utilized extra-cinematic materials to strengthen the likelihood of audience engagement and action. For example, Michael Moore, through his website, connects readers to various causes by directly linking citizens to petitions and information on current issues of the day. The website becomes an important part of filling the networking and information gaps on political and social issues to transform how citizens approach civic engagement (Barrett and Leddy). For example, "Try this on" is a webpage located on Moore's website which invites visitors to engage in current events. External links, such as "find your polling place," to promote the importance of voting, are some of the many ways that Moore uses technology for coalition building.

Moore does have celebrity status that has pushed countless numbers of movements forward and continues to do so; however, the celebrity persona can only go so far in stabilizing a movement. I echo Thomas Goodnight's claim that celebrity advocacy is "a complex discourse that minimally inscribes a dialectical opposition between the modes of televisualized criticism and the stylistic vision of film production" (430). Thus, while the celebrity persona acts as a catalyst to forward a cause's movement, such as the multiple celebrities that were arrested during the Standing Rock protests (e.g., Shailene Woodley), the celebrity does not necessarily sustain it. Indeed, the celebrity persona is not there to make change but instead communicate the need for it. This is where online portals and how-to-do sites become vital components in the bigger movement.

While it's true that many of these techniques have been utilized for some time, it is necessary to acknowledge the possibilities that have been created from the existence and use of these online spaces in public discourse. For example, the website for the film *How to Die in Oregon* (2011) connects users to information about Death with Dignity laws (DwD). Users are also invited to participate in a weekly "TweetChat Conversation" to raise awareness about the DwD laws and to connect with others who have the same interests. Users who want more information about the movement at a national level are able to look at the state-by-state breakdown of laws both passed and attempted throughout the United States. Similarly, the website for the film *Blackfish* links to other wildlife organizations for more information on wildlife exploitation and captivity. Users are also linked to pages that allow them to make donations to the movement. The accessibility to information about a specific cause and similar issues at hand allows the audience to make educated decisions regarding their commitment to the issues at many levels, even if it is a simple donation.

Campaigns also frequently provide resources for the audience. For *Gasland* and *An Inconvenient Truth* (2006), the films' websites provide tool kits to use for national distribution. On the "take action" webpage on the *Gasland* website, users are instructed to follow specific steps to get involved. These steps include the common "get connected" through social media sites as well as give materials or "tool kits" to use on a wider scale. *Gasland*'s website gives the option to send an electronic postcard to the White House informing former President Obama about the "I'm not from Gasland" movement that opposes Obama's support of natural gas and fracking. *An Inconvenient Truth*'s website "takepart.com" offers similar steps which include a list of environmentally friendly companies to be involved with, as well as the importance of self-awareness about our own carbon footprint. The website "climaterealityproject.org" (which houses the AIT sequel, *An Inconvenient Sequel: Truth to Power* [2017]) offers similar materials for activists such as the "I Am Still In" action kit, which includes information regarding the U.S.'s role in the Paris Agreement and the climate movement.

Of course, there can never be a guarantee that all films which fall into the category of this genre or the events, materials, and actions used to aid the genre will produce a mobilized partisan audience; however, the campaigns of these films work in one or two ways—either the audience who is already committed to the cause is reaffirmed in their commitment, or on the other side of the spectrum, new followers are encouraged to engage in the cause. What is significant about this function is not whether or not an audience is successfully persuaded, but instead the creation of an open space for which public deliberation and dialogue is made possible, because the paths to "how to get there" have to come before potential outcomes or solutions. Indeed, similar to the meeting spaces that Habermas claimed were vital to healthy public spheres, these campaign networks provide audiences with both the opportunity to engage issues as a community, and the mechanisms by which members of those communities might act in concert with one another. Though there are real reasons to doubt the efficacy of the public sphere and its ability to translate outcry into successful collective action (Phillips), there can be little doubt that such a platform has reorganized a landscape of possibilities for activist media. Thus, the formation of this space allows citizens to gather openly to discuss and deliberate, which is a crucial part in how publics form.

If we look at the function of these spaces (filmic texts and the networks in which they circulate), we can see that the campaign trait of advocacy documentary "constitute the 'people' as a potential historical actor" (Laclau 74). Identities change as the cost of these demands as individuals are called into a collectivized union of people—a mobilization caused by the shared feeling that people are unheard and disenfranchised. The opportunity that a campaign provides allows the audience to gain agency within a space that is "one of discursive relations, a theater for debating and deliberating" (Fraser 75). Through these campaign techniques, we can better speculate the rhetorical possibilities of an argument for change through understanding the extent to which these networks function individually and collectively as the call for civic engagement circulates in public discourse.

It is clear that significant changes have taken place in how activists organize their efforts. While it may be too early in these developments to assess the overall impacts such efforts have in producing social change, there can be no doubt that by expanding the audience reached by the campaign—by offering more robust opportunities for citizen action and by providing a platform for interested parties to affiliate with one another—this approach to activist messaging has fundamentally changed the discursive potential of documentary and the activism it supports. Regardless of the final actions of the audience, campaign networks play a significant role because their functions work rhetorically to provide a space for which a public can mobilize through distribution of information that to an extent may inform and motivate towards action.

NOTES

1. I want to extend my appreciation to my colleagues Mai Xiong (North Carolina State University) for her extensive feedback on this essay and Bill Trapani (Florida Atlantic University) with whom I'm collaborating on related ideas for a different project.
2. See Bitzer, Lloyd F. "The Rhetorical Situation." *Philosophy & Rhetoric*, 1968, pp. 1–14.

WORKS CITED

Barrett, Diana, and Sheila Leddy. "Assessing Creative Media's Social Impact." *The Fledgling Fund*, January 2009, http://www.thefledglingfund.org/wp-content/uploads/2012/08/Impact-Paper-Abridged.pdf.

Estes, Nick. "Awake: A Dream from Standing Rock. Directed by Myron Dewey, Josh Fox, and James Spione." *Environmental History*, vol. 23, no. 2, 2018, pp. 383–386.

Fox, Josh. Interview by Jordan Chariton. *Josh Fox on New Standing Rock Documentary AWAKE.* 1 May. 2017, https://www.youtube.com/watch?v=Wzx3JVD8540.

Fraser, Nancy. "Rethinking the Public Sphere: A Contribution to the Critique of Actually Existing Democracy." *Between Borders: Pedagogy and the Politics of Cultural Studies*, edited by Henry A. Giroux and Peter Mclaren, Routledge, 1994, pp. 74–98.

Goodnight, Thomas G. "The Passion of the Christ Meets Fahrenheit 9/11: A Study in Celebrity Advocacy." *American Behavioral Scientist*, vol. 49, no. 3, 2005, pp. 410–435.

Kaufman, Gina, and Robert Allen. "Standing Rock Protesters Now Protesting Line 5 Pipeline." *Detroit Free Press*, 11 August 2018, Accessed 27 September 2018.

Kellner, Douglas. "Habermas, the Public Sphere, and Democracy: A Critical Intervention." *Perspectives on Habermas*, edited by Lewis E. Hahn, Open Court, 2000, pp. 259.

Laclau, Ernesto. *On Populist Reason*. Verso, 2007.

Merry, Stephanie. "A New Standing Rock Documentary Shows How Film Can Give Voice to Those Who Feel Powerless." *The Washington Post*, 13 April 2017, https://www.washington post.com/entertainment/a-new-standing-rock-documentary-shows-how-film-can-give-voice-to-those-who-feel-powerless/2017/04/12/e2da02d4-1dfb-11e7-ad74-3a742a6e93a7_story.html.

National Public Radio. "Tougher Laws on Pipeline Protests Face Test in Louisiana." *National Public Radio*, 19 September 2018, https://www.npr.org/2018/09/19/648029225/tougher-laws-on-pipeline-protests-face-test-in-louisiana.

Neate, Rupert. "SeaWorld Sees Profits Plunge 84% as Customers Desert Controversial Park." *The Guardian*, 6 August 2015, https://www.theguardian.com/us-news/2015/aug/06/seaworld-profits-plunge-customers.

Palczewski, Catherine H. "Cyber-movements, New Social Movements, and Counterpublics." *Counterpublics and the State*, edited by Robert Asen and Daniel C. Brouwer, State University of New York Press, 2001, pp. 161–186.

Parrish, Will. "Standing Rock Activist Faces Prison After Officer." *The Guardian*, 4 October 2018, https://www.theguardian.com/us-news/2018/oct/04/standing-rock-marcus-mitchell-shooting-charges.

Pazerski, Gayle. "Four Years Later, the Impact of 'Waiting for Superman' Carries On." *Artwith impact.org*, 3 July 2014, https://www.artwithimpact.org/four-years-later-the-impact-of-waiting-for-superman-carries-on/.

Phillips, Kendall R. "The Spaces of Public Dissension: Reconsidering the Public Sphere." *Communication Monographs*, vol. 63, no. 3, 1996, pp. 231–248.

Rouge, Rene. "Solidarity with Marcus Mitchell." *go fund me*, https://www.gofundme.com/solidarity-with-marcus-mitchell.

"Stop the Dakota Access Pipeline." *Defunddapl.org*, 2019. https://www.defunddapl.org.

Gillard of Thrones

Using Popular Culture to Resist Misogyny

Ana Stevenson

In May 2013, Australian prime minister Julia Gillard surprised her constituents by tweeting in Dothraki, a fictional language created for HBO's hit television series *Game of Thrones* (2011–2019). Her tweets followed a video interview with *Guardian Australia* in which she expressed much enthusiasm for the series. "It's not just us plebs who enjoy a rollicking, premium-cable sex drama," a columnist for popular U.S. feminist blog *Jezebel* flippantly observed; "super important world leaders also like to watch hour-long rape and murder spectacles as a diversion from their comparable uninteresting lives" (Barry).

Game of Thrones (*GoT*) debuted in the United States on HBO during April 2011 and on Australian cable television in July that same year. After *Lord of the Rings* (2001–2003) and in anticipation of *The Hobbit* (2012–2014), film audiences worldwide were primed for high fantasy. *GoT* achieved resounding popularity for bringing the fantasy world of Westeros to life. Its unpredictable narrative depicts key dynasties—House Lannister, House Stark, and the exiled princess of House Targaryen—engaged in power struggles to be seated as monarch upon the Iron Throne, yet nearly all the characters are oblivious to the impending doom coming from supernatural forces beyond the realm (Gjelsvik and Schubart 5–7). HBO created an effective adaptation of George R.R. Martin's *A Song of Ice and Fire* fantasy series, begun in 1996 yet still unfinished, by embracing the aesthetic and discursive practices which have come to define premium cable television (Hassler-Forest 161).

Far from being just entertainment, audiences worldwide learn about global politics not from academic disciplines such as international relations but through popular culture (Clapton and Shepherd 5). Since *GoT* "displays power-politics in the raw," Britain's *Telegraph* reflected in 2015, it holds particular interest for politicians: "The characters are trying to do what they consider to be their best ... while fighting a pervading sense of doom as 'winter is coming.' How very like our own dear world, as our politicians squabble about who can offer us the most secure future" (Boulton). Former world leaders such as U.S. president Barack Obama, British prime minister David Cameron, and Dutch minister for foreign affairs Frans Timmermans have all expressed their appreciation for *GoT*.

So did Julia Gillard, the first woman to serve in Australia's highest office. Politicians and their parties now regularly use popular culture to communicate with voters and mediate their political ideology. Gillard began to discuss her enjoyment of *GoT* publicly in 2013. Projecting "normality"—in this case, by watching a celebrated television series—enables politicians to "foster highly positive affinities with voters (at least temporarily)" (Wood et al. 582). Since this occurred towards the end of Gillard's political career, it might be seen as a media adviser's attempt to help a struggling leader better engage with the Australian public. But Gillard continued to discuss *GoT* in the years after her prime ministership. Through fannish television reviews, published by *The Guardian* in 2014 and 2015, Gillard developed a covert response to the Australian media's sexist coverage of her prime ministership. In so doing, Gillard used *GoT* and its female characters to resist the mainstream media's misogynistic treatment of women leaders.

Julia Gillard became prime minister of the Commonwealth of Australia in June 2010. Since 2007, she had served as deputy prime minister to Prime Minister Kevin Rudd. The Rudd-Gillard years inaugurated more than a decade of leadership instability. Between 2007 and 2019 Australia has witnessed a whirlwind of seven prime ministers, four of whom were internally deposed by their party. When Malcolm Turnbull became the third prime minister to rise to power via this increasingly turbulent process in 2015, U.S. news website *Vox* declared: "Australia is basically turning into a real-life Game of Thrones" (Lind).

This leadership instability began in December 2006, when Rudd challenged veteran Australian Labor Party (ALP) leader Kim Beazley to become Leader of the Opposition in federal parliament. Rudd then became prime minister in a landslide 2007 federal election against John Howard, who had been prime minister since 1996. After successfully campaigning as a "political celebrity"—complete with the slogan Kevin '07—Rudd represented a moment of political change (Wilson 203). In June 2010, Gillard colluded with the ALP Caucus to push an internal party vote to remove the increasingly embattled Rudd and hence become prime minister. Soon after, the Australian media villainized Gillard, framing her political ascent as underhanded and unfeminine (Stevenson 55–56). After being unseated as prime minister, Rudd repeatedly tried to regain power by destabilizing and undermining Gillard

(Wilson 213). Following the federal election of August 2010, the Gillard government was faced with a hung parliament: the ALP only held a small majority and therefore had to foster inter-party coalitions. In spite of these difficulties and not without controversy, the Gillard government passed an impressive amount of legislation between 2010 and 2013. But it also faced media coverage characterized by increasingly intense sexism and misogyny. By early 2013, the beleaguered Gillard government was faced with the prospect of a loss in the upcoming federal election. Rudd finally deposed Gillard in June 2013.

GoT premiered in 2011, the year after Gillard became prime minister, and became HBO's biggest hit by 2014. Only as the series gained greater cultural resonance globally did some Australian commentators begin to use *GoT* as a political metaphor. In April 2013, during season three and the Gillard government's decline, public affairs magazine *Eureka Street* published "Gillard's game of thrones," a satirical political commentary featuring *GoT* aliases and tropes:

> The place: Parliament House, Canberra
> The Time: The Present
> The Inhabitants: Soon to be History
> *Queen Julia struts into her office, blood dripping from her battle axe. Within, she is met by her aide-de-camp, diminutive Lord Tyrian Lannister* [McDermott 24].

Eureka Street imagined a dialogue not between a prime minister and fellow politician, but between a tyrannical ruler and her advisor. Journalist Jim McDermott's Queen Julia begins by uttering the words "Moving forward..."—the same banal political slogan as Gillard. "Tell me you did not dispatch *all* of the rebels," Lord Tyrian responds (McDermott 24, emphasis in original). This exchange satirized what the Australian media viewed as Gillard's most controversial, divisive, and unfeminine political maneuver: her so-called political "stabbing" of Rudd in June 2010 (Trimble 57–58, 165–166). The piece supported Rudd's self-styled image as the quintessential celebrity politician. "Milady, your people loathe you, and the court still comes for your head," Lord Tyrian continues; "Lord Rudd," he acerbically remarks, "stands alive outside your gates, doing an interview for the ABC [Australian Broadcasting Corporation]" (McDermott 24). Using Westerosi politics as metaphors for existing media discourses, *Eureka Street* recast Gillard as a violent, undemocratic ruler whose dynasty is about to crumble but still let Rudd emerge as a sly but astute man of the people.

An exciting new pop cultural touchstone, *GoT* offered a compelling framework through which to envisage Australia's leadership instability. Building on the media's existing tendency to visualize politics through metaphors of war and combat (Trimble 152–168), the series' themes of violent politicking and war offered pertinent metaphors for what once might have been merely described as a "game of musical chairs" (Jokovich 10). As a *Sydney Morning Herald* headline about the 2013 federal election proclaimed: "Candidates and hopefuls line up for the game of thrones" (Kenny and Maley). Some commentators even saw Canberra, the nation's capital, as surpassing the scheming surrounding the Iron Throne. "There has been a surreal element to federal politics over the past three years and each month has thrown political intrigue that made the fantasy series *Game of Thrones* seem more like *The Wizard of Oz*," journalist Eddy Jokovich reflected (10). The sense of fatality pervading the world of Westeros thus paralleled what many perceived as the destructive spiraling of Australian politics in the 21st century.

Only a month before being deposed as prime minister, Gillard revealed herself to be a *GoT* enthusiast in a video interview with *Guardian Australia*. "It's a bloody tale of warring clans fighting for control of the throne—so it should perhaps come as little surprise to Game of Thrones fans that Julia Gillard is an avid viewer," journalist Lenore Taylor (et al.) editorialized. *Guardian Australia* was launched on 27 May 2013 with the aim of offering a "fresh and independent view" in the lead-up to the 2013 federal election (Sweney). Its articles about Gillard's pop cultural predilections, published online between 26 and 28 May 2013, effectively helped launch this national news outlet. Gillard's interview became so newsworthy that, in addition to *The Guardian*'s cross-promotion and coverage in overseas news outlets such as *Jezebel*, excerpts were replayed on Australian free-to-air television stations such as Channel Ten ("Julia Gillard: Khaleesi?").

In the *Guardian Australia* video interview of 26 May, Gillard and Taylor explored the nature of fandom as well as the thematic relationship between politics and the television series. "I'm told that you're a bit of a *Game of Thrones* fan," Taylor (et al.) began. "Is that because it's even more bizarre than Australian politics?" "Ah. Well! I hadn't thought about it like that," Gillard laughingly replied. "I was given the DVDs over the summer period when I did get a little bit of time off," she recalled; "I watched them one after the other. I don't get many lazy afternoons, but I managed to have a few!" (Taylor et al.). Gillard seemed reticent to position herself as too much of a television devotee lest her dedication to her job be questioned. Indeed, the stereotype of consuming too much television is often associated with women and the working classes. However, HBO itself has a connection with "Quality TV," a premium cable genre designed to appeal to a "coveted audience of upper-middle class subscribers with abundant disposable income" (Hassler-Forest 163). To adapt the original fantasy novels, HBO embraced highbrow (rather than lowbrow) entertainment and production values; narrative complexity through character development; and "televisual transgression" through violence and nudity (Hassler-Forest 163–164). "Quality TV" is aimed at exactly the affluent and educated viewers epitomized by the prime minister.

In the context of Gillard's direct access to this premium cable drama, her classed and gendered concerns about being criticized for watching too much television appear misplaced. As Gillard ultimately revealed, "now I'm a bit of an addict and I anxiously await the new episode each Monday night" (Taylor et al.). Though a Sunday evening ritual in the United States, each *GoT* episode only became available across the international date line on Monday—legally in the morning and illegally sometime thereafter. Describing *GoT* as the "most illegally downloaded TV series of all time," Channel Ten went on to joke: "Not sure whether [Gillard] got it illegally or not!" ("Julia Gillard: Khaleesi?"). In reality, Gillard likely experienced none of the difficulties that defined her fellow citizens' attempts to access the series. Australia is, notably, a prosperous nation reputed to be "among the most prolific non-paying users of digital entertainment content" (MacNeil 545). Due to strict international licensing agreements, *GoT* was only screened in Australia via Foxtel subscription on the channel Showcase on Monday mornings and evenings; on iTunes, with intermittent availability; or on DVD, if purchased months later (MacNeil 552–553, 556). On account of the series' growing cultural capital, many viewers considered it imperative to watch each new episode promptly. Gillard, in contrast, appeared to directly access each new episode both via cable television subscription and DVD. "While it'd be fun to implicate the PM as a GoT pirate," U.S. tech website *Gizmodo* jibed, "it's highly doubtful she'd be that silly" (Hopewell).

What Gillard actually said about the series' characters had the potential to create disadvantageous double entendres for the politically engaged observer. This was principally true of her comments about one particularly unfortunate character, who, in light of Gillard's political history, could easily be read onto Rudd:

> GILLARD: Oh, I was a little bit shocked when Ned Stark got killed off so early on!
> TAYLOR: It seemed premature, right?
> GILLARD: It did, because he sort of had *hero* written all over his forehead. ... I assumed he was going to be the central, sort of, *heroic character* for all of it— or most of it—so I didn't expect the *grizzly end* so early. But yes, Ned Stark was obviously a good character [Taylor et al., emphasis added].

The death of Ned Stark, a noble character "torn between ambition, vengeance and family loyalty" (Frankel 41), is indeed a surprising narrative outcome. But Rudd—who'd had *change* written all over his forehead in 2007—also experienced a premature demise. For fans who had identified with Ned Stark and interpreted his execution as unjust, Gillard's reflections had the potential to frame Rudd's removal from the office of prime minister as illegitimate.

The prime minister's favorite character offered the possibility of far more positive overtones. "I'm barracking for the khaleesi, the mother of dragons," Gillard gleefully divulged (Taylor et al.). To fervently support the avenging Daenerys Targaryen is hardly surprising. Described by one scholar as the "Hero Queen" (Frankel 147), the *khaleesi* is able to prevail and even thrive in the face of misogynistic forces. In spite of the series' questionable feminist credentials, Daenerys has been celebrated as a symbolic force for feminism (Gjelsvik and Schubart 4, 7–9). Her character arc follows her progression from a powerless pawn to a young woman destined to be queen (Frankel 158). The character is clearly a fan favorite, which trends in baby names from the last few years reveal. "Khaleesi, a title given to the wife of a fictional Dothraki khal—it basically means queen—falls in at No. 48 and is more popular than traditional names like Jane, Lydia, and Anna," explains *Business Insider Australia* (Oswald). A fictional royal title—rather than the character's forename—has been embraced as a girl's name.

As a powerful but imperfect female leader, Gillard had much in common with this character. While in office, the Australian media pursued increasingly incessant references to Gillard's so-called "stabbing" or "knifing" of Rudd and gave endless attention to her de facto relationship, childlessness, and sartorial choices (Trimble 57–58, 96–103, 121–130). Her conservative political opponents publicly denounced Gillard as a "bitch," a "witch," and "JuLIAR" (Stevenson 55). In October 2012, Gillard finally responded by delivering a parliamentary speech in which she decried misogyny in politics. This speech gained international acclaim in news outlets such as the *New York Times*, *Telegraph*, *New Yorker*, *Huffington Post*, *Irish Times*, and *Jezebel* (Stevenson 58). In contrast, prominent Australian media outlets cynically interpreted the speech as a political ploy, accused Gillard of "playing the gender card," and delegitimized her attempts to discuss sexism within political discourse by reinvigorating the "gender wars" metaphor (Trimble 85, 152–168). Given the depth of vitriol the Australian media expressed in response to Gillard's first major foray into decrying sexism in politics, Gillard, like Daenerys Targaryen, would have to confront the forces of sexism creatively.

But Gillard's personal and symbolic identification with the khaleesi also had shortcomings. Daenerys Targaryen emerges as an unambiguously monarchical figure, regally self-styled as "Daenerys Stormborn of the House Targaryen, First of Her Name, the Unburnt, Queen of the Andals and the First Men, Khaleesi of the Great Grass Sea, Breaker of Chains, and Mother of Dragons." An exiled princess and heir to the Iron Throne, the khaleesi is no democratic sovereign. Her single-minded desire to rule Westeros offered particularly uncomfortable parallels for Gillard's own rise to power. Despite her actions being far from unprecedented and the Gillard government's democratic reelection in August 2010 (Trimble 47–61), Gillard's role in unseating Rudd as ALP leader and prime minister could easily recall the whims of monarchical rule. Neither did other less savory aspects of the khaleesi's character encourage positive overtones for real-world leadership. Daenerys, who ruthlessly conquers territories across Essos, is a messianic white savior figure who does not fully appreciate the structural abuse and exploitation suffered by enslaved people of color (in Gjelsvik and Schubart 187–188). Her dragons—the "equivalent of nuclear weapons"—signify the extent of her aggression, while her willingness to use such overwhelming firepower is the source of her authority (Clapton and Shepherd 12).

Pros and cons aside, the parallels between the prime minister and Daenerys Targaryen could not be curbed once Gillard began to discuss *GoT*. In the *Guardian Australia* interview, Taylor asked Gillard: "Khaleesi's not a name you'd like to be known by in the office?" "Ah, well, I don't have any pet dragons!" Gillard replied. "Maybe they'd come in handy from time to time. But no-one's given me any dragon eggs. And given she had to walk into fire in order to hatch them, I'm not sure that I *particularly* want that bit of it!" (Taylor et al., emphasis added). Although Gillard herself remained unconvinced, Channel Ten subsequently described its piece about the interview as "Julia Gillard: Khaleesi?" Perhaps surprised by the success of its original interview, *The Guardian* asked its readers: "[W]ould you join Julia Gillard in House Targaryen?" (Hughes). It featured a photograph of Gillard giving an address alongside a screenshot of the khaleesi emerging naked from the pyre, a newly hatched baby dragon on her shoulder. Proceeding to describe the characteristics of each major Westerosi House, *The Guardian* highlighted the Targaryen motto, "Fire and Blood" (Hughes).

Soon after Gillard's fan status was revealed, one Perth-based fellow fan took to Twitter to share her sense of pop cultural kinship: "Julia Gillard confirms she is addicted to Game of Thrones. ONE OF US! ONE OF US!" (Bader).[1] This tweet did not go viral but was widely quoted in *The Guardian*'s commentary, which superimposed a photograph of Gillard onto the Iron Throne. Gillard responded by tweeting in Dothraki, a fictional language derived from Martin's novels. While her interview certainly facilitated positive public engagement, her tweets in Daenerys' second language went a step further. Gillard replied: "Not addicted—me allayafa anna! #gameofthrones JG" (Gillard). Anticipating readers' interest, *The Guardian* offered a translation: "Not addicted—it pleases me" ("Julia Gillard's Dothraki tweets"). But this fan had not independently postured the prime minister as a television addict; only days previous had Gillard herself asserted that she was "a bit of an addict" (Taylor et al.). In this personally signed tweet ("JG"), however, Gillard avowed that she was *not* a television fanatic—though perhaps in a knowing in-joke between fellow fans. But her repeated willingness to tweet in Dothraki, a highly specialized language, actually implicated Gillard not just as a *GoT* fan but as an addict indeed. When popular Perth-based commercial radio station

Nova 937 ran a campaign for Gillard to be cast in the series' next season, she replied: "Yer chomoe anna—but being Prime Minister keeps me pretty busy. JG." "You honour me," *The Guardian* again translated ("Julia Gillard's Dothraki tweets"). For Gillard, asserting a busy schedule spoke as much to her actual competence as a politician (Wilson 213) as to the image she sought to cultivate prior to the 2013 federal election. At the same time, discovering how to convey simple phrases in Dothraki expressed deep personal interest in *GoT*. In the coming years, Gillard would again personally attest to the series' "addictive power" ("Game of Thrones has parallels").

Popular culture offered Gillard the opportunity to shape her own narrative in response to the harsh reporting, parody, and satire to which politicians are almost always subject in open democracies. "Perhaps it's not so much Dothraki as GOT fandom she is counting on to deliver her and voters a common language," a tactic by no means limited to Gillard, Taylor remarked ("Julia Gillard's Dothraki tweets"). Since her womanhood meant she could not access the benefits of political celebrity in the same manner as men like Rudd (Wilson 212), Gillard instead channeled *GoT* to venture into this contested terrain. But this only offered Australia's first female prime minister a brief reprieve from a particularly high degree of scrutiny. When Rudd finally spearheaded a successful leadership challenge against Gillard just ahead of Australia's 2013 federal election, one journalist reported, "Rudd wins the game of thrones" (Grattan). As *GoT* fans know, however, "When you play the game of thrones, you win or you die" ("You Win or You Die"). After Rudd lost the 2013 federal election, Melbourne's *Herald Sun* embraced war metaphors to position his "battle" with Gillard as taking "cues" from her "TV indulgence" (Carlyon).

At this juncture, Gillard undertook a career transformation from an Australian political leader to an influential international commentator and spokesperson for girls' education. Following the success of her 2013 *Guardian Australia* interview, Gillard took an unusual step into extended cultural commentary by penning two fannish *GoT* television reviews for *The Guardian*. Her analysis highlighted the political capacities of powerful women in the imaginative realm of Westeros to reject the mainstream media's skepticism about women's capacity for leadership in the real world. Gillard's subsequent commentary about women in real-world politics has appeared in outlets such as the *New York Times* and *The Atlantic*. Her advocacy for girls began in 2014 as chair of the Global Partnership for Education, while in 2018, Gillard became the inaugural chair of the Global Institute for Women's Leadership at King's College London.

The Guardian published Gillard's first *GoT* television review after episode one of season four aired in April 2014. Not only did her piece, entitled "Game of Thrones has parallels with my time as Australian prime minister," unambiguously signal a personal perspective and encourage direct comparison with her own leadership, it also appeared months before the September 2014 release of her political memoir, *My Story*. Its tagline—"Power is relentlessly pursued in both worlds"—set the tone for her pointed criticisms: not of the series, which she continued to enjoy, but of real-world politics. Gillard began by again recounting her first encounter with *GoT*, a series which had already hooked many of her staff. "Drawn in, I binged on series one over three days on brief Christmas leave in 2012," she regaled. "Fiction and reality started to collide" in March 2013, when Gillard was faced by an internal party leadership challenge from ALP veteran Simon Crean. As early as February 2012, Rudd had pursued a leadership challenge against Gillard; before finally succeeding in June 2013, he considered standing alongside Crean only months earlier in March 2013. Although these events might be seen as a political reckoning, many of Gillard's colleagues and staffers appreciated her leadership. "Returning to my office," Gillard recalled of March 2013, "I was greeted with posters of sword fighting with the slogan: 'What do we say to the god of death? Not today.'" ("Game of Thrones has parallels"). Paraphrased from master swordsman Syrio Forel's advice to Ned Stark's daughter Arya ("A Golden Crown"), this quote has become a fannish shorthand for tenacity— a will for survival that Gillard, as prime minister, certainly possessed. In embracing fan language to offer Gillard solidarity, her supporters celebrated her fortitude in the face of political uncertainty.

Gillard's television reviews also juxtaposed Westerosi politics with real-world attitudes towards gender and power. *GoT* is "not a story of Everyman," Gillard reflected; indeed, its narrative is not primarily concerned with the fate of soldiers, laborers, serfs, sex workers, or enslaved people. Rather, she realized, the "lot of the everyman and everywoman forms only a backdrop to the story of would-be rulers and their clashes for power." Of specific interest was women's political influence. "In this world of constant war, female characters have never been relegated to the sidelines," Gillard emphasized; a woman can "confound the stereotypes" and be far more than "a bit player in a male drama" ("Game of Thrones has parallels"). But the power of such female characters is far from guaranteed. Since Westerosi society is both feudal and misogynistic, critics question whether *GoT* actually endorses or condemns patriarchal and patrilineal power structures (Clapton and Shepherd 10). A certain type of lone woman such as Daenerys Targaryen might prevail but might equally struggle to bring other women along with her. Still, Gillard found inspiration in "The Khaleesi," the "Wildling, Ygritte," and the "child combatant, Arya Stark" ("Game of Thrones has parallels"). If fictional women and girls can defy gender conventions in television's imaginary fantasy realm, she seemed to imply, why is there so much consternation about women's leadership in the real world? By highlighting the strong female characters widely appreciated by fans, Gillard invited audiences to think about the alternative possibilities these archetypes created.

Gillard's second television review appeared a year later in April 2015, after the release of episode one of season five. Here, she recalled media repartee from 2013 by mentioning the illegal download scandals which continued to surround the series. Again, Gillard reflected on the experiences and agency of powerful women. Although Cersei Lannister is "mourning both her father and her eldest son," Gillard suggested that their deaths offered her both "freedom from being directed against her will but also the anger that accompanies vicious grief." The "tension" between Cersei and her soon-to-be daughter-in-law Margaery Tyrell, she continued, "vibrates ominously" to create a "deliciously dangerous" interplay. Interested in representations of the complexities of female power, its capabilities and limitations, Gillard described how her favorite character continued to prevail in spite of Westeros' patriarchal culture. "The Khaleesi, Daenerys Targaryen, has always baked in warmth, even fire. But she has done so in complete isolation from all the other major characters," Gillard observed. In season five, Daenerys encounters "resistance all around, from large dragons who will not be mothered, and from freed slaves and angry slavers who will not easily be ruled." Recalling Gillard's own need to negotiate effectively to lead a hung parliament, she implied that such struggles to generate unity might be the very lessons of leadership. The women of Westeros are both powerful and flawed, "defying simple characterization as goodies or baddies" ("Julia Gillard on Game of Thrones").

The representation of women in *GoT* broadens media visibility at the same time as affirming existing political norms. The series certainly challenges the convention that men should have exclusive access to power, yet it also reinforces gendered assumptions about political authority (Clapton and Shepherd 12). The khaleesi does offer alternate visions of society. Monarchs are "all just spokes on a wheel," Daenerys proclaims: "I'm not going to stop the wheel. I'm going to break the wheel" ("The Winds of Winter"). But Gillard's favorite character has not been able to bring about such a revolution: Daenerys' actions reify the centrality of the state and she relies upon force to achieve her goals—explicitly rendered in the show's final season. As Gillard noted of season four, however, "there are signs everywhere that the kaleidoscope that constantly shifts the pieces of this puzzle" was about to change ("Game of Thrones has parallels"). Gillard applauded the groundbreaking potential for audiences to encounter female characters who are autonomous political forces.

In the years since 2013, journalists have embraced parallels between national politics and *GoT* far more frequently. "Australians have not been backward in likening the revolving door of prime ministerial power to the show's treacherous dynastic politics," medievalist academics proclaimed in literary magazine *Meanjin* (D'Arcens and Monagle 108). The series' exponential popularity has rendered it an ever more potent political metaphor. *GoT* entered the "collective consciousness like no other show in recent memory," another commentator reflected in 2017; by sharing her enthusiasm for Daenerys Targaryen, Gillard had, if only momentarily, harnessed this "zeitgeist in a way that must have made Kevin Rudd see Lannister red" (Bastow 14, 17). Yet, by inviting fans to consider not just the aptness of the metaphor but also the gender politics of Westeros versus the real world, Gillard's use of *GoT* was far more defiant.

Despite being a *GoT* fan and a Gillard voter, the events described in this essay seemed, at the time, to be a fairly heavy-handed attempt to resonate with the Australian electorate. Only in retrospect have I come to appreciate Gillard's astute embrace of the *GoT* universe to broaden the international discussion about women's leadership. When *GoT* was gaining international acclaim in 2013, Gillard's fannish conversation with *Guardian Australia* laid the groundwork for the media and her constituents to draw—hopefully affirming—parallels between herself and Daenerys Targaryen. Across 2014 and 2015, Gillard's television reviews for *The Guardian* highlighted the powerful women of Westeros to encourage her fellow fans to think beyond the series and consider the lack of latitude bestowed upon 21st-century women leaders. As Australia's first female prime minister harnessed popular culture on her own terms, the imaginative possibilities offered by the fictional realm of Westeros became a site of resistance against misogyny in contemporary politics. However, the transformation Daenerys Targaryen undertook—from benevolent emancipator to ruthless, vindictive monarch—during the 2019 season finale makes it seem likely that no politician will ever purposefully channel this character again.

NOTE

1. The textual complexity of this phrase stems from Tod Browning's controversial film *Freaks* (1932): a conniving able-bodied trapeze artist becomes frightened when her fellow sideshow performers chant, "We accept her. One of us! One of us!" upon her sham marriage to the little person Hans.

WORKS CITED

Bader, Jordan (@JordanBader1). "Julia Gillard Confirms She Is Addicted to Game of Thrones. ONE OF US! ONE OF US! #gameofthrones" *Twitter* 27 May 2013, 1:40 a.m.

Barry, Doug. "Australian PM Julia Gillard Backs House Targaryen, Because Dragons." *Jezebel*, 28 May 2013. https://jezebel.com/australian-pm-julia-gillard-backs-house-targaryen-beca-510056579.

Bastow, Clem. "Let the Game Begin." *Big Issue Australia*, vol. 541, 2017, pp. 14–17.

Boulton, Adam. "I Can See Why Politicians Love Game of Thrones." *Telegraph*, 18 April 2015. https://www.telegraph.co.uk/culture/tvandradio/game-of-thrones/11545259/I-can-see-why-politicians-love-Game-of-Thrones.html.

Carlyon, Patrick. 2013. "Sheer Treachery and Delusion: The Kev and Julia Show." *Sunday Herald Sun*, September 8. Factiva Database.

Clapton, William, and Laura J. Shepherd. "Lessons from Westeros: Gender and Power in *Game of Thrones*." *Politics*, vol. 37, no. 1, 2017, pp. 5–18.

D'Arcens, Louise, and Clare Monagle. "Mad Monks and the Order of the Tin Ear: The Medievalism of Abbott's Australia." *Meanjin* vol. 74, no. 4, 2015, pp. 106–113.

Frankel, Valerie. *Women in* Game of Thrones: *Power, Conformity and Resistance.* Jefferson: McFarland, 2014.

Gillard, Julia (@JuliaGillard). ".@JordanBader1 Not addicted—me allayafa anna! #gameofthrones JG." 27 May 2013, 7:01 a.m.

_____. "*Game of Thrones* Has Parallels with My Time as Australian Prime Minister." *Guardian*, 7 April 2014. https://www.theguardian.com/tv-and-radio/2014/apr/07/game-of-thrones-parallels-prime-minister.

_____. "Julia Gillard on *Game of Thrones* Series Five: 'Enjoy, Carefully.'" *Guardian*, 13 April 2015. https://www.theguardian.com/tv-and-radio/2015/apr/14/julia-gillard-on-game-of-thrones-series-five-enjoy-carefully.

Gjelsvik, Anne, and Rikke Schubart, eds. *Women of Ice and Fire: Gender,* Game of Thrones *and Multiple Media Engagements.* New York: Bloomsbury, 2016.

Grattan, Michelle. "Rudd Wins the Game of Thrones." *The Conversation*, 26 June 2013. https://theconversation.com/rudd-wins-the-game-of-thrones-15573.

Hassler-Forest, Dan. "*Game of Thrones*: Quality Television and the Cultural Logic of Gentrification." *TV/Series*, vol. 6, 2014, pp. 160–177.

Hopewell, Luke. "Julia Gillard Is a Big *Game of Thrones* Fan." *Gizmodo*, 27 May 2013. https://www.gizmodo.com.au/2013/05/julia-gillard-is-a-big-game-of-thrones-fan/.

Hughes, Sarah. "*Game of Thrones*: Would You Join Julia Gillard in House Targaryen?" *Guardian*, 27, May 2013. https://www.theguardian.com/tv-and-radio/australia-culture-blog/2013/may/27/game-of-thrones-gillard-targaryen.

Jokovich, Eddy. "Once Upon a Time in Canberra…" *Armedia*, 18 July 2013. https://www.armedia.net.au/once-upon-a-time-in-canberra.

"Julia Gillard: Khaleesi?" *YouTube*, uploaded by Channel Ten. 28 May 2013. https://www.youtube.com/watch?v=jsDpX7YGwbA.

Kenny, Mark, and Jacqueline Maley. "Candidates and Hopefuls Line Up for the *Game of Thrones*." *Sydney Morning Herald*, 27 April 2013. https://www.smh.com.au/politics/federal/candidates-and-hopefuls-line-up-for-the-game-of-thrones-20130426-2ikll.html.

Lind, Dara. "Vox Sentences: Australia Is Basically Turning into a Real-Life *Game of Thrones*." *Vox*, 14 September 2015. https://www.vox.com/2015/9/14/9327159/malcolm-turnbull-vox-sentences.

MacNeil, Kate. "Torrenting *Game of Thrones*: So Wrong and Yet So Right." *Convergence*, vol. 23, no. 5, 2017, pp. 545–562.

McDermott, Jim. "Gillard's *Game of Thrones*." *Eureka Street*, vol. 23, no. 6, 2013, p. 24.

Oswald, Anjelica. "Thanks to 'Game of Thrones,' Khaleesi Is a Now More Popular Baby Name Than Sophia or Jane," *Business Insider Australia*, 8 July 2016. https://www.insider.com/game-of-thrones-inspires-baby-names-2016-7.

Stevenson, Ana. "Making Gender Divisive: 'Post-Feminism,' Sexism and Media Representations of Julia Gillard." *Burgmann Journal*, vol. 1, no. 2, 2013, pp. 53–66.

Sweney, Mark. "Guardian Australia Launches with Promise of 'Fresh and Independent View,'" *Guardian*, 26 May 2013. https://www.theguardian.com/media/2013/may/26/guardian-australia-launch-julia-gillard.

Taylor, Lenore. "Julia Gillard Reveals *Game of Thrones* Addiction," *Guardian*, 26 May 2013. https://www.theguardian.com/world/2013/may/26/julia-gillard-game-of-thrones.

_____. "Julia Gillard's Dothraki Tweets Translated." *Guardian*, 28 May 2013. https://www.theguardian.com/politics/australia-culture-blog/2013/may/29/julia-gillard-dothraki-language.

Taylor, Lenore, Christian Bennett, and Oliver Laughland. "Julia Gillard on *Game of Thrones*: A Vote for the Khaleesi—video." *Guardian*, 26 May 2013. https://www.theguardian.com/world/video/2013/may/26/julia-gillard-game-of-thrones-video.

Trimble, Linda. *Ms. Prime Minister: Gender, Media, and Leadership.* Toronto: University of Toronto Press, 2017.

Wilson, Jason. "Kevin Rudd, Celebrity and Audience Democracy in Australia." *Journalism*, vol. 15, no. 2, 2014, pp. 202–217.

Wood, Matthew, Jack Corbett, and Matthew Flinders. "Just Like Us: Everyday Celebrity Politicians and the Pursuit of Popularity in an Age of Anti-Politics." *British Journal of Politics and International Relations*, vol. 18, no. 3, 2016, pp. 581–598.

Come from Away

Resistance in the 2017 Film Wonder Woman

MARY F. PHARR

For women, the need to resist is surely a natural response to the massive social mores that demand female obedience in a supposed man's world. For much of history, women without the luxury of wealth or position were expected (and not just by men) to accept their secondary position on Earth and (presumably) in eternity. Since men were usually physically stronger than women, ipso facto, men were superior in other ways as well. The roles of birthing and nurturing other humans were necessary for the survival of the species—but not, apparently, significant enough to give women equal stature to men. In 1776 when Thomas Jefferson boldly asserted that a set of American colonies had the right to break away from their English rulers, he justified America's rebellion by claiming, "All men are created equal" (U.S. Declaration of Independence, 2nd para.). Jefferson's remarkable paean to the rights of man does not mention any rights of woman. Only when the Industrial Revolution had progressed enough to indicate a gradual shift of power from the physical to the technological did various women's movements find the internal and external means to demand recognition of their basic human rights.

More often than not, the demand for recognition had to be backed by the action of resistance. In 1956, Rosa Parks changed history by refusing to give up her seat to a white man on a Montgomery, Alabama, bus. Parks said later that she was not too physically tired to give up her seat; she "was tired of giving in" (qtd. in Wood).[1] By refusing to obey an inappropriate demand, Parks became an emblem of resistance for women of every color. Yet more than 60 years after Parks' defiant act, resistance remains a necessary response to gender injustice. The movement toward worldwide gender equality continues to be a grindingly slow process, meaning that for untold masses of women, equality is still a concept come from away rather than a human birthright.

Ironically, the creation of the Amazonian comic-book heroine Wonder Woman itself reflects this "come from away" concept. Although initially drawn by artist Harry G. Peter, the character of Wonder Woman was actually created and written by William Moulton Marston (under the pen name Charles Moulton) in 1941. Marston was not a particularly successful psychologist, but he did contribute significantly to the development of a functional polygraph machine, a somewhat ironic accomplishment given that Marston himself has been described by Jill Lepore as someone who "loved nothing so much as fantasy" (315). He was, however, also committed to improving the 20th century's perception of capable women, perhaps because he was equally committed to his wife, Elizabeth Holloway Marston, and to their mutual life partner, Olive Byrne. By all accounts, this unconventional polyamorous family arrangement worked well. After Marston's death in 1947, Elizabeth and Olive remained together for decades separated at the end only by their own mortality. As depicted in Lepore's book *The Secret History of Wonder Woman* (2014) and (less successfully) in the biopic *Professor Marston and the Wonder Women* (2017), Marston's determination to walk a line between the mores of the world he lived in and the possibilities of the world he saw embodied in the women of his household suggests both the potential and the tension inherent in Wonder Woman—a role model for girls created by a not entirely liberated man who yet loved and was loved by two remarkably liberated women.

If Marston's home was something of an island of resistance in an ocean of conventional relationships, the character he created for DC Comics was also, from the beginning, a paradoxical figure of resistance. After being hired by National Periodicals (later to evolve into DC) as a consultant, Marston suggested (apparently at the urging of his wife) that the company develop a female superhero. That hero proved to be Marston's own creation: Diana, Princess of Themyscira. Better known in popular culture as Wonder Woman of Paradise Island, Diana first appeared in *All-Star Comics* in late 1941. Like all comic book superheroes, Wonder Woman has a curious in-story origin: she is not born from the womb; instead, she comes to life (through the power of Zeus) as a child sculpted from clay by Hippolyta, Queen of the Amazons. With such an origin, Diana is destined to be extraordinary, but her gender makes her even more extraordinary: it allows her to be compassionate without fear of looking weak even when she enters the male-dominated world.

The early comic book version of the adult Wonder Woman also focused—not infrequently—on episodes of bondage and whippings. In his essay for Lupoff's and Thompson's classic *All in Color for a Dime* (1970), Jim Harmon goes so far as to call the environment in which the early Wonder Woman stories were set "a very sick scene" (192). As an older woman who still remembers the America of 1970, I find myself thinking that Harmon's essay implicitly says as much about the often-confused gender expectations of men in the early '70s as it does about Marston's personal vision of strong women in 1941. Marston himself insisted that the *Wonder Woman* comic book "was a form of feminist propaganda" (Lepore 220). In a press release Marston ghost wrote, he announced that "Dr. William Moulton Marston, internationally famous psychologist and inventor of the widely-publicized 'Lie Detector Test,'" had just created a female hero "to combat the idea that women are inferior to men..." ("Noted Psychologist Revealed as Author," qtd. in Lepore 220). The irony in a male-created female role model seems not to have concerned Marston—but he did understand that women needed an emblem of female resistance to the evils prevalent in a male-dominated world.

As a new superhero, Wonder Woman quickly became a major figure in the DC canon. Granted, the character never really challenged the primacy of the top male heroes: Superman and Batman. For example, while neither Supes nor Bats bothered joining the original Justice Society of America (DC's predecessor to today's Justice League of America), Wonder Woman served a seemingly endless term as the JSA's secretary without (as far as I know) complaining about the sexist implications. Yet while male JSA characters like Sandman, Doctor Fate, Hourman, Doctor Mid-Nite, and Starman are only occasionally referenced in the apparently infinite permutations of the modern DC universe, Wonder Woman has continued to be showcased in DC publications for more than 75 years. She remains a fantasy, yes, but also an inspiration for girls who want to be both good and hard-hitting. Retaining her status among so many male superheroes—and among their mostly male writers, artists, fans, and critics—has never been easy, however. In 1954 she was condemned as a lesbian in Frederic Wertham's reactionary denunciation of the comic book industry, *Seduction of the Innocent*. Happily, the industry and Wonder Woman both survived the overwrought controversy Wertham created. In 1968 DC executives tried (rather belatedly) to bring Diana into the Swinging Sixties by first letting her surrender her superpowers, then having her exchange her Amazonian costume for a mod outfit clearly influenced by the wildly popular BritTV character Emma Peel (*The Avengers* 1961–1969). No longer associated with Paradise Island, the mod Diana (guided by a blind martial arts master) used her newly honed kung fu skills to fight evil by kicking the crap out of bad guys in the name of peace. But mod Diana Prince was not nearly as intriguing as Princess Diana of Paradise Island. When DC eventually returned its signature heroine to an updated version of her old Wonder Woman costume and her old powers, I, for one, was glad that Diana's birthright had been confirmed.

Interpretations of Wonder Woman on television also varied in both quality and fidelity when compared to Marston's original. In 1974, ABC presented a pilot starring Cathy Lee Crosby as a blond Diana Prince with a predilection for jumpsuits. It was not bad TV; it just lacked audience appeal, presumably because it essentially deleted the wonder from the woman in question. A year later, ABC premiered a far more traditional (and appropriately cast) *Wonder Woman* starring Lynda Carter, who looked like the comic book Diana, right down to the skimpy but patriotic uniform. This time, the series lasted from 1975 to 1979—not quite a major hit but still a clear reminder that Marston's concept of a female superhero defying evil still held appeal.

In America, of course, success on film still holds sway over success on television (just think about the different audience response to the Oscars and the Emmys). Princess or not, only when Diana conquered the silver screen could she really be said to be media royalty. In 2016, Israeli actress Gal Gadot made her first appearance as Wonder Woman in a supporting role in Zac Snyder's *Batman v Superman: Dawn of Justice*. Snyder said he cast Gadot because she projects a "combination of being fierce but kind at the same time..." (qtd. in Pringle). In a similar vein, after Patty Jenkins' *Wonder Woman* film came out, Andrew Barker's review noted that "a huge factor in [the film's] ability to convey a note of inherent goodness lies in Gadot, whose visage radiates dew-eyed empathy and determination—and whose response to the iniquity of human nature isn't withdrawn cynicism but rather outrage" (*Variety*). Gadot is certainly the most convincing Princess Diana I have seen. To begin with, she bears a strong physical resemblance to the comic book character. More importantly, Gadot's performance consistently conveys a sense of the character's appealing combination of naïveté, courage, and strength. Finally, she is literally "come from away" but still serves as an emblem of hope for "man's world" when it is caught in a conflict that has already injured or killed millions.

Set during World War I in Europe, the film emphasizes the resolve with which Gadot's Princess Diana resists evil in the physical form of her half-brother, Ares, the god of war; however, both the film's script and its visuals make clear that the evil is also inherent in the particularly twisted nature of World War I itself—the "war to end all war"—that set historical lows for its lack of justifiable cause, its technological horror, and its human waste. According to the *Chronicle of the World*, during World War I "a whole generation of men was lost, and future generations were blighted as a result" (1072). Even now, it's hard to explain with any certainty just why the War happened. Fantasizing an angry god seems as sensible as all the usual political reasons.

The use of Ares as the ultimate villain both in and beyond the War also makes sense against his half-sister's role as the ultimate hero: a universe precariously balanced between male violence and female resistance to the ultimate cause of that violence. In the film's most famous scene, Diana literally—and symbolically—crosses the dreaded No Man's Land between the armies of the Allies and the Axis on a mission to rescue the hapless residents of a village called Veld. While doing so, she faces a torrent of machine-gun fire, which she deflects with her bracelets and her shield—Amazonian symbols of feminine strength and endurance. The crossing is the moment when Diana is first seen in man's world doing something extraordinary on behalf of ordinary humans. Although this crossing scene was apparently difficult for everyone but Jenkins to envision before it was shot, it is impossible to forget once seen—a triumph of active female opposition to the horrendous obstacles inherent in male-created warfare and (in a different sense) in male-dominated filmmaking.

Of course, the film's chronology does not begin with Diana's defiance of the Great War. The narrative opens with a brief, elegant prelude set in 21st-century Paris. In a voiceover, Diana explains that "I used to want to save the world. This beautiful place. But I knew so little then." She goes on to say, "What one does when faced with the truth is more difficult than you think. I learned this the hard way. A long time ago. And now.... I will never be the same" (*WW* 2017). With these few words, the audience begins to empathize with the title character, a hero whose reflections on her own limitations make her immediately sympathetic to her innately fallible viewers. Visually, of course, Diana Prince is another matter: utterly chic and apparently timeless. In contemporary Europe, while working as a curator of antiquities at the Louvre, Ms. Prince receives a delivery from Bruce Wayne: a package containing an old monochrome photo that shows four soldiers and Wonder Woman (her star-spangled costume partially covered by a great cloak) standing amid a village's war-created rubble. It is this picture that takes Diana (and us) back to her past. Ironically, the scene in which the World War I photographer takes the photograph of Captain Steve Trevor's team was shot on the first day of the movie's principal shooting. Producer Deborah Snyder recalls the day "as a passing of the torch" from *Batman v Superman* to the Wonder Woman origin film (qtd. in Gosling 166). Batman's indirect but significant input in *Wonder Woman* also heralded the *Justice League* movie that came out (to much less critical acclaim) later in 2017. Like its rival Marvel Studios, DC is clearly creating a cinematic universe of intertwined heroes and villains to keep its audience involved in an increasingly complex narrative.

One of *Wonder Woman*'s narrative strengths is that while it refuses to ignore the dark side of reality, it also presents a clear awareness of the existential need to believe that something can be done to change or at least ameliorate that grim reality. In a remarkably effective early flashback structure, Diana's childhood is shown, with the only dissension on the Island seeming to come from the arguments between her mother and her aunt over just how intense Diana's warrior training should be. Eventually, Hippolyta explains the Amazons' origin to her daughter so that she will understand "that war is nothing to hope for" (*WW*). Hippolyta tells the young Princess that after

Zeus created beings in his image for the gods to oversee, his son Ares grew jealous of the new beings and "turned them against one another" so that "war ravaged the Earth" (*WW*). In response, the gods created the Amazons "to restore peace." But Ares' followers enslaved the Amazons. With the encouragement of Zeus and the other gods, Hippolyta led a revolt to free her people. In response, Ares killed all his fellow gods. But just before he died, Zeus wounded Ares enough to make him retreat. Zeus also left the Amazons the Godkiller (supposedly a sword so strong it might even slay a god) and the island Themyscira. Given this history, Diana's hard training seems justified—enough so that between heritage and training, Diana's "might makes sense" (Williams).

Years later, in a neat reversal of traditional romantic meetings, her training also comes in handy when Diana rescues AEF pilot Steve Trevor from the sea. Very soon, however, all of the other Amazons must also prove their mettle in an extraordinary defense made with spear and shield, bow and arrow against invading German soldiers with guns. Her Aunt Antiope's death during this battle is a significant factor in Diana's subsequent realization that she must do something about the evil that has engulfed the world beyond Themyscira. After the battle, Hippolyta uses the magic Lasso of Hestia to force Steve to explain why the Germans followed him to Themyscira. Admitting that he is an American spy assigned to British Intelligence, Steve tells the Themyscirians that he stole Dr. Maru's notebook from a lab he found in a secret military installation in Turkey and then flew off in a German Fokker—only to be shot down near their secret island. Of course, the notion of an isolated idyllic society is a staple of utopian fiction, not just in Thomas More's *Utopia* but also in the Shangri-La of *Lost Horizon* and the island of Bali Hai in *South Pacific*. While it may be that most people feel "there's no place like home," most people also sometimes wish there were.

Fearing that the corruptibility of men could disrupt the safety and well-being of her Island, Hippolyta is unwilling to interfere in human affairs. But against her mother's will, Diana decides to join Steve in the war that she believes Ares controls. Although Steve does not press Diana to join the fight, he does admit that his father told him, "You see something happening in the world, you can either do nothing, or you can do something." And then (making the audience love him), Steve hastens to add, "And I already tried nothing." Despite her mother's admonition against leaving the Island, Diana, in her initial act of resistance, decides that she, too, will do something. After telling Hippolyta, "If no one else will defend the world against Ares, I must," Diana takes the Godkiller and leaves with Steve (*WW*).

This journey to action initially promises to be a crusade for justice, but it's actually presented as something closer to a journey of self-discovery, an odyssey wherein Diana confirms both her heritage and her independence.

The odyssey succeeds cinematically not only because of the film's exceptionally good cast and direction but also because the script mercifully includes unexpected touches of humor. Sometimes the humor is, paradoxically, both obvious and subtle. As they sail from Themyscira to England, Steve tries to explain just how bad this particular war is. Calling it a "great big mess," he adds that "there's not a whole lot you and I can do about that. We can get back to London and try to get the men who can" (*WW*). Diana's response is immediate: "I'm the man who can!" (*WW*). The line is funny and touching, but it also notes just how much of a foreigner Diana is: she has no sense of value determined by gender. If we refer to all humans as "mankind," why not refer to a female warrior as a man?

Some of the best moments in the film are connected to Diana and Steve's discovery of each other. There's almost a fairy tale quality involved here. For example, the night voyage from Themyscira to England lets the audience see the couple's mutual sexual attraction while still keeping the film's visuals and dialogue true to the PG-13 rating required for the widest theatrical release and largest audience possible. Despite their "above average" looks and intelligence, despite their exceptional skills as warriors, both Diana and Steve evince a charming diffidence when they talk about the very different societies that gave them their values. When Steve explains the concept of marriage to Diana, she asks if married couples really do love each other "until death"; Steve's nervous response is "Not very often"—which just confuses them both (*WW*). Then when he asks about her father and she explains her "sculpted from clay" origin, he can think of nothing more profound to say than "Well, that's neat" (*WW*). However odd the situation may be, it's a great romantic setup.

As if to remind the audience that the movie is about more than romance, the scene shifts to German-occupied Belgium, where the two characters who serve as polar opposites to Steve and Diana plot against peace in favor of war at its most inhumane. General Ludendorff mourns the likely approach of peace, until his favorite mad scientist, the disfigured Dr. Maru restores his vitality with some kind of amphetamine-like gas; it makes him feel stronger but also destroys what shreds of sanity he once had. Pleased by what she has done for Ludendorff, Maru (whose ruined face is apparently the result of an earlier experiment) exultantly declares that she has now come up with something else that's "going to be terrible" (*WW*).

Patty Jenkins has noted that Ludendorff is the only one in the movie "based on a real historical figure," who "genuinely believed that war was humanity's natural state" (qtd. in Gosling 142). Maru (better known by her nickname, Dr. Poison) is a character from the World War II-era *Wonder Woman* stories. While both villains seem melodramatic, 20th-century history includes even worse real-life villains: e.g., Adolf Hitler and Dr. Mengele.

Diana blames Ares for the War and its horrors, but the introduction of Luden-dorff and Maru remind the audience that humanity is quite capable of creating its own horrors.

Once in London, Diana is amazed at its pollution but delighted by a glimpse of a baby (the first she's ever seen). With the help of Etta Candy, Steve's secretary, Diana finds "suitable" clothes and even dons a pair of prescription-free spectacles. Despite being sartorially encumbered, the Amazonian (with a bit of help from Steve) still easily fends off a street attack by Ludendorff's minions, who are seeking Maru's notebook. Clothes, apparently, do not unmake the Woman. But they do seem to limit her influence in a War Office council, where Sir Patrick Morgan argues for peace even as he accepts Dr. Poison's notebook, offering to share it with the War Cabinet. Despite the proof found in the notebook regarding a terrible new gas, the Cabinet decides to follow Sir Patrick's plan to negotiate an armistice. Knowing that Ares will allow neither negotiation nor surrender, Diana tells everyone present, "You should be ashamed" (*WW*). Beyond the immediate story, the male/female division in the World War I era is openly represented in this scene by the dozens of older white males brimming with authority at odds with one young female disgusted with them all. Even more crucially, the scene resonates beyond its own narrative, suggesting the disgust millions of unknown females must have felt through the millennia while trapped on the sidelines of "man's" history.

Yet the film is no diatribe against the male species. Too often, Wonder Woman adaptations have presented Steve as an amiable lightweight, but Chris Pine's Captain Trevor is something more: handsome and charming, yes, but (like Diana herself) also utterly focused on resisting an evil that threatens the entire world. So, when the Council ignores the threat of the new gas, Steve assures the angry Amazon that despite his orders to do nothing, they are going to do something. On the way to the Front, they team up with a few of Steve's less respectable but more reliable cohorts. Meanwhile, Ludendorff has used Maru's terrible new death gas to assassinate the German generals who want to negotiate peace. High on Maru's "other" gas, he now plans a demonstration of the effects of the death gas so that the Kaiser will know Germany can still win the war.

With all the major players in front-line Belgium, Diana discovers the horrors of trench warfare. The German army is just two hundred yards away in another string of trenches, but Diana becomes fixated on the plight of a young mother from the village Veld, now enslaved by invading Germans. When Steve explains the concept of "No Man's Land" to her, she remains adamant about helping Veld. Frustrated, Steve tells her, "We can't save everyone in this war. This is not what we came here to do"; "No," she replies, "but it's what I'm going to do" (*WW*). Uncloaked, Princess Diana of Themyscira becomes Wonder Woman and—followed by Allied soldiers—conquers No Man's Land. Metaphorically, this scene is the perfect emblem of female resistance to the ultimate folly that is male-created war. It also confirms the revitalization of Marston's superhero. Referencing both Gadot and Pine, A.O. Scott refers to the movie as "a star vehicle all the way" (rev.), but it's not just the actors, nor even the actors along with director and writers, who are the stars. It's also the cinematographers, the effects specialists, the stunt people, the sound team, the location finders, the prop specialists, the costume designers, the support crew—pretty much the entire company. And in this single action scene, they set their place in cinematic history.

Nothing else in the film is likely to be remembered as much as the crossing of No Man's Land, but the liberation of Veld and the culmination of the heroes' relationship humanize the narrative, making it not just Diana's story but also Steve's. Reviewer Justin Chang has observed that "the real pleasure, and novelty" of the film "is in the delicacy with which Jenkins teases out the love story at the movie's core…" (rev. *LA Times*). Even though Steve and Diana were attracted to each other on first sight, Steve must still win his girl's respect. By using Amazonian battle tactics to help the Princess destroy a sniper's nest in a bell tower, Captain Trevor proves that he is a soldier Hippolyta herself would respect—a worthy partner for the Queen's daughter. For a few hours after this small victory, everyone is happy. A photographer takes the picture that will galvanize Diana's memory a hundred years later, and Veld prepares to celebrate its liberation. But the war is always present. On the field phone, Steve learns that Ludendorff and Maru will soon attend a gala at the nearby headquarters of the German High Command. He's also warned by Sir Patrick not to jeopardize the "peace accord." At this moment Diana has a revelation: Ludendorff, that most warlike of German generals, must be Ares in disguise. War or not, however, the celebration goes on, and that night, Steve and Diana dance while Diana experiences snow for the first time in her life. So, when the couple finds a private room in which to share a romantic embrace, the scene cuts off, and the PG-13 rating remains undisturbed.

To me, the German gala sequence seems a bit too reminiscent of the "corrupt rich folks'" bashes so common in 007 movies to work as well as the earlier scene depicting the "decent poor folks'" party held in Veld. Disguised as a German officer, Steve tries for that longest of long shots: to charm Dr. Maru into revealing something about her work. But when he inadvertently gapes at Diana as she enters the gala in a stolen dress that fits as if it were designed only for the Princess, Maru loses interest. Diana fares no better when she approaches Ludendorff, who assures her that "war gives man purpose, meaning"—words that convince Diana she is dancing with Ares (*WW*). But before she can assassinate Ludendorff, they are interrupted, and Steve reminds her that their immediate mission is to find the gas Maru has been developing. The noise of a rocket going off pulls everyone outside, where they see a projectile headed toward Veld. Ludendorff has deployed the gas in hopes of delaying peace. Veld is—as so often happens in war—just unlucky.

Diana alone is immune to the poison gas. In a surreal scene that stretches the PG-13 rating to its limits, she walks in horror through the gas, through the dead town that she thought she had saved from the worst of the war. Coming out of the death zone, she finds Steve, but when he reaches for her, she pushes him away, blaming him for not letting her kill Ares. Hysterical with horror, Diana berates not just the God of War but also all mankind: "It isn't just the Germans he's corrupted; it's you too. All of you" (*WW*). There's no special emphasis given to this condemnation in the movie, but it resonates with the truth about war: it ruins not just those who are inherently evil but also all too often those who started out good.

Driven beyond reason, Diana finds Ludendorff and—despite his use of Maru's mad gas—she kills him, all the while thinking she is killing Ares. This moment of supposed triumph is actually proof of Wonder Woman's own fallibility. She has made a double error: mistaking Ludendorff for Ares and thinking that Ares alone is the cause of World War I. Steve has to tell her that human beings are themselves responsible for the war, and in her disillusionment, she says that "people don't deserve our help" (*WW*). Desperate, Steve pleads with her: "It's not about deserve.… It's about what you believe" (*WW*). But moving from the extreme idealism she first felt about humanity to complete disillusionment, Diana abandons Steve's cause. After Steve leaves to try and stop the release of the poison gas without Amazonian help, Diana is confronted by Sir Patrick, whom she suddenly recognizes as the true Ares. Seeing her disillusionment with humanity, Ares expects Diana to join him; instead, she tries to use the Godkiller sword against him, but he simply destroys it with a flick of his hand. And in what is surely the most chilling line in the entire movie, Ares tells Diana that she is the real Godkiller, the daughter Zeus left as a weapon that could one day be used against Ares. Ironically, Ares now expects Diana to join him in wiping out mankind, thus returning the Earth to a paradise fit for the gods. In his confident attempt to convert Diana to his side, Ares seems to me to prove rather that he is not the most perceptive of gods. He has let Diana live among and even love the beings he now wants her to destroy. Unsurprisingly, she refuses to join his cause, and so he tries to destroy her, but like most males, he underestimates female resistance. However naïve Diana may be, she is inherently resolute when it comes to protecting others. And so, after her lover has sacrificed himself in the air to save thousands of lives by destroying the poison gas bomb high in the atmosphere, she fights her brother to save millions more. Steve dies a true hero, while Diana lives out her destiny as the Godkiller, destroying Ares like an avenging angel to finish Steve's mission. And humanity stumbles on, imperfect but still alive.

Scriptwriter Heinberg, director Jenkins, and actress Gadot all seem to interpret Wonder Woman as a model of feminine resistance to the temptations of individual hubris and hegemonic power. And whenever I view this film, I find myself wishing that in these tumultuous times we had a real Wonder Woman to balance out the scales of justice. But if we cannot always rely on powerful heroes, we can still find small but meaningful ways to resist injustice—not merely against women but also against all creatures great and small. Meanwhile, the cinematic Wonder Woman is slated for at least two sequels, although it's impossible to tell if the follow-up films will sustain the grace of the first movie's Diana. Still, if these films make Wonder Woman more and more relevant in contemporary culture, they may bring a few of Diana's values—come from away, remember—into our world as well. That in itself would be a fine act of resistance.

NOTE

1. Rosa Parks is the most famous example of this specific Civil Rights era type of resistance; however, it was 15-year-old Claudette Colvin who is noted at the first to resist giving up a seat for a white person on a Montgomery city bus, in March 1955, several months prior to Parks.

WORKS CITED

Barker, Andrew. "Film Review: *Wonder Woman*." *Variety*, 24 May 2017. https://variety.com/2017/film/reviews/film-review-wonder-woman-1202446320/.
Chang, Justin, *Wonder Woman* Movie Review." *LA Times*, 31 May 2017. https://www.latimes.com/entertainment/movies/93460203-132.html.
Chronicle of the World. Ed. Jerome Burne. Paris: Jacques Legrand, 1989.
Gosling, Sharon. *Wonder Woman: The Art and Making of the Film*. Titan Books, 217.
Harmon, Jim. "A Swell Bunch of Guys." *All in Color for a Dime*, edited by Dick Lupoff and Don Thompson, Arlington House, 1970, pp. 171–97.
Lepore, Jill. *The Secret History of Wonder Woman*. 2014. Vintage Books-Penguin Random House, 2015.
Pringle, Gill. "Some Kind of Wonderful." *Filmlink*, 5 Jan. 2016. https://www.filmink.com.au/some-kind-of-wonderful/.
Professor Marston and the Wonder Women, directed by Angela Robinson, Annapurna Pictures, 2017.
Scott, A.O. "Review: 'Wonder Woman Is a Blockbuster That Lets Itself Have Fun." *New York Times*, 31 May 2017. https://www.nytimes.com/2017/05/31/movies/wonder-woman-review-gal-gadot.html.
Williams, Zoe. "Why *Wonder Woman* Is a Masterpiece of Subversive Feminism." *The Guardian*, 5 Jun. 2017. https://www.theguardian.com/lifeandstyle/2017/jun/05/why-wonder-woman-is-a-masterpiece-of-subversive-feminism.
Wonder Woman, directed by Patty Jenkins, screenplay by Allan Heinberg, performances by Gal Gadot and Chris Pine, Warner Bros., 2017.
Wood, Jennifer M. "15 Inspiring Quotes from Rosa Parks." *Mental Floss*, 4 Feb. 2018. http://mentalfloss.com/article/91801/15-inspiring-quotes-rosa-parks.

"We are the spark that will light the fire"

Hope, the Cyclical Pattern of Resistance and Concrete Dystopia in Disney's The Last Jedi

ANNIKA GONNERMANN

An original 1980 poster for *Star Wars V: The Empire Strikes Back* sold in an August 2018 auction for a whopping $26,400 (Spiegel). This makes it one of the most expensive collectible movie posters ever sold, adding to *Star Wars'* impressive list of records. Holding at least 10 records, among them "highest box-office film gross by a science-fiction film series" and "most valuable movie franchise" (Swatman), *Star Wars* constitutes an unprecedented pop cultural phenomenon and for the time being, stands as the "most influential science fiction film[s] in history" (Booker 109). The story continues to lure fans into the cinema, thriving on George Lucas' successful postmodern pastiche compiled of "culturally inherited myths and symbols synonymous with the very roots of western civilisation" such as the ever-present David vs. Goliath narrative, depicting the fight between a small, under-equipped rebellion movement and a hegemonic Empire (Geraghty 191).

Having been a fan myself ever since my parents took me to see *Episode I: The Phantom Menace* in 1999 when I was eight years old, my analysis builds on the premise that the underdog narrative thread is *the* defining hallmark of the entire franchise. Every trilogy initiates a new story arc of rebellion thriving on the characters' hopes for a better future, sometimes even explicitly repeating and recycling motives, plots, and topoi of earlier movies. While some of the success of the franchise surely has to do with the spectacular visual effects and likeable characters, I argue that it is *Star Wars'* continued alliance with *hope* as a narrative device that secures its position as a long-standing and instrumental popular media franchise on and off screen. I argue that the films are so successful because they have monetized the fundamental character trait of humanity: the need and ability to hope for a better world. According to Ernst Bloch, hope resonates within every human being, thereby identifying it as a universal point of reference for global audiences (3). While evil, hope, and non-acceptance of the status quo do of course feature in many popular narratives (J.R.R. Tolkien's *The Lord of the Rings* and J.K. Rowling's *Harry Potter*), *Star Wars* installs the concept of hope at the heart of its narrative like no other, making sure to never run low on the urge for creating a better world. I am therefore going to examine the concept of hope, its connection to the motif of rebellion, and the influence of its presence in the series, focusing on the penultimate film addition to the canon. *The Last Jedi* (2017) is yet the latest movie in a series of many that depicts the world on the brink of destruction. It can be read as a "concrete dystopia," presenting its audience the fate of the rebellion on a razor's edge.

In order to grasp the concept of the "concrete dystopia," it is vital to understand its counterpart—the "concrete utopia." German Marxist philosopher Ernst Bloch (1885–1977), known for his life-long dedication to the analysis of hope, works with this term in his opus magnum *The Principle of Hope* (1954–1959); Bloch claims that the desire for a better life is what distinguishes humans from animals, since only humans are capable of "throw[ing] themselves actively into what is becoming" (3). Therefore, hope and the necessity to strive for a better future are the defining impulse behind every aspect of human life—or, as Bloch states: "Nobody has ever lived without daydreams" (3). One of his most influential achievements is his elaborate analysis of a concept he calls "concrete utopia"—a term with which he tries to describe the positive potential the future holds at a given time. "Concrete utopias" in the Blochian sense are defined by a "Not-Yetness" (Thompson 34), i.e., their anticipatory nature, meaning that they signal that reality is not "a fixed, unchanging object of human inquiry [but rather a progress that] incorporates future possibilities" (Varsam 208). They denote a specific time frame—say a day, a week, or a month—during which a utopian dream is implementable in the here and now. German LGBTQ-activists might list the year 2017 as an example for a "concrete utopia," when debates were held about the legalizing of same-sex marriage. It is not simply wishful thinking—a process Bloch tried to capture by the term "abstract utopia"—but rather an actual, concrete option for social improvement. This opportunity is often created by revolutions—moments in time when people actively try to change the future for the better. Quoting from Bloch himself, Tom Moylan in his *Locus of Hope* (1982) gives examples for "concrete utopias," listing the Peasants' Revolt alongside the French and Russian Revolution, concluding with the events of 1968.

Moylan claims that these are moments in time when human hope reaches beyond the status quo, connecting the present "with the [future] potentiality within the world" (159). Revolutions, hence, are understood as opportunities to change human life for the better; inspired by the American Revolution, the French Revolution, for instance, resulted in the abolition of absolutism and coined the Western understanding of what it means to be human to this day by championing universal human rights. It can thus be rightfully evaluated as a concrete utopia, a moment in time when opportunity came to change history for the better (disregarding for a moment its more dystopian side effects like the Reign of Terror).

Just as there are concrete utopias, there exist concrete dystopias. Maria Varsam argues that both concepts share "an emphasis on the real, material conditions of society that manifest themselves as a result of humanity's desire for a better world" (208). They fundamentally differ, however, in terms of atmosphere and prospects for the future: "In opposition to concrete utopia, concrete dystopia designates those moments, events, institutions, and systems that embody and realize organized forces of violence and oppression. [...] Whereas concrete utopia is a manifestation of desire and hope for a better world and an 'unalienated order' that upsets that status quo, concrete dystopia delineates the crushing of hope and the displacement of desire for the purpose of upholding that status quo" (Varsam 209). The term concrete dystopia constitutes the opposite to the aspiring potential of concrete utopia and denotes exactly those moments in history when the situation is about to deteriorate, giving rise to oppression, violence, and a heightened societal climate of terror. It "delineates the crushing of hope" (Varsam 209), offering a glimpse at a dystopian future.

Combined with hope's universal appeal as diagnosed by Ernst Bloch, concrete dystopia offers audiences insight into the unprecedented success of *Star Wars*. Since hope is a universal need, it stands to reason that, broadly speaking, audiences around the world enjoy watching stories that feature hope as a central narrative device. Additionally, revolutions and rebellions constitute a handy narrative element, since they not only provide the necessary background for an action-packed and thrilling storyline, but also because they are propelled by the rebels' belief and hope in a better world. All three *Star Wars* trilogies are cases in point: they combine revolutions with hope and can all thus be classified as concrete utopias or concrete dystopias respectively, depending on which side is closer to gaining victory. Consequently, when focusing on the most recent *Star Wars* movie, one cannot fail to notice that *The Last Jedi* portrays a historical moment in time that can be adequately described by the term concrete dystopia for it displays a timeframe when the forces of oppression and violence seem to be gaining the upper hand.

It is noteworthy that *The Last Jedi* is in fact the movie with the shortest intradiegetic story time. While the earlier *Star Wars* movies usually span a fortnight or even more, most of *The Last Jedi* concentrates on six hours that determine the future of the entire galaxy, presenting the Rebels and the First Order in battle. *The Last Jedi* is thus the *Star Wars* movie closest to Bloch's theory, cultivating its potential and continuing the multi-million-dollar franchise. Throughout the two and a half hours of running time, the resistance movement is on razor's edge, closer to destruction than ever before. The audience witnesses an intergalactic life-or-death race between the First Order and the rebels, the latter running low on weapons and, what is worse, fuel. Indeed, it seems to be, in General Hux's words, "just a matter of time" until the First Order "snuff[s] out the Resistance once and for all" (*TLJ*). Both the characters and the audience are presented with the prospect of the final "crushing of hope and the displacement of desire for the purpose of upholding that status quo" (Varsam 209)—a concrete dystopia threatening to turn the entire galaxy into an authoritarian nightmare. Moreover, this set-up also generates tension and excitement for the audience members, who want to know how the movie will end: Will the Rebels be able to oppose the First Order, or will the authoritarian movement be victorious after all?

Indeed, the two forces fighting over the future of the galaxy could not be more different; while the Resistance strives to return to the Galaxy's democratic past, the First Order claims to bring civilization and order to the galaxy in the form of one-party rule. However, the audience knows that "order" and "civilization" are mere euphemisms for oppressive reign of terror. Or, as the bar owner Maz Kanata phrases it, "through the ages, I've seen evil take many forms. The Sith. The Empire. Today, it is the First Order. Their shadow is spreading across the galaxy. We must face them. Fight them" (*The Force Awakens*). The First Order thus descends directly from prior authoritarian systems that have already attempted to bring the galaxy under their control; the difference is that the First Order is the closest to achieving an unchallenged hegemony. Having depleted the Resistance to the very last "400 of [them] on three ships," the First Order "will control all the major systems within weeks" (*TLJ*) if they manage to eliminate the rest of the fleet.

Three times it looks as if the First Order might succeed, only to be detrimentally detained by desperate kamikaze-maneuvers by individual members of the resistance, most notably Vice Admiral Holdo's heroic decision to sacrifice herself by ramming one of the last remaining Resistance ships into a Star Destroyer. Despite her ultimate sacrifice, defeat seems inevitable. General Leia Organa is forced to concede that "the galaxy has lost all its hope. The spark is out" (*TLJ*). Metaphorically, hope is synonymous with fire, and consequently, defeat with quenching the flame. Moreover, Leia's metaphor for defeat is emphasized by the construction of space. The Rebel Alliance maintains an outpost on the desolate planet Crait. Its surface is covered in white salt and the texture and color of the mineral, as well as the ice-blue, crystalline appearance of the Vulptex, an indigenous canid, reminds the audience of ice, the opposite of fire. Indeed, the barren starkly colored landscape also likely reminds audiences of the planet Hoth, home of yet another Alliance base that saw a crippling battle with the then-named Galactic Empire. That imagery is further cemented as the First Order's General Hux describes the destruction of the Resistance as a "snuffing out." *Star Wars* thus employs a well-established metaphor, alluding to the passion and dedication of its members, the most important resource of the Resistance.

But of course, although the odds seem bleaker than ever, *Star Wars* cannot let the First Order win—in fact it could, but it is doubtful whether the fans would accept this. After all, *Star Wars* is a narrative of hope, of offering a way out, and of having the good ones win. The movies narrativize Bloch's claim, meaning that they use hope as a central device, which will ultimately promote victory, sooner or later. In fact, the moment of the rebels' almost defeat becomes the moment the Resistance is revived by giving them back hope. Turning the tide, Luke Skywalker appears to hold off the First Order's attack by dueling with Kylo Ren, which procures the surviving rebels enough time to flee: "The Rebellion is reborn today. The war is just beginning. And I will not be the last Jedi" (*TLJ*). The movie ends by foregrounding the renewed hope of the Rebellion; after all, Rey, the female protagonist of the recent trilogy, has risen above her status as an orphaned garbage collector to be the equal to the dark forces. Her unique position as an embodiment of hope is expressed through the same metaphor Leia used to describe defeat. Other characters comment on her "fiery spit of hope," most notably Supreme Leader Snoke, the tyrannical ruler of the First Order, to whom Rey refuses to capitulate. Rey thus becomes the very symbol of hope for the Resistance, metaphorically rekindling the spark, which Leia fears has been quenched. The metaphor of fire, heat, and burning thus links hope, Rey, and the resistance movement, establishing her as the driving force. While the rebels of course depend on massive supplies of weaponry, armor, food, and other bare necessities such as uniforms and fuel, their hope is the most important resource. It is what keeps them going in the face of their seemingly omnipotent enemy, the First Order. Without it, they would long have abandoned their suicidal mission, which has already killed so many of them.

While no movie has come closer to the total defeat of the resistance movement, all *Star Wars* movies thrive on the concept of hope as the central narrative device. And since hope and overcoming evil resonate deeply within us, the audience, because they strike a note within a universal human character. We enjoy stories that continue to satisfy this need to see a better future arise. The makers of *Star Wars* demonstrate a genuine understanding of Bloch's claim that hope is an emotional need nobody can live without. They, therefore, employ it excessively and turn it into the driving force behind the characters' actions.

This famously begins in the first movie of the franchise *Star Wars* (1977), later retitled *Star Wars—Episode IV: A New Hope* to fit the overall chronology. With the concept of hope added to the title, the movie starts in medias res, with then-Princess Leia's starship under attack by the Galactic Empire. At the last minute she manages to send an SOS message to Obi-Wan Kenobi: "I have placed information vital to the survival of the Rebellion into the memory systems of this R2 unit. [...] You must see this droid safely delivered to him on Alderaan. This is our most desperate hour. Help me, Obi-Wan Kenobi, you're my only hope" (*ANH*). It is, then, a plea for help that initiates the plot of *A New Hope* and thus Luke's journey away from Tatooine. Indeed, Leia gives her appeal more emphasis by calling Obi-Wan her "only hope," indicating the seriousness of the situation. Without explicit confirmation that Obi-Wan has received the message and with herself in captivity, Leia has only hope that the construction plans of the Death Star have safely arrived.

The entire existence of the Resistance, then, is closely connected to the concept of hope right from the start of the first trilogy. To emphasize this connection, the movie makes sure to replay Leia's final words, "Help me, Obi-Wan Kenobi, you're my only hope," four times in total (*ANH*). The message for both characters and viewers, however, becomes clear: the Rebellion has little to offer in opposition against the Galactic Empire—apart from hope, which becomes the defining force behind the narrative. Optimism against all odds and the desire for a better future away from the authoritarian terror regime nourishes the rebellion and brings the audience on board. After all, the film explicitly tells the audience where its loyalties should lie; the distribution of sympathy is firmly established from the start, introducing Darth Vader as the nicely identifiable villain in black armor and Princess Leia in her white dress as the pretty damsel in distress (Charles 285–287). The Rebellion's cause thus becomes the audience's cause by glorifying the rebels as a bunch of idealists and likeable heroes.

Hope in the Blochian sense of wishing for a better future, though, exists throughout the film franchise and often makes explicit connections from one episode to another. For example, Leia's holographic entreaty for help has become an iconic scene and is significant in the context of the recent *Star Wars* trilogy, starting with *Episode VII: The Force Awakens* (2015). It reappears in *Episode VIII: The Last Jedi*, linking both movies thematically. Set approximately 35 years after *A New Hope*, *The Last Jedi* initially presents the same "basic scenario: rebel forces are currently engaged in a civil war against '[an] evil Galactic Empire'" (Booker 110). In both films, Leia sends out messengers to allies, hoping for their help. Yet again, her hologram plays a crucial role: When Luke Skywalker refuses to enter the fight, R2-D2 replays Leia's original message in its entirety, ending again with "you are my only hope." Although Luke protests, claiming that this "was a cheap move" on R2-D2's part, the words resonate with both him and the audience (*TLJ*). The repetition of the scene helps to establish a thematic and structural connection between the two movies, both of which show the rebellion on the brink of failure. It demonstrates the repeated introduction of hope as a central force behind the rebellion and establishes it as its defining characteristic against all odds.

Moreover, the inclusion of the hologram-scene is not only useful in terms of narrative coherence, connecting the two movies thematically and chronologically; it invites the readers to abandon their reservations regarding the third trilogy. After all, many fans were afraid that Disney might ruin the "feel" of the franchise, turning it into a soulless money-printing machine (Child), a similar situation compared to when the second trilogy was released in 1999. Internet forums such as *Reddit* overflow with discussions about how and why Disney destroyed *Star Wars*. Even the renowned *Guardian* published a piece on that matter, pleading to get all of the coming *Star Wars* movies, sequels, and prequels "right," or "millions of voices will suddenly cry out in horror—and it will probably be several decades before they shut up" (Child). The re-introduction of the iconic scene is the production team's attempt of welcoming the old movies back while simultaneously trying to launch a new narrative 30 years later—or as it was phrased in an official statement released by Disney: "Rian Johnson, the cast, and the Lucasfilm team have delivered an experience that is totally *Star Wars* yet at the same time fresh, unexpected and new" (Sheperd). What constitutes a "*Star Wars* experience" is encompassed and transmitted by the concept of hope, a narrative stabilizer in the first trilogies, and consequently in the new one as well.

Hope for a better future, then, is what connects viewers watching on screen to the Resistance movement and the civilians in the galaxy, who although passive in terms of armed rebellion nevertheless wish for the end of the rule of tyranny exercised by the First Order. As the final shot of *The Last Jedi* demonstrates—showing an almost Dickensian nameless slave boy on the planet Cantonica wearing a ring emblazoned with the symbol of the Resistance—the movement is characterized by ordinary, often anonymous people wishing for a better future without the First Order. In Vice Admiral Holdo's words "in every corner of the Galaxy, the downtrodden and oppressed know [that] symbol and they put their hope in it" (*TLJ*). It is the exploited who are shown to be part of the Resistance in some way or another, be it the slave children of Canto Bight, or years earlier, the teddy bear-like Ewoks, whose forest moon the Empire invaded in *Episode VI: The Return of the Jedi* (1983). It is notable that both of these groups possess neither sufficient weaponry nor superior technological advancements to seriously threaten the galactic military superpower. The Ewoks famously attack the imperial stormtroopers with their slingshots, thereby explicitly repeating the David vs. Goliath imagery established when Luke single-handedly blew up the Death Star. Hope and the determination of its members are their only resources, becoming the unifying factor connecting the forces of the rebellion.

I have argued that the *Star Wars* movies agree with Bloch. Both postulate hope as the driving force behind human actions—to be more precise behind revolutions, which open up the concrete potential for betterment in the future. In order to keep this incredibly successful movie recipe alive, *Star Wars'* entire mythology is designed to preserve that narrative element, cultivating it for yet more movies of the franchise to come. As Leah Deyneka has argued, "*Star Wars* becomes a cyclical monomyth," stating the importance of repetition (45). Although *Star Wars* has grown to become an intergenerational saga, which would account for a linear timeline, every generation's story is a mirror and repetition of the preceding one, introducing a historical dimension to the imperial forces and the resistance against them. To put it bluntly, the characters are never done with resisting—every generation needs to fight for their own better future[1]; Jyn Erso, introduced in *Rogue One* (2016), redeems her father's assistance in constructing the Death Star by joining the Resistance. Additionally, *The Force Awakens* establishes Poe Dameron whose parents fought in the first resistance movements, paving the way for his fight against the First Order. Luke and Leia, most notably, fight the system that their father, Anakin Skywalker—aka Darth Vader—has helped to build. Leia's son, Kylo Ren, in turn wants to establish the reign of the First Order. *Star Wars* is a world in which "happily ever after" does not and cannot exist. If the galaxy were ever to arrive at a point where authoritarian rule and despotism are impossible, hope, as a narrative device, would no longer be necessary. After all, in a perfect society, what is there to hope for?

This cyclical nature of *Star Wars* becomes also apparent by looking at the titles of the episodes. Words like "revenge" (*Revenge of the Sith*), "striking back" (*The Empire Strikes Back*) or "return" (*Return of the Jedi*) indicate a back-and-forth structure, hinting at the reactionary nature of *Star War*—for in order to take revenge, one must have been wronged or treated unfairly before. *Star Wars* is therefore based on an action-reaction pattern, initiating a spiral of back and forth between a totalitarian empire and a liberal opposition: "They blow you up today, you blow them up tomorrow" (*TLJ*) is how the master decoder DJ phrases this push and pull dichotomy, thus commenting aptly on the cyclical nature of the narrative. Furthermore, it is impossible to install a perpetual equilibrium of forces. One of the two opposite movements will always have the upper hand for a certain amount of time.

Tellingly, the movies rarely depict times of peace, meaning the makers actively decided against setting the narratives within the periods of relative political and economic stability—a choice certainly indebted to *Star Wars'* status as action movies. Instead, the movies present a totalitarian world without providing an explanation for how this order came about (with the exception of the Episodes I, II, and III; yet, arguably, these movies are not usually the fans' favorite films for it is much more interesting to watch totalitarian systems get overthrown); *A New Hope* shows the Galactic Empire at its height, while *The Force Awakens* presents the First Order as the ruling elite, without explaining how Supreme Leader Snoke or General Hux have achieved their position and power. This is due to the fact that *Star Wars*, at least from episode IV onwards, is not interested in how authoritarian systems come into being. On the contrary, it is interested in how these systems can be overcome, thriving on the principle of hope expressed as a longing for a better future. This interest though does not remain a mere theoretical mind game to be depicted on screen. *Star Wars* has some very real influences on contemporary resistance movements around the world, firstly due to its role in identifying the systems worthy of fighting against.

Reacting in accordance to the *zeitgeist*,[2] since its beginning *Star Wars* has always inspired and encouraged its audience to work against certain tendencies and developments deemed negative in the real world. While episodes IV through VI engaged in anti-imperialist criticism showing genuine interest in guerrilla movements, the subsequent episodes I through III contained "a not-so-subtle indictment of the Bush administration" (Lowry). The final trilogy has spotted yet another target of criticism: It engages with economic themes, indulging in pretty obvious anti-capitalist critique. Introducing the desert planet Cantonica with its capitalist playground city Canto Bight full of the "worst people in the galaxy" (*TLJ*), *Star Wars* explicitly addresses the topics of environmentalism, animal rights, as well as ethics and responsibility in neoliberal capitalism. While one could easily accuse *Star Wars* of not practicing what it preaches—after all, "there's obvious irony in a money-making enterprise like *Star Wars*, fattening the coffers of the Disney empire, decrying capitalism run amok" (Lowry)—the movie encourages people to protest the current economic and political situation. As Booker comments on the movies' status as harbinger of hope in the 1970s: "The success of *Star Wars* announced a new desire for an optimistic, reassuring message that announced the possibility of a better future […]" (115).

Secondly and even more importantly, by embracing a diverse cast, by siding with anti-fascist and anti-capitalist egalitarian thoughts, and by rejecting elite politics as demonstrated by Luke Skywalker's curse to not count on "that mighty Skywalker blood" (Aronoff), *The Last Jedi* champions the nobodies and seemingly powerless of this world. This has led real-world protesters to increasingly channel their protest through images taken from *Star Wars*, choosing characters and symbols from the franchise to give voice to their thoughts and feelings. "Following the release of *Rogue One: A Star Wars*

Story, whose message 'rebellions are built on hope'" (Loughrey) protesters have increasingly relied on *Star Wars,* its characters, symbols, and catch phrases. This development was especially prominent during the protest marches against Donald J. Trump's inauguration as 45th president of the United States, for example, most notably during the Women's March in 2017. Internet platforms such as *Pinterest* abound in pictures showing (mostly women) protesters holding signs with overt *Star Wars* content, explicitly referenced by the design and type face of the posters. Signs reading "The Women Strike Back," "Women Against the Dark Side," "Nasty Women Lead the Rebellion," and "A Woman's Place Is in the Resistance" are prominent. "We are the Resistance" posters showing the face of Leia as a symbol of the rebels are often carried by young women, sometimes even dressed in Leia's iconic white costume to drive the point home. It seems as if Leia has transformed from a powerless damsel in distress into a general in combat and a global symbol of resistance.

The advantages of using *Star Wars* imagery and characters (condensing the message of resistance and hope through a popular and well recognized symbol of pop culture) seem to appeal to protesters in the U.S. and around the world. Increasingly, these people identify with *Star Wars'* message of female empowerment, social resistance, and hoping for a better future, a theme readopted by *The Last Jedi.* After all, it is, Rey, an apparently parentless, unimportant, unheard of woman(!) collecting garbage to make ends meet, who is burdened with standing up against the First Order despite her humble origins. The message seems to be: "Anybody can be a hero, so there's no excuse not to get involved in the fight" (Moses). Rey is a placeholder for all those men and (especially) women who live on the crumbs falling off the table. Yet, she has the power to change the status quo and succeeds in giving hope to the downtrodden of the galaxy, cultivating hope as the central narrative device and advocating its power. The movies champion the opinion that real change is actually possible if we never stop fighting for it, both in *Star Wars* and in the real world. Thus, *Star Wars* stays true to its core: to kindle one spark of hope—or to say it in the words of Leia Organa: "Hope is like the sun. If you only believe in it when you can see it, you'll never make it through the night" (*TLJ*).

Notes

1. Interestingly enough, many fans feel that they are never "done" with *Star Wars* either. Having grown up with the franchise and being used to revisit the previous movies with every new incarnation, fans experience this cyclical nature as familiar and rewarding, structuring their lives, too. At the same time, it is them who keep the cyclical structure alive by craving for new stories and thus encouraging those in charge to produce more and more *Star Wars* movies, books, etc.

2. The *Encyclopaedia Britannica* defines the German loanword *zeitgeist* as "the nature

of a historical period" ("novel," *EB*). The *zeitgeist* expresses the peculiar characteristics of one epoch, most and foremost its dominating ideology and worldview.

Works Cited

Abrams, J.J., director. *Star Wars: The Force Awakens.* Walt Disney Studios, 2015.
Aronoff, Kate. "*Star Wars: The Last Jedi* Takes a Side in the Class War." *The Intercept*, 24 Dec. 2017. https://theintercept.com/2017/12/24/star-wars-last-jedi-class-politics/.
Bloch, Ernst. *The Principle of Hope* [1959]. Basil Blackwell, 1986.
Booker, M.K. *Alternate Americas: Science Fiction Film and American Culture.* Praeger, 2006.
Charles, Michael B. "Remembering and Restoring the Republic: *Star Wars* and Rome." *Classical World*, vol. 108, no. 2, 2015, pp. 281–98.
Child, Ben. "Disney Will Truly Know the Power of *Star War's* Dark Side if It Ruins Darth Vader and Han Solo." *The Guardian*, 29 Jan. 2016. https://www.theguardian.com/film/2016/jan/29/star-wars-disney-expanded-franchise-dark-side-darth-vader-han-solo.
Deyneka, Leah. "May the Myth Be with You, Always." *Myth, Media, and Culture in Star Wars: An Anthology*, edited by Douglas Brode and Leah Deyneka, Scarecrow Press, 2012, pp. 31–46.
Edwards, Gareth, director. *Rogue One—A Star Wars Story.* Walt Disney Studios, 2016.
Geraghty, Lincoln. "Creating and Comparing Myth in Twentieth-Century Science Fiction: 'Star Trek' and 'Star Wars.'" *Literature/Film Quarterly*, vol. 33, no. 3, 2005, pp. 191–200.
Johnson, Rian, director. *Star Wars: The Last Jedi.* Walt Disney Studios, 2017.
Loughrey, Clarisse. "Women's March: How *Star Wars'* Princess Leia Became a Potent Symbol of Resistance." *The Independent*, 22. January 2017. https://www.independent.co.uk/arts-entertainment/films/news/womens-march-on-washington-star-wars-princess-leia-carrie-fisher-a-womans-place-is-in-the-resistance-a7539916.html.
Lowry, Brian. "*Star Wars: The Last Jedi* Leans into Political Fray." *CNN.com*, 19 Dec. 2017. https://www.cnn.com/2017/12/18/entertainment/star-wars-politics/index.html.
Lucas, George, director. *Star Wars: Episode I—The Phantom Menace.* Twentieth Century Fox, 2004.
Lucas, George, director. *Star Wars: Episode IV—A New Hope.* Twentieth Century Fox, 1977.
Moses, Toby. "Anti-Empire, Pro-Activist... *The Last Jedi* Is as Left Wing as Jeremy Corbyn." *The Guardian*, 19 Dec. 2017. https://www.theguardian.com/commentisfree/2017/dec/19/last-jedi-left-wing-jeremy-corbyn-star-wars-champion-grassroots.
Moylan, Tom. "The Locus of Hope: Utopia versus Ideology." *Science Fiction Studies*, vol. 9, no. 2, 1982, pp. 159–66.
"Novel." Britannica Academic, *Encyclopædia Britannica*, 5 Jul. 2018. academic.eb.com/levels/collegiate/article/novel/110453#50986.toc.
Shepherd, Jack. "*Star Wars: The Last Jedi*: Do Audiences Actually Hate Episode 8?" *The Independent*, 18 Dec. 2017. https://www.independent.co.uk/arts-entertainment/films/news/star-wars-the-last-jedi-audience-cinemascore-rotten-tomato-user-score-a8116166.html.
Spiegel. "'Star Wars'-Plakat zur Rekordpreis versteigert." *Spiegel Online*, 02 Aug. 018. https://www.spiegel.de/panorama/gesellschaft/star-wars-filmplakat-fuer-rekordpreis-versteigert-a-1221163.html.
Swatman, Rachel. "Star Wars Day: The Force Is Strong with These Ten Records." *Guinness World Records*, 04 May 2017. https://guinnessworldrecords.com/news/2017/5/star-wars-day-10-world-records-that-have-the-force-470827.
Thompson, Peter. "What Is Concrete About Ernst Bloch's 'Concrete Utopia'?" *Utopia: Social Theory and the Future.* Ed. Michael H. Jacobsen and Keith Tester. Ashgate, 2012, pp. 33–46.
Varsam, Maria. "Concrete Dystopia: Slavery and Its Others." *Dark Horizons: Science Fiction and the Dystopian Imagination*, edited by Raffaella Baccolini and Tom Moylan, Routledge, 2003, pp. 203–23.

About the Contributors

Jason **Buel** is an assistant professor of communication at North Carolina Wesleyan College. He has a Ph.D. in communication, rhetoric, and digital media from North Carolina State University. His research focuses on the politics of documentary and digital media, particularly in and around contemporary social movements. His article "Assembling the Living Archive" is available in *Public Culture* 30.2 (May 2018).

Leisa A. **Clark** is an adjunct professor of humanities and communication at various colleges. She is coeditor (with Amanda Firestone and Mary F. Pharr) of *Harry Potter and Convergence Culture*; *The Last Midnight*; and *Of Bread, Blood and* The Hunger Games. Her book, *From Welcoming Feasts to Trolley Treats*, was published in 2018.

S. Katherine **Cooper** is an assistant professor of sociology at the University of Tampa. Her research examines popular women's stand-up comedy and audience reactions to those performances. Her previous work has been published in *Sociological Focus* and *The Communication Review*.

Elizabeth J. **Dickhut** received an MA in English from the University of Northern Iowa. She is an adjunct faculty member at Hawkeye Community College. Her scholarly interests include digital humanities, embodied performance, social activism, and voice access, which she plans to pursue further through an MM program in music history.

Corinne E. **Fanta** is a student at the University of Tampa pursing a degree in applied sociology and nursing. She has conducted research on etiology regarding pneumonia in children with Dr. Lilliam Ambroggio, Ph.D., MPH, discussed medical diagnosis uncertainty with Dr. Shivani Patel, and expanded medical knowledge through simulations with Dr. Brian Herbst as a part of the Summer Undergraduate Research Fellowship at Cincinnati Children's Hospital. She presented her research at the University of Cincinnati's Capstone Symposium.

Amanda **Firestone** is an assistant professor of communication at the University of Tampa. Her research broadly examines children's and young adult literature as it pertains to the heroine's coming of age. While international best-selling series like *Harry Potter* and *The Twilight Saga* have been her intensive sites for analysis, she has also published about apocalyptic media, ruin porn, and monstrosity.

Annika **Gonnermann** specializes in utopian and dystopian literature; her Ph.D. dissertation was on dystopian fiction of the new millennium. Her work embraces an interdisciplinary approach, combining literature, philosophy, and political and social sciences. Her further research interests include Gothic literature, contemporary TV series, superhero narratives, and popular culture in cinema and TV.

Brittany M. **Harder**, Ph.D., is an assistant professor of sociology at the University of Tampa. She specializes in medical sociology, race, ethnicity and immigration as well as research methods and her research addresses issues of minority health/well-being, politics and profits in (U.S.) health, and media representation of minority groups. Her work has been published in *The Journal of Pediatrics*, *Qualitative Health Research*, and *Critical Public Health*, among others.

Caroline **Hovanec** is an assistant professor of English and writing at the University of Tampa, where she teaches writing courses about television and pop culture. Her research focuses on animal studies, modernism, and contemporary literature. She is the author of *Animal Subjects* (2018).

Jeana **Jorgensen** is a feminist folklorist, alt-ac scholar, blogger, sex educator, and dancer. She teaches at Butler University. Her research focuses on gender and sexuality in fairy tales and folklore, body art, dance, digital humanities, feminist and queer theory, and the history of sex education. Her work has appeared in *Marvels & Tales*, *The Journal of American Folklore*, *Cultural Analysis*, and elsewhere.

Kristi **Kouchakji** is a Ph.D. student in communication studies at McGill University, examining the daily experiences and public expectations of urban technological networks in contemporary Montreal. Her other research interests include documentary and social activism. Her work has appeared in *Participations*, *Rally!*, *Synoptique*, *Film Matters* and *POV* as well as on *Art Threat*.

Amanda K. **LeBlanc** is a visiting assistant professor in the Department of English and Communication at Adams State University. She received a Ph.D. in communication from the University of South Florida. She is a feminist media scholar who studies media representations of race, gender, sexuality, and monstrosity. She has written about violence and post-race in *American Horror Story: Coven* (2018).

Chandra A. **Maldonado** received a Ph.D. in communication, rhetoric, and digital media from North Carolina State University. Her work focuses on presidential memory and commemoration and visual rhetoric and other projects include the rhetorical functions of contemporary advocacy documentary films as well as gender and the labor movement. She has been published in multiple peer-reviewed venues such as *Recovering Argument*, *Networking Argument*, *Trespassing Journal*, and *Rhetoric Society Quarterly*.

Alisha **Menzies** received a Ph.D. from the University of South Florida. She is an assistant professor of communication from the University of Tampa. Her research intertwines media culture texts such as the film *Precious* (2009), Marvelyn Brown's website (marvelynbrown.com), and Magic Johnson's *The Announcement* (2012) to interrogate the relationship between lived experiences and media representations of HIV in connection with race, class, and gender.

Sabrina **Mittermeier** earned her Ph.D. in the field of American cultural history at Ludwig Maximilian University of Munich. She is the coeditor of an essay collection on *Star Trek: Discovery* (forthcoming) as well as the volume *Here You Leave Today* (2017). She has also published on other diverse topics of American popular culture and history such as the history of Disney theme parks, *Star Trek*, and constructions of temporality.

Mary F. **Pharr** is a professor emeritus of English at Florida Southern College. She received a Ph.D. from Vanderbilt and has published and presented extensively on speculative film and fiction. In 2012, she coedited (with Leisa A. Clark) *Of Bread, Blood and* The Hunger Games, and in 2016, she coedited (with Leisa A. Clark and Amanda Firestone) *The Last Midnight*.

Jessica **Stanley** is an English instructor at John Tyler Community College, where she teaches composition, literature, and developmental writing. She completed an MA in English at Longwood University. Her research interests include children's and young adult literature, popular culture, and gender studies. She is also a contributor to the edited collection *Age of the Geek* (2017).

Ana **Stevenson** is a postdoctoral research fellow in the International Studies Group at the University of the Free State, South Africa. Her research examines media representations of the political woman and the development of feminist rhetoric in transnational social movements. She has published articles in *Camera Obscura: Feminism, Culture, and Media Studies*, and *The Journal of Popular Television*, among others.

Kwasu David **Tembo** received a Ph.D. from the University of Edinburgh's Language, Literatures, and Cultures Department. His research interests include comics studies, literary theory and criticism, philosophy, particularly the so-called "prophets of extremity"—Nietzsche, Heidegger, Foucault, and Derrida. He has published on Christopher Nolan's *The Prestige* in *The Cinema of Christopher Nolan* (ed. Jacqueline Furby and Stuart Joy, 2015) and on Superman (*Postscriptum* [2017]).

Meagan **Thompson** is a Ph.D. candidate in American studies at the College of William & Mary. She earned an MA in English from Old Dominion University. Her interests include trauma and performance studies, critical race theory, queer theory, storytelling, and contemporary literature. She has presented at several conferences on topics related to writing center pedagogy, gender and queer theories, and cultural studies.

Index